W9-CHO-940

CREATING GAME ART FOR 3D ENGINES

BRAD STRONG

CHARLES RIVER MEDIA

Boston, Massachusetts

Copyright 2008 Career & Professional Group, a division of Thomson Learning Inc.
Published by Charles River Media, an Imprint of Thomson Learning Inc. All rights reserved.

No part of this publication may be reproduced in any way, stored in a retrieval system of any type, or transmitted by any means or media, electronic or mechanical, including, but not limited to, photocopy, recording, or scanning, without *prior permission in writing* from the publisher.

Publisher and General Manager, Charles River Media: Stacy L. Hiquet
Associate Director of Marketing: Sarah O'Donnell
Manager of Editorial Services: Heather Talbot
Marketing Manager: Jordan Casey
Marketing Assistant: Adena Flitt
Project/Copy Editor: Karen A. Gill
Technical Reviewer: Mike Duggan
CRM Editorial Services Coordinator: Jennifer Blaney
Interior Layout Tech: Judy Littlefield
Cover Designer: Sherry Stinson
Cover Images: Brad Strong
CD-ROM Producer: Brandon Penticuff
Indexer: Joan Green
Proofreader: Sybil Fetter

Charles River Media, Inc.
25 Thomson Place
Boston, MA 02210
617-757-7900
617-757-7969 (fax)
info@charlesriver.com
www.charlesriver.com

This book is printed on acid-free paper.

Brad Strong. *Creating Game Art for 3D Engines.*
ISBN-10: 1-58450-548-6
ISBN-13: 978-1-58450-548-8
Library of Congress Catalog Card Number: 2007933886
3ds Max is a registered trademark of Autodesk, Inc. Photoshop is a registered trademark of Adobe Systems Incorporated. All other brand names and product names mentioned in this book are trademarks or service marks of their respective companies. Any omission or misuse (of any kind) of service marks or trademarks should not be regarded as intent to infringe on the property of others. The publisher recognizes and respects all marks used by companies, manufacturers, and developers as a means to distinguish their products.

Printed in Canada
08 09 10 11 12 TC 10 9 8 7 6 5 4 3 2 1

Charles River Media titles are available for site license or bulk purchase by institutions, user groups, corporations, etc. For additional information, please contact the Special Sales Department at 800-347-7707.

Requests for replacement of a defective CD-ROM must be accompanied by the original disc, your mailing address, telephone number, date of purchase, and purchase price. Please state the nature of the problem, and send the information to Charles River Media, Inc., 25 Thomson Place, Boston, MA 02210. CRM's sole obligation to the purchaser is to replace the disc, based on defective materials or faulty workmanship, but not on the operation or functionality of the product.

This book is dedicated to my wife, Åsa,
who was an encouragement and a blessing
from the time this book was just an idea until the final edit.

CONTENTS

CHAPTER 11   CHARACTER ANIMATION   251

ACKNOWLEDGMENTS

I wish to thank the editing team at Charles River Media (Emi Smith, Karen Gill, Jennifer Blaney, and Jenifer Niles) for their help in getting this book publish-ready. Thanks, too, to my technical editor, Mike Duggan. Also deserving recognition are the guys who make the Torque Game Engine available, GarageGames, who directly or indirectly made this book and the accompanying CD possible. In particular, I want to thank Joe Maruschak at GarageGames for the great articles and forum answers that have helped me and many others get a handle on this engine. I also want to thank Autodesk for a great product (3ds Max) and for the experience I gathered while there; thank you David Koel for making me a better AE. Cuneyt Ozdas deserves recognition for writing Texporter, the handy UV renderer. Thanks also to Matt Summers for writing the Dark Industries exporter, and to Sam Bacsa for writing Codeweaver, which helped me to work through some of the scripting challenges. Finally, thanks to Steve Smith at the Art Institute of Colorado for freely sharing his knowledge while I taught there.

ABOUT THE AUTHOR

Brad Strong, a former Autodesk application engineer, has more than 18 years of experience using and teaching digital design software in the Rocky Mountain region. He holds a master's in computer information systems from Denver University/University College, where his thesis and capstone project was on game-based learning; a master's in management from the University of Phoenix, where his thesis was on effective CAD utilization; and a bachelor's in art from the University of Colorado at Denver.

Brad has developed and taught a range of courses on programming, art, and game development at art and technical colleges in the Colorado area. Most recently, he taught 3D modeling, materials and lighting, 3D animation, and online game development for the Art Institute of Colorado. Since 2002, he has been developing 3D learning games. He is the president of 3dCognition, a game-based learning development studio, based in Karlskoga, Sweden. The 3dCognition Web site can be found at http://www.3dcognition.com.

When he's not working, Brad enjoys theology, philosophy, bass guitar, and composing fusion-lounge-gospel music with his wife.

INTRODUCTION

This book focuses on how to create game art properly for a game engine, as well as how to export that art to the engine and make script changes so that the art becomes a viable part of the game.

Although many of the processes and techniques will apply to specific modeling, texturing, animation, and game software solutions, this book will use 3ds Max release 8 to generate models and animations, and the Torque Game Engine for the game-side examples. These two solutions are at the forefront of their class; 3ds Max has more than 200,000 registered users and is used by more top-selling game developers for modeling and animation than any other solution. The Torque Game Engine enjoys a solid reputation as the most powerful and affordable solution for the small game development studio, in addition to being a viable choice for students and hobbyists.

Much of this book comes from my own tribulations as an instructor for modeling, texturing, animation, and game development courses. A good instructor learns over a period of semesters and years how to get the information across as efficiently as possible to minimize everyone's (his own included!) frustration.

An equal part of this book stems from my own frustrations as a game developer for the past five years. It was from my own notes on what was working and what wasn't, combined with my own interpretation of the resources at the Torque Web site (http://www.GarageGames.com), that many of these pages were birthed.

Because this book covers so many aspects of game art (modeling, unwrapping, texturing, rigging, animation, exporting, scripting), it will be impossible to drill too deeply into any one area. However, the goal of this book is to provide step-by-step exercises and video tutorials that a serious student can use to create and successfully import game art, from simple shapes to full-blown characters. There should be more than enough here for the accomplished or aspiring artist/animator to gain an understanding of how to create game art and how to make it come alive in a 3D engine.

Multimedia is a powerful medium because it engages so many of our senses. 3D games are the highest and most compelling form of multimedia, because they add competition, instant feedback, immersion, and adventure. We are motivated, challenged, and empowered to do things we could not do otherwise. The future of game development is promising, and I believe that the future for game-based learning and interactive simulations is particularly bright. Math, for example, is a dry subject, but if solving a few equations will help me fly to a far star, I might be interested.

If you have questions or comments on this book, feel free to e-mail them to brad@3dCognition.com. As feedback is generated from this book, any noteworthy corrections or additions will be available at http://www. 3dCognition.com.

I hope that this book is instrumental in making your game ideas real.

CHAPTER

1

INTRODUCTION TO 3DS MAX

In This Chapter

- Examining the 3ds Max Interface
- Creating, Viewing, and Modifying Primitives
- Box Modeling a Chair
- Working with the Material Editor
- Managing Files

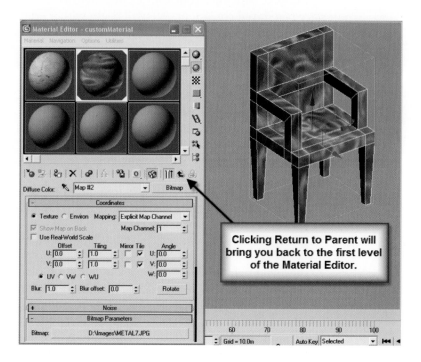

Clicking Return to Parent will bring you back to the first level of the Material Editor.

T his chapter introduces some of the foundational features of 3ds Max for the benefit of those who have limited or no experience. Please keep in mind that for complete coverage of 3ds Max, you should work through a book that is focused solely on that product. Even then, the vast majority of 3ds Max users do not use or understand the entire functionality of the product. Because the goal of this book is to generate game assets and make them functional in the game, we will only discuss those foundational aspects of 3ds Max that directly pertain to our goal.

We will overview the 3ds Max interface, primitives, viewing tools and options, transforms, properties, Editable Polys, and basic materials. Each version of 3ds Max adds a vast amount of functionality; however, on the whole, the look and feel of 3ds Max has not changed for several releases. This tutorial and the files on the CD-ROM are being made with Release 8. The features used are primarily found in Release 7 and earlier; Release 8 features will be noted when used. If you are using a version of 3ds Max as early as 4 or 5, you should still be able to follow and apply the majority of what will be discussed in this book.

EXAMINING THE 3DS MAX INTERFACE

The features of 3ds Max continue to improve with each release, but the general interface has stayed consistent. We will begin with a brief overview of the interface, and then we'll jump right into creating some 3D primitives. The intent here is to stay laser-focused on those foundational tools and techniques that will help us to build pickups, weapons, and characters in the following chapters. This walk-through will be done project-style, so we will discuss the different tools as we come to them in each project. Our first project will be to model a simple chair.

In Figure 1.1, at the top of the screen, you have drop-down menus with a Standard toolbar immediately below. If your screen resolution is 1024 × 768, the entire toolbar will not fit on the screen; therefore, you will need to drag it to the right and left as you work so that you can see the entire set of tools. To the right are the panels. There are panels for Create, Modify, Hierarchy, Motion, Display, and Utilities. This is typically one of the most heavily used areas of the interface. In this image, the Create panel is focused on the Geometry tools. This is where you find primitives, such as boxes, cylinders, and spheres.

At the bottom of the workspace is the animation area, where you can set and modify keyframes.

At the lower right are the viewing tools. These tools will change based on whether you are in a perspective view, an orthographic view (such as front, right, back, or top), or if you are looking through a camera.

The area in the middle is the workspace. By default, you have four viewports. You can activate any viewport by right-clicking in it. At any time, you can toggle between four viewports or one viewport by clicking the Maximize Viewport toggle, which resides in the lower right-hand corner of the screen. If you click the Maximize Viewport toggle while a particular viewport is active, that viewport becomes maximized. Clicking the toggle again returns you to a four-viewport interface. Click this button a

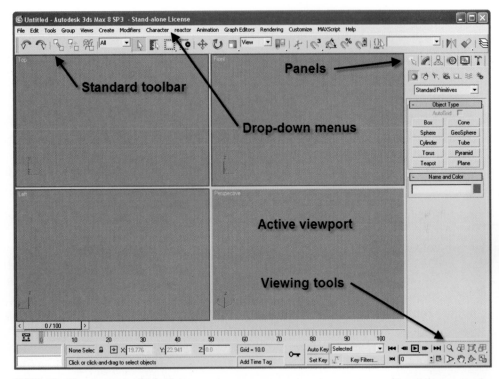

FIGURE 1.1   The anatomy of 3ds Max.

few times to see what happens. In general, it is best to have as big a viewport as possible when working with a model, but at different times during the development process, you will need to switch to multiple viewports to see how the model is shaping up from different points of view.

Depending on what you are doing and where in the interface you click, a right-click will generate different menus. A right-click on the viewport area will give you access to the Move, Rotate, and Scale tools, as well as the option to hide selected objects or hide unselected objects, for example. You also have hotkeys such as F for front view, L for left view, P for perspective view, U for user view, Alt+W to toggle between one big viewport and multiple viewports, and G to toggle Grid mode on and off.

Using Drop-Downs and Panels

3ds Max is set up primarily with two means of creating and editing: drop-down menus and panels, located to the right of the workspace. For the majority of our work, you will be using the Create panel and the Modify panel. If you cannot find the tool you are looking for, try these panels first.

Adjusting Grid and Snap

Grid and Snap are related. You can set the size of the grid on the screen by right-clicking the Snaps toggle and accessing the Grid tab. You can toggle the grid off and on by using the G hotkey. You can set the default Snaps by right-clicking the Snaps toggle and accessing the Snaps tab. Check the box next to the type of snap you want enabled, and close the dialog box by clicking the X in the upper-right corner. Then, as long as the Snaps toggle is enabled, the mouse cursor will snap accordingly. The Snaps toggle is a tool that should be deactivated most of the time and used only when you have a specific need for it. Most of the time, having this tool turned on will get in your way. Likewise, having the Grid turned on will often just add confusion to your viewport.

Setting Preferences

A few adjustments to the Preferences in 3ds Max can make your work more productive. From the Customize drop-down menu, click Preferences; then select the General tab. Setting the Scene Undo level to 100 enables you to click the Undo button up to 100 times if you've made a wrong move. In the Viewports tab, under Mouse Control, make sure that Middle Button is set to Pan/Zoom and that Zoom About Mouse Point is checked for both Orthographic and Perspective. This setting allows you to spin the mouse wheel and zoom in or out on a viewport while causing the zoom to target wherever your mouse cursor is.

CREATING, VIEWING, AND MODIFYING PRIMITIVES

To become familiar with 3ds Max, start by creating some primitives from the Create, Standard Primitives panel. Create the geometry by clicking on the shape and then clicking and dragging in your perspective viewport. Depending on the shape, when you release the mouse the first time, you may have to define another desired dimension. (For example, after you define the base of the Box primitive, you define its height.) You can name a primitive and adjust its object color at the time of creation by accessing the Name and Color rollout on the Create, Standard Primitives panel. In Figure 1.2, some of the standard primitives have been created on the screen. Create these on your own screen to get a feel for how primitives are created. The green box has just been created, so you can still change its parameters in the menu at the right. The most important things to consider for now are the size and number of segments in the primitive. Create some primitives of your own, and try changing length, width, and height values. Also, try changing the number of segments. You will see the number of segments change in the orthogonal viewports (top, front, left), but the number of segments for each primitive will not show up in the perspective viewport until you make an adjustment. If you want to clear the screen without saving changes, click File, Reset.

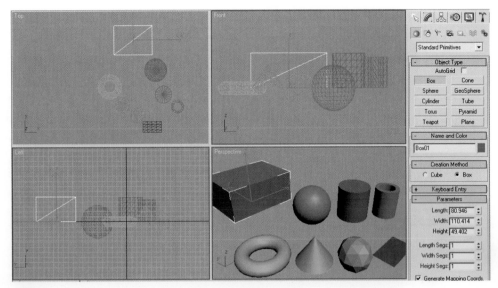

FIGURE 1.2   The Create panel gives you access to standard primitives and their parameters.

Now that you have seen the standard primitives, take some time to look at the extended primitives as well. Being aware of the basic shapes that can be achieved with a few button clicks can save you modeling time later.

Using Viewport Controls

The ability to see segments (or edges) on your models will become very important as you begin to model. If you want to turn on Edged Faces for any particular viewport, you need to right-click on the viewport name (the name for each viewport is in the upper left-hand of the viewport) and make sure that Edged Faces is checked. Likewise, you may want the contents of a viewport to be Smooth+Highlights or Wireframe. The Views flyout on this right-click menu allows you to change the kind of view you are looking at; top, front, right, left, user, and perspective are all useful options. If you use the Arc Rotate tool in any of your orthogonal viewports, the viewports will become user views. They will lose their straight-on orthogonal quality; any view that is skewed in any way is either a perspective view or a user view.

Modifying Primitives

As long as your Select tool is active, you can select different primitives by clicking on them. The Select tool button looks like a white arrow and resides on the Standard toolbar. When a primitive is selected, the edges of the primitive will turn white, and there will be a white selection box around it. You can delete selected objects by pressing the Delete key. Even after you've created the primitive, you can change its size and number of segments by selecting the object and clicking the Modify panel.

If we want to move this box, we can click the Select and Move button on the Standard toolbar. Alternatively, you can select the object first and then activate the Move tool, or you can perform a select and move simultaneously. The Move tool has a gizmo (a directional indicator) that is red, green, and blue and is made up of three axes and three planes. The red axis corresponds to the X direction, the green axis to Y, and the blue axis to Z. The axes and planes will highlight (turn yellow) as you pass the mouse over them. Dragging on an axis will move the box only in that axis, and dragging on a yellow plane of the Move gizmo will move the box only in one of the three planes: XY, YZ, or XZ. When you release the mouse button, you'll notice that the object moved. The Rotate and Scale tools have similar gizmos, where selected objects can be rotated or scaled in an axis or a plane.

In Figure 1.3, a box that was created is being modified via the Modify panel, the number of segments has been changed to 2 in each direction, and Edged Faces have been turned on for the perspective viewport. Note also that in this figure, the Move tool has been turned on in the Standard toolbar, and the Move gizmo is near the box.

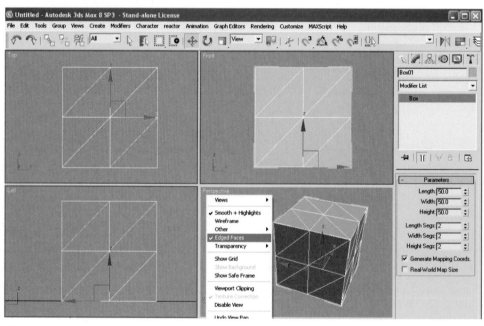

FIGURE 1.3   Setting viewports to show Edged Faces, adjusting segments, and the Move gizmo.

Using Viewing Tools

The Zoom, Pan, Arc Rotate, and Maximize Viewport buttons reside in the lower-right corner of the screen. Practice zooming in and out in different viewports by right-clicking on the viewport to activate it and then spinning the mouse wheel to zoom. Pressing and holding the mouse wheel causes a pan. In the lower-right corner of the screen, the Maximize Viewport button is a toggle that maximizes whatever viewport is current so that it is a single large viewport; clicking this button again returns to a multiviewport state.

The Arc Rotate tool allows you to do a left-click-drag to change your view of the model. Figure 1.4 displays this process in action; you can see the Arc Rotate tool turned on in the lower-right corner of the screen. The yellow circle that is displayed on the screen during Arc Rotate is called a *trackball*. By clicking inside the trackball, you can intuitively change the viewpoint of your object. Arc Rotate flyouts are gray for general purposes, white to focus on selected objects, and yellow to focus on selected sub-objects. In this figure, the Arc Rotate Selected button is active, meaning that as you click and drag, the selected object will be the center of the rotation.

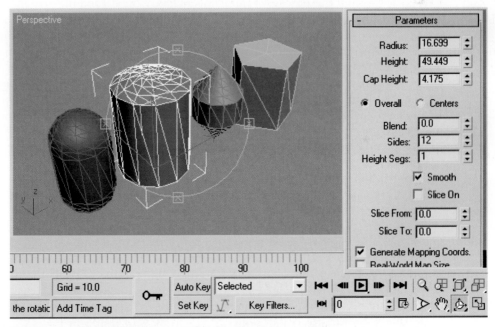

FIGURE 1.4   Using the Arc Rotate tool to change the viewing angle.

Do not mix up the Arc Rotate tool with the Rotate tool. You use the Arc Rotate tool for rotating the view of the model, whereas you use the Rotate tool for rotating the model. Do not use the Rotate tool, located next to the Move tool on the Standard toolbar, to change your view of the object. Doing so will make your model more difficult to edit, because it will be in an inconvenient orientation for editing.

Using Selection Windows

The Selection button on the Standard toolbar in 3ds Max toggles between activating a Window Selection mode and activating a Crossing Window selection mode. Every time you left-click-drag on the screen in 3ds Max, you define one corner of a selection window. When you release the mouse button, you define the opposite corner of the selection window. All objects within that window will be selected. This describes the behavior of a standard selection window. A Crossing selection window selects not only the objects within the window but also the objects that are even partially in the window; that is, it also selects the objects that the selection window *crosses*.

BOX MODELING A CHAIR

ON THE CD

Walking through the process of modeling a chair will be good practice for the models we will build later in this book. You can find the video ModelingAChair.wmv in the Videos folder on the companion CD-ROM. Start by creating a simple chair from a box primitive. Do this by going to the Create panel, activating the Geometry menu, verifying that you have standard primitives selected from the drop-down list, and selecting Box from the list of primitives. To create the box, use a click-drag-release action with the mouse. Perform this drag action in the perspective viewport. The first click-drag creates the base of the box; when you release and move the mouse again, you are defining the height of the box. When you click the mouse button, the box is complete. If this is your first time creating primitives with 3ds Max, spend a few minutes creating primitives such as spheres and cylinders. When you want to delete a primitive, select it with left mouse button and press the Delete key. Test some of the viewing tools that are built into your mouse; spin the mouse wheel to zoom in and zoom out, and do a click-drag on the middle mouse button/mouse wheel to pan the screen around.

To modify the box, select it first. Figure 1.5 depicts four important things. First, the Select button is active in the Standard toolbar. If you find that you cannot select an object, first check to see that the Select button is active. Second, the box we just created is selected. This is indicated by a selection box with white edges that highlights the box. Third, the Modify panel is selected. If you have an object selected and you select the Modify panel, you will generally find that you have access to the parameters or sub-objects of that selection. In this case, because our object is a box, we have access to the Length, Width, and Height, as well as the number of segments for each of these values. Adjust the dimensional values of your box to mimic the image seen in Figure 1.5 so that your box more clearly resembles the seat of a chair. Notice that our current viewport is perspective. (The name is in the upper-left corner.) To display edges in this viewport, right-click on the name of the viewport (Perspective) and click Edges. Now we are ready to add edges. This is the fourth important thing to notice from the figure. We want three segments for length and three for width so that we have enough edges to create legs and a back for the chair.

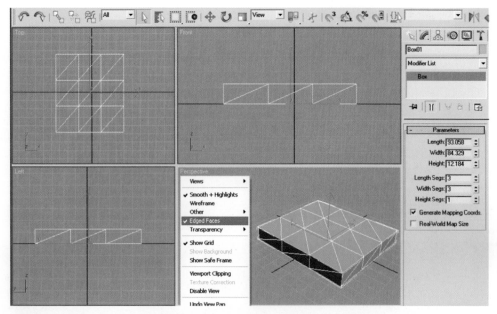

FIGURE 1.5   Edged faces are turned on for the viewport, and edges are added for the box.

 If your Move gizmo (or the other transform gizmos, for that matter) is not visible, there are two possible causes. The first is that you accidentally pressed the X button on your keyboard, which turns off the transform gizmo. Press X again and see if this corrects the problem. The second possible cause is that your preferences may have somehow been set to turn the transform gizmos off. If this is the case, try going to the Customize drop-down menu, select Preferences, select the Gizmos tab, and make sure the check box for Gizmos is selected.

Converting to an Editable Poly

Our next step in going from a box to a chair is to convert the box into an Editable Poly. When we do this, we lose the ability to parametrically adjust the length, width, and height, but we gain the ability to modify sub-objects such as vertices, edges, and polygons. To convert the box to an Editable Poly, right-click on the box and select Convert to Editable Poly. When you do this, you will see the Modify panel change; the Editable Poly modify menu allows the user to select a sub-object type, each of which has its own specific modification options. Figure 1.6 displays what the Convert to Editable Poly menu looks like, as well as the Editable Poly menu to the right.

Moving the Vertices of the Editable Poly

The Editable Poly has five different sub-object types: Vertex, Edge, Border, Polygon, and Element. Our objective at the moment is to move the vertices of the Editable

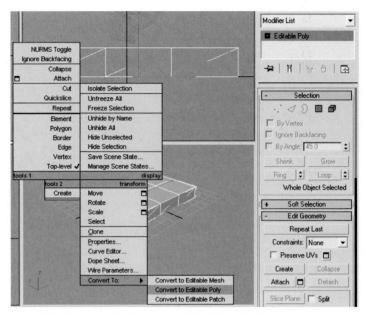

FIGURE 1.6   Where to find Convert to Editable Poly. This box has already been converted.

Poly so that we can extrude the legs and the back of the chair. Click on the Vertex sub-object type to activate it. You will know it is active when you see the word *Vertex* highlighted in yellow.

Working in sub-object mode can be tricky the first few times you do it. You will not be able to select any other objects until you properly exit sub-object mode. This involves clicking on the yellow highlighted bar. The disappearance of the yellow highlight means you have exited sub-object mode, and you can treat this model as a regular model or select another model. When you are in sub-object mode, you are in a sense "locked" inside that model.

Activate the top viewport by right-clicking in it. We will use the top viewport because it is easier to select a complete row of vertices when all the geometry is flat to the screen. We can use what can be called an "implied window" technique to select a row of vertices. This involves doing a click-drag-release from one corner of the selection area to the other. When you release the mouse button, you should see a row of red vertices, indicating that all of them have been selected. After you've selected these vertices, you can use the Move tool to move them to the left. Figure 1.7 shows the four stages of this process. The implied window is used to select the vertices; they will then turn red when selected. The Move tool is activated and used to move the entire row of selected vertices closer to the edge of the Editable Mesh. Continue this process on the other vertices so that all of the vertices are near the edge of the object. This creates small polygons in each corner, which we can use to extrude the legs.

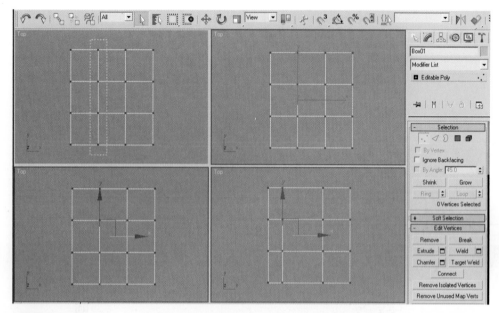

FIGURE 1.7   Four stages of moving vertices in Vertex sub-object mode, from within the top viewport.

Maximizing the Viewport and Using Arc Rotate

Up until now, we have had all four standard viewports displayed. When we maximize a viewport, whatever viewport is currently active will enlarge to fill the screen. Right-click on the perspective viewport to activate it, and then maximize it by clicking on the Maximize Viewport button in the lower-right corner of the screen. The hotkey for this is Alt+W. Pressing the button or entering the hotkey again will return you to the four default viewports. After you have the Perspective viewport maximized, use the Arc Rotate tool to move your view of the model so that you are looking at it from the bottom, where you will extrude the legs. Rotate the view of the object until your screen looks like Figure 1.8.

Extruding the Legs of the Chair

To generate four legs of the chair, first click on Polygon sub-object mode. (This mode is the one that looks like a red square under the Selection sub-menu.) Just as Vertex sub-object mode allowed us to modify vertices of the model, Polygon sub-object mode will allow us to modify polygons. When we are in the right mode, we can left-click to select the four corner faces for the legs; to select all four polygons at once, hold down the Ctrl key. The polygons should turn red when selected. If they do not, make sure your viewport is set to Smooth+Highlights; if the polygons are still not shaded, try pressing F2 to toggle Highlight Selected Faces. Click on the Extrude Settings button to the right of the Extrude button, as shown in Figure 1.8, and change the Extrusion height until you like the result. When you are satisfied, click OK.

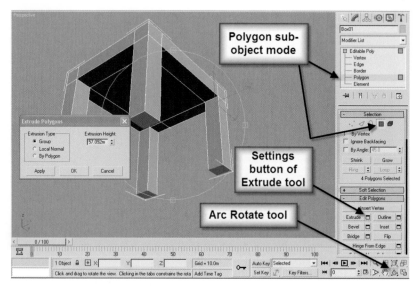

FIGURE 1.8   Selecting four polygons and using Extrude Settings to adjust their length.

Extruding the Back of the Chair

Rotate the view of the chair again using the Arc Rotate tool so that you are once again looking down upon it. Select the three polygons at the back of the chair and extrude them to form the back of the chair. You may want to left-click once on the gray background of the screen to make sure that the ends of the chair legs are not still selected; otherwise, they will be extruded again, along with the chair back.

Creating the Arms of the Chair

The Editable Poly modification menu is rather extensive, so it is sometimes useful to pull the menu out so that more of it can be seen at one time. To do this, click on the edge of the menu and drag toward the left until another panel width is visible, as shown in Figure 1.9. Make sure you are back in Vertex sub-object mode, and from the Edit Geometry rollout, click the Slice Plane button. This will generate a yellow preview plane, which you can move with your Move transform tool. Move this slice plane into a position as shown, and click the Slice button. You have more vertices and polygons available now.

Before you actually rotate the slice plane, activate the Angle Snap toggle so that your rotation can be more precise. When you are ready to rotate the slice plane, click the Rotate button. Click-drag on the Rotate gizmo, where you see a green circle corresponding to the Y axis, until the slice plane has rotated 90 degrees. When the slice plane has the right orientation, use the Move tool to bring it closer to the front of the chair and click Slice to complete your final slice for this model. Figure 1.10

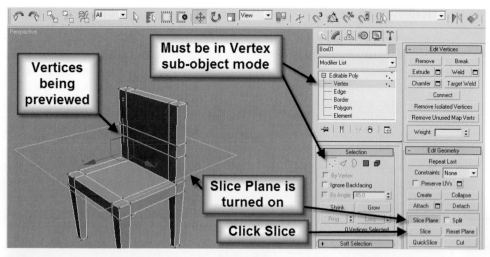

FIGURE 1.9   Cutting new edges with the Slice Plane tool.

shows the chair with appropriate slices made. In this figure, we are in Polygon sub-object mode and have selected the four polygons we will build the chair arms from. Each of these polygons is extruded a short distance to give us something to work with.

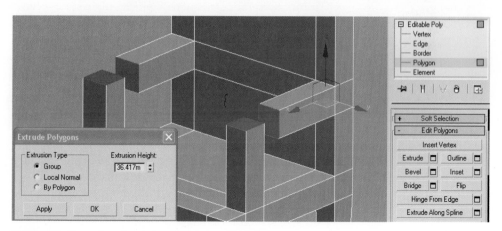

FIGURE 1.10   Extruding the chair arms.

If we were designing a chair for a movie or almost any other purpose than as a real-time game asset, we would likely add more details and additional edges to refine the appearance and prepare the model for adding a MeshSmooth modifier. However, this process would quickly bring the chair's polygon face count to over 1,000 faces. Because we are rendering all faces real-time, we need to keep our models simple and make up for that simplicity with believable textures.

Welding Vertices

There are two basic kinds of welds: general and target. To use either one, you have to be working with an Editable Poly (or an Editable Mesh), and you must be in Vertex sub-object mode. Also, for both types of welds, you need to be sure that there are no polygons between the two vertices. If there are polygons or faces between the two vertices you want to weld, you have to delete these obstructions first by selecting them in Polygon sub-object mode and pressing Delete. In Figure 1.11, we have deleted the polygons at the end of each chair arm extrusion so that we can weld the arms together.

The general weld works by selecting or windowing a group of vertices and then clicking the Weld button. If the threshold is set to 0.25, any of the selected vertices that are within that distance of each other will be welded together. The target weld is accomplished by dragging from one vertex to the vertex where you want it to be welded. It is a left-click-drag-release type of action.

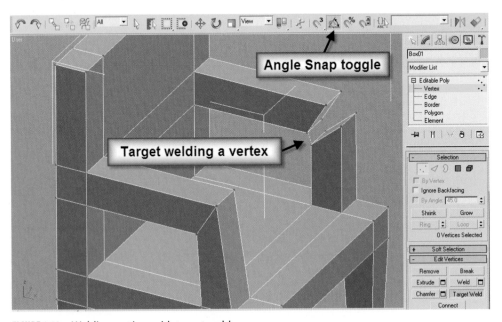

FIGURE 1.11   Welding vertices with target weld.

Manipulating Vertices

Just as we moved vertices in the segmented box at the start of this chair design, we can move vertices from an orthographic view (a straight-on view) to fix the chair arm vertices so that they are straighter. Depending on how you created the chair, you should be able to see a clear view of the side of the chair from the front or the left viewport. Viewed from the side, there are really only two sets of vertices that might need to be moved so that the chair arm is straight. By using an implied window, you can select these vertices and move them where you think they should be.

WORKING WITH THE MATERIAL EDITOR

The Material Editor is an interface that is dedicated solely to creating, applying, and modifying materials. Although it cannot be used like Photoshop to manipulate pixels and create bitmaps, it does allow us to select and use those bitmaps in a variety of ways.

Applying a Standard Material to an Object

It is a good idea to select the object that you want to apply the material to first and then launch the Material Editor. You can launch the Material Editor from the Standard toolbar or by pressing the hotkey M. Click the Get Material button to launch the Material Browser (see Figure 1.12). Set the Browse From group in the Material Browser to Material Library so that you can see the standard materials. Double-clicking on a material will place it in the sample slot of the Material Editor. Then you can apply the material to the object by clicking the Assign Material To Selection button. The material will not be visible on the model until you click the Show Map in Viewport button. Also, you may need to make sure your viewport is set to Smooth+Highlights so that you can see the shaded image in the viewport.

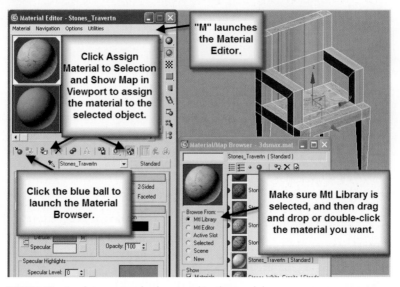

FIGURE 1.12   Applying a standard material to the model.

Look at the material and the way it lies on the model. It looks fine on some faces but is streaking on others. It is always a good idea to add a UVW Map modifier to any modeled object so that you have more control over how the material lies on the model. To apply a UVW Map modifier to the chair, make sure the chair is selected and that you are not in sub-object mode. Then click the Modifiers drop-down list described in Figure 1.13 and select UVW Map modifier from the end of the list.

Select Box for the map type, and note that the appearance, while still not perfect, is now at least more consistent than before. Note the modifier stack on the right. By selecting an object and clicking on the Modify panel, we can quickly understand what kind of object this is (an Editable Poly in this case) and what modifiers have been added to it. (The UVW Map modifier has been added.) Note that you can click the plus sign next to any modifier in the modifier stack to open that same modifier to access deeper levels.

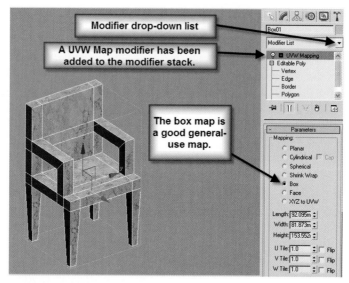

FIGURE 1.13   Applying a UVW Map modifier to the model to control the way the material looks.

Applying a Custom Material to an Object

Standard materials are okay for tutorials or traditional texturing work, but for real-time rendering, we will almost always need to create custom textures for our assets. Create the material by locating a copyright-free image on the Internet, creating it in Photoshop, scanning an image, using a digital photo, or using some combination of these methods. Launch the Material Editor and select an empty sample tile. Then give your new material a name. Scroll down to the Maps section and check the box that says Diffuse Color. Click the button to the right that normally says None. After that, double-click on Bitmap and find the material you made (see Figure 1.14). Using maps other than diffuse is covered in Chapter 4, "Texturing Game Art."

After you have selected the bitmap, you can close the Material Browser. Your Material Editor interface will now reflect the parameters of the bitmap you just added. Here you have access to the Parameters rollout for the bitmap; this is the area where you can turn on the Alpha channel for reflective or transparent materials, for

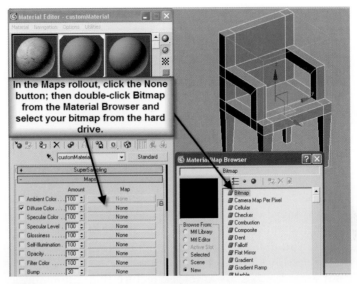

FIGURE 1.14 Applying a custom material to the model.

instance. To get back to the general Material Editor interface, click the Go To Parent button (see Figure 1.15). If you ever want access to bitmap parameters again, simply click on the bitmap name in the Maps rollout.

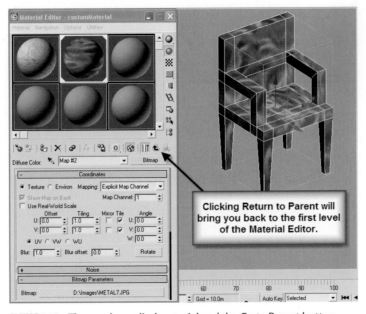

FIGURE 1.15 The newly applied material and the Go to Parent button.

MANAGING FILES

A big part of art asset development is managing the data. Consider implementing file-naming conventions, system backups, offsite storage, and a means of tracking which assets were used for different iterations of a game. At a minimum, being able to save your work and being able to merge and import files are important skills.

Saving Your Work

You can save your work by selecting File, Save; use File, Save As to give the file a new name; or use File, Save Copy As to make a copy of the file. The most important thing is to save your work regularly in case you encounter a crash or lose your work. The File, Save As dialog has a plus sign (+) to let you automatically save and incre-ment your saved copy to Filename01.max, Filename02.max, and so on. Incremental file saves are an excellent idea because they not only back up your work, but they also allow you to backtrack to specific signposts in your design process if you inad-vertently destroy your work.

3ds Max also has an Autoback feature that automatically backs up your files. The setup for Autoback is in Customize, Preferences, Files, in the Auto Backup group. This feature is especially helpful if 3ds Max crashes; 3ds Max will attempt to save a backup copy of your work to the Autoback folder where 3ds Max is installed.

Merging and Importing Files

What if we want to bring our chair into a room that has other furniture? First, it would be a good idea to name this model chair rather than its default name of Box01. Then we can save this file (let's call the name of the file chair as well) and open our room file. Once room is open, select File, Merge from the drop-down menus and find the chair file. Upon merging the files, you will have the choice of what objects within that file you want to merge. This is where names are helpful. You can also export and import 3ds files; 3ds files are a file format that saves only the mesh information of your models.

SUMMARY

In this chapter, we started by looking at the general interface of 3ds Max and its viewing tools. We then looked at the model creation process, working from a prim-itive box to a more refined Editable Poly. We closed this chapter with examples of how to add UV maps and materials to an object. In the next chapter, we will build upon these tools and techniques to model the noncharacter components of our game.

LOW POLY MODELING

In This Chapter

- Creating Structurally Sound Models
- Keeping a Low Polygon Budget
- Modeling a Simple Shape
- Modeling a Health Patch
- Modeling a Power Charger
- Modeling a Weapon

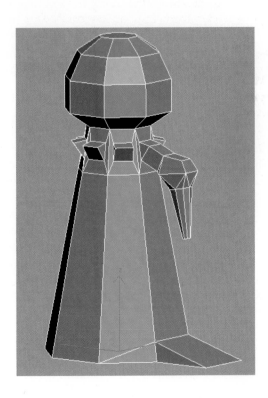

T he goal for this chapter is to cover the basics of low poly modeling in 3ds Max. This includes learning how to repair a model that has problems and how to minimize the number of faces that a model has. Models for a simple shape, a health patch, a power charger, and a weapon will be created. Each of these models will ultimately be unwrapped, textured, and exported to the Torque Game Engine. More advanced low poly techniques will be presented in Chapter 7, "Character Modeling."

When it comes to low poly modeling, there are two primary modeling features: Editable Mesh, and Editable Poly. Editable Poly is in most cases the best tool because it has been enhanced so much over the years, and it allows you to handle more geometry more effectively because you are dealing with polygons instead of triangles. You can convert a model from Editable Poly to Editable Mesh or vice versa, as often as you wish. In fact, ultimately it will be necessary to convert all geometry you are going to import to the Torque engine to Editable Mesh. Editable mesh geometry is made up of triangle faces, which are necessary for the Torque engine. For this reason, it is not necessary to model exclusively in quads. Because you are dealing with a real-time rendering engine that breaks down all mesh geometry into triangles anyway, triangles are acceptable in the model wherever you want to place them.

CREATING STRUCTURALLY SOUND MODELS

As you work, it is important to build upon structurally sound models. In this section, we will look at some of the components of a model and how to make sure they work together properly.

Figure 2.1, on the left side, shows two related issues: unwelded vertices and overlapping faces. Wherever there are overlapping faces, there are overlapping edges. A vertex was not properly welded to its neighbor, creating chaos in the model. This is also apparent on the right side of the box, where a weld is needed to repair the model. Simply making sure every vertex is welded and that there are no stray vertices will help to ensure that your models have integrity. In addition, this model demonstrates what a *T-junction* is. Whenever you have an edge that stops abruptly, without flowing into another edge, a T-junction is formed that creates ambiguity in the model. There should be no dead-ends in the model; all edges should flow into another edge. To repair a T-junction, you either need to remove the edge that is causing the T-junction, or you need to add one or more edges to connect it to an existing vertex. *Stray vertices* are also a problem. If a vertex does not tie at least three edges together, it is probably a stray vertex. Stray vertices can be easily removed when in Vertex sub-object mode by selecting the vertex and pressing the Backspace key, or selecting Remove from the Edit Vertices rollout. In addition to these issues, keep on the lookout for *sliver faces*. These are faces that are unusually long and thin and usually point to the need either to cut additional edges or to turn an interior edge. If given the choice between one long, thin face or two more normally proportioned faces, go with the more normally proportioned faces.

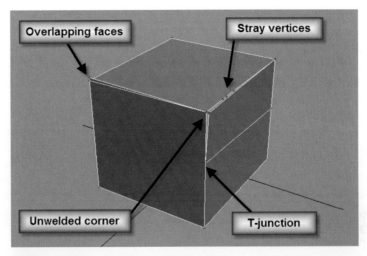

FIGURE 2.1   Things to avoid: overlapping faces, unwelded corners, stray vertices, and T-junctions.

The problems with the model in Figure 2.1 are exaggerated for clarity. Usually you will have to zoom in to see these kinds of issues; it may also be necessary to enter sub-object mode and begin to poke and prod with the Move tool until the issue becomes apparent. For example, if you are not sure if the vertices are welded in the corner of a model, you can enter Vertex sub-object mode and try selecting and moving the vertex to see what happens.

KEEPING A LOW-POLYGON BUDGET

It stands to reason that the fewer faces you have, the better your game performance, particularly for machines that are on the slow side. The manufacturers of the Torque engine recommend a maximum of 500 faces for weapons and a maximum of 2,250 faces for characters. All other objects in the scene should be kept to a minimum face count. Face counts should be made based on triangle counts, not polygon counts. An Editable Poly is based on polygons, which are actually two triangles, whereas an Editable Mesh is based on triangles, so it pays to know which type of model you are working with. To arrive at the correct number, count the faces in an Editable Mesh, or double the face count in an Editable Poly. One way to count faces is to use the 7 hotkey, which displays face counts of any selected model. A good tool for counting faces is the Polygon Counter; to launch it, go to the Utilities panel, click on More, and select Polygon Counter. This counter lets you choose whether you want to count triangles or polygons for selected objects as well as the entire scene. It also lets you set size limits. Finally, you can find an overall summary of the faces used in the scene by going to File, Summary Info.

Thinking low poly is really an acquired state of mind. You are on a serious budget, where exceeding the budget can mean you must remove other meshes from the game or pay a performance penalty. Making your assets low poly is much more effectively done early on, rather than having to remove polygons later. The Multires and Optimize modifiers can help you simplify a model quickly, but the resulting mesh is never as clean and ordered as you can achieve by hand, by doing it the right way initially.

Typically, a low poly model starts as a box primitive. This depends on the geometry of the shape you are trying to achieve, however, and it is a good idea to be familiar with all the primitives (box, sphere, cone, plane, and so on) and extended primitives (capsule, oil tank, and so on) available from the Create panel so that you can save modeling time. In Chapter 1, "Introduction to 3ds Max," a box primitive was used to start the modeling process. This was because the box has characteristics that make it suitable for modeling a chair. For an oil drum, a different sort of primitive must be used.

MODELING A SIMPLE SHAPE

The first model to create will represent an oil drum. A cylinder primitive will work well because it already has the general shape necessary. Later you can use a texture to make this look like an oil drum, so you don't need a lot of detail. The model itself can be a simple cylinder with 12 sides. In Figure 2.2, note that the drum at the left is wasting a huge number of faces, because it has 5 height segments that do not appreciably affect the shape of the drum. The cylinder in the middle is wasting faces also, because it has more than enough side segments to suggest roundness. For the purposes of a game, 12 sides and 1 segment is more than adequate.

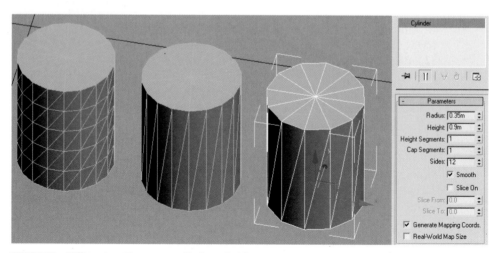

FIGURE 2.2   Different settings on a cylinder primitive.

Another thing to note in Figure 2.2 is the size of the cylinder. The units for this session of Max have been set to meters as the default unit type. Because the Torque Game Engine considers every unit a meter, it makes sense to design in meters. You can set units in 3ds Max from the Customize drop-down menu by clicking on Units Setup and then selecting Metric. Because the average character in Torque is about two meters high, the oil drum should be only a meter or so high. Create a cylinder similar to the one shown on the right in Figure 2.2 that is a little over one meter tall, and make sure your viewport is set to Shaded with Edges so that you can see what you are doing. Save the model as `OilDrum.max`. A completed version of this file is available on the companion CD-ROM. It is named `OilDrumTextured.max` and is located in `Files\OilDrum`.

ON THE CD

MODELING A HEALTH PATCH

Our next model will be made of three meshes and will be used as a health pickup in the game.

Figure 2.3 shows the first four steps to creating this model. Start with a cone that has 6 sides and 2 height segments. Make the cone a little less than 1 meter high. Then convert it to an Editable Poly by right-clicking on it and selecting Convert to Editable Poly. In the Editable Poly menu, go into Polygon sub-object mode, and select all the polygons on the object. In the Polygon Properties group, under Smoothing Groups, click the Clear All button. This should turn off any inherent smoothing and give you some nice, faceted faces as are apparent in stage B. At stage C, the model is in Vertex sub-object mode, and all the vertices along the waistline of

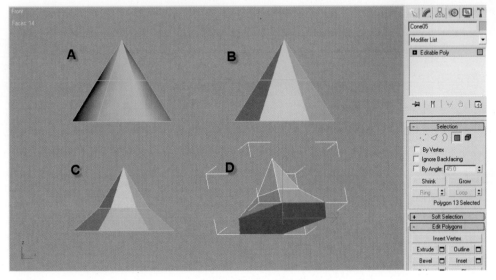

FIGURE 2.3   Four stages in the development of a simple pickup model.

the object have been selected with a selection window and scaled down slightly. You may also want to move the vertices up or down a bit to get the look you want. Stage D involves getting into Polygon sub-object mode again, using Arc Rotate to look underneath the model, clicking on the bottom polygon, and pressing the Delete key on your keyboard to delete it.

When the bottom is open, we can go to the front view and, using Edge sub-object mode, select all six edges at the bottom of the model, hold down the Shift key on the keyboard, and simultaneously move the edges down. This technique copies the edges, in effect forming new polygons. It is important to note that copying these edges only works if you delete the polygon under the model first, as indicated in Figure 2.3. Edges must be "free" or open to be copied. Figure 2.4 depicts the process of moving the selected edges (while the Shift key is held down) to create additional polygons.

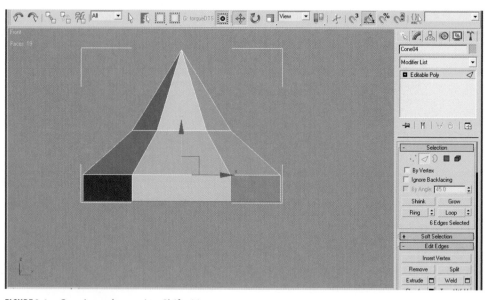

FIGURE 2.4   Copying edges using Shift+Move.

The view in Figure 2.5 is from under the model. Make sure to use Arc Rotate to arrive at new viewpoints. Do not make the mistake of using the Rotate tool for this. The Rotate tool will actually rotate your model, and you will end up with a misaligned model. However, if this misalignment does happen to you, create a box primitive and use the Align tool on the Standard toolbar to align your model to the box. Select the misaligned object, and then go to Tools, Align; pick the box primitive; and from the Align dialog box, check the boxes for X, Y, and Z axis in the Align Orientation group.

In this last phase, you are once again copying edges, but this time using Scale+Shift instead of Move+Shift. This enables you to close the opening in the base of the model, or at least get most of the way there. Continue scaling the edges even beyond what is shown in Figure 2.5, until you end up with a very small opening, which you can weld together in the next step.

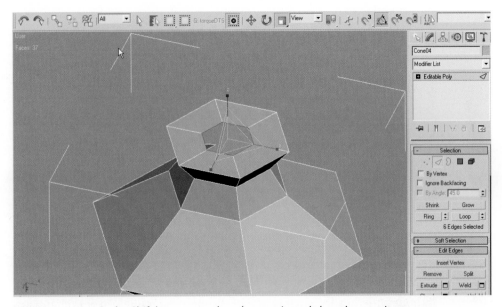

FIGURE 2.5   Using Scale+Shift key to copy the edges again and close the opening.

Welding Vertices with Weld Threshold

Looking at Figure 2.6, the opening is quite small, but still apparent. To completely weld this hole shut, you need to select the vertices. If you still have the edges selected, try holding down the Shift key while you click on Vertex mode. This should convert the selection set from edges to vertices. Depending on your version of 3ds Max, this may not work, in which case you can select the vertices with a selection window. In this image, you can see the number of vertices selected listed in the Selection rollout; this feedback can help you stay on track.

Now that you are in Vertex sub-object mode, go to the Edit Vertices rollout and click the Weld Settings button (to the right of the Weld button). This should bring up the dialog box you see in Figure 2.6, which allows you to set a threshold for welding. This process only works for the *selected* vertices. Notice the setting Number of Vertices, Before and After. In this example, there are 42 vertices in the entire model. When you move the Weld Threshold value up, it zeros in on the selected vertices and, if they are within the threshold distance, welds them together. Use this tool by moving the Weld Threshold value higher and higher as you watch both the vertices and the number readout. In this case, when the six vertices seem to become one vertex, or when Number of Vertices goes down to 37, you know you are done.

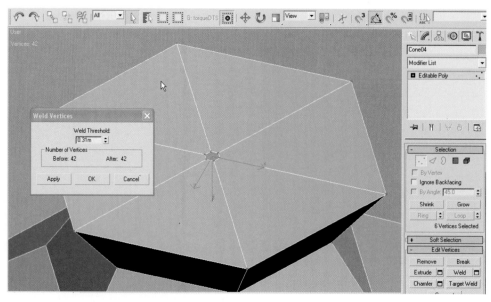

FIGURE 2.6   Adjusting a weld threshold.

Creating a Pickup with Three Parts

Although the health patch is one of the simplest models in this chapter, it will ultimately have some of the most complex materials. Torque allows you to have more than one mesh in a shape, which presents some interesting possibilities when it comes to materials. In Figure 2.7, the top of the health patch model has been collapsed by moving the upper vertex down, and two additional cones have been placed against the main model. Both of these have faces removed where they meet

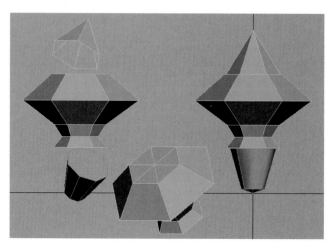

FIGURE 2.7   Three separate meshes make up our health pickup.

the main body of the health pickup. These faces are removed because they will not be seen, and you don't need them. To remove faces, get into Polygon sub-object mode, select Polygons, and press the Delete key on your keyboard.

Finally, convert the model to an Editable Mesh, and save the file as `HealthPatch. max`. A copy of this file with texturing applied is located on the companion CD-ROM. It is named `HealthPatchTextured.max`, and it is located in `Files\HealthPatch`.

ON THE CD

MODELING A POWER CHARGER

The majority of this geometry will be modeled using an eight-sided cone. Refer to Figure 2.8 for the approximate size and shape of the cone; the completed model is shown at the left, and the starting primitive is shown at the right. Here, more height segments make sense, because you need varying diameters to follow the shape in the finished example. Note that the height of this model is only 16, but that refers to 16 meters. In the game, this model will be about the size of a four-story building.

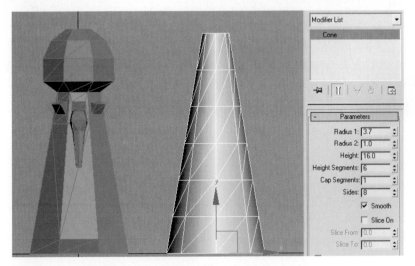

FIGURE 2.8   Starting the power station with an 8-sided cone.

Figure 2.9 shows the process of selecting all the polygons in the model and clearing any smoothing that may already exist. This is always a good idea because you are better able to see what you are doing, and you don't want to operate under any random assumptions. If you want to use smoothing later, you can do so as a deliberate choice when the model is ready for it.

In Figure 2.10, in Vertex sub-object mode, the vertices are being windowed, one row at a time, and moved up toward the top of the model. Then each row of vertices is scaled with the Select and Uniform Scale tool. In the image, you can see that the Scale button is turned on, and the Scale gizmo is active on a set of vertices. At this point, the model is almost ready for additional features.

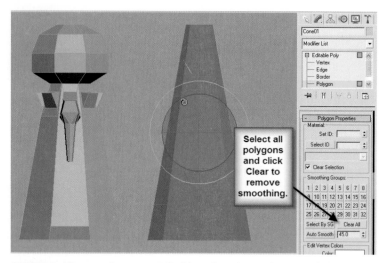

FIGURE 2.9   The cone is now an Editable Poly. Select Polygon and Clear All under Smoothing Groups.

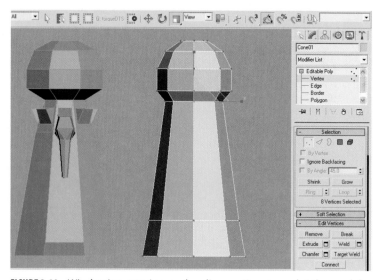

FIGURE 2.10   Windowing, moving, and scaling vertices to sculpt the model.

One of the first things to notice is that there is a different rotation on the two models. The finished model at the left has flat polygons facing the front view, whereas the primitive on the right has its edges facing the front view. If you are going to build on to this model, it makes sense to do it in a way that is easily editable from the established orthographic views. That is, you should try to set up this model so that you can easily add and edit different features by going to the standard viewing modes—that is, top view, left view, front view, and so on.

Figure 2.11 shows the same two models from the top view, so that the different rotations of the models are more apparent.

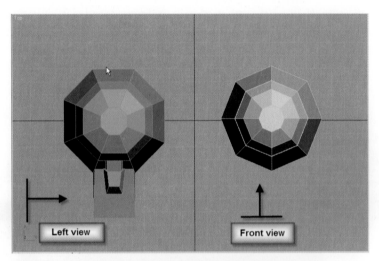

FIGURE 2.11   From the top view, you can see the different orientations of the two models.

To set up the new model in the proper orientation, you need to figure out how many degrees each segment of the eight-sided cone includes. If you start with 360 degrees and divide that by 8, you get 45 degrees for each side. This means that if you rotate the model 45 degrees, it will still have edges lined up to the standard views instead of polygons as we would prefer. To get the polygons to face the front view, rotate the model *half* of 45 degrees, or 22.5 degrees. See Figure 2.12.

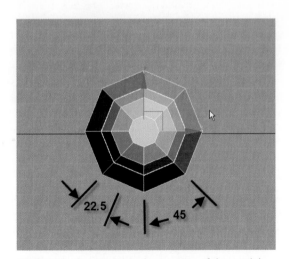

FIGURE 2.12   Determining the rotation of the model.

Before rotating the model, make sure you are out of sub-object mode, and that the model is selected. To rotate the model 22.5 degrees, you need to adjust the Angular Snap value so that when you rotate the model, it will snap to that value. To do this, right-click on the Angle Snap toggle on the Standard toolbar. Adjust the Angle setting to 2.5 degrees, as shown in Figure 2.13, click the red X at the upper-right corner of the dialog box to close it, and then rotate the model 22.5 degrees.

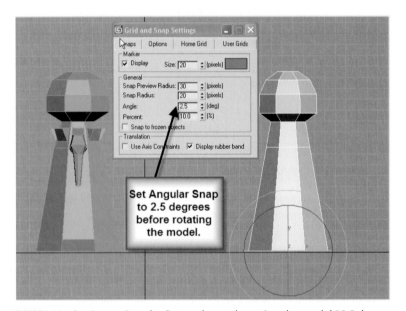

FIGURE 2.13   Setting an Angular Snap value and rotating the model 22.5 degrees.

Use the F hotkey to get into the Front view. Make a cut in this front polygon so you can create a ramp for the character to stand on when he is charging his weapon. Select the polygon and extrude the ramp; now that you have a good orthogonal view of the ramp, meaning you can look at it straight-on from the Front view, you can go to Vertex sub-object mode and move vertices to make the ramp line up.

Finally, go ahead and weld the vertices at the end of the ramp so it makes a smooth transition to the ground (see Figure 2.15).

Convert this model to an Editable Mesh and then inspect it, looking for how the topology has changed from when the model was an Editable Poly. Depending on how you worked, you may find a flaw similar to Figure 2.16 on the right side of the model. The edge that was cut for the ramp left two T-junctions in the model. An edge has been exposed that is not as effective for unwrapping or proper shading and lighting as if the edge were going the other way. You can turn this edge now, or you can take care to remove the T-junction before you convert the model to an Editable Mesh. If you want to turn the edge, look ahead to Figure 2.31 for an example of how this is done. Be warned that this takes a little practice. Handle these ambiguous

FIGURE 2.14   After the ramp is extruded, adjust the vertices from the Left view.

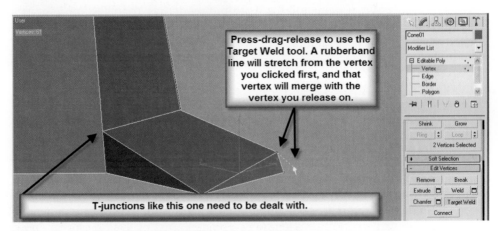

Press-drag-release to use the Target Weld tool. A rubberband line will stretch from the vertex you clicked first, and that vertex will merge with the vertex you release on.

T-junctions like this one need to be dealt with.

FIGURE 2.15   Using Target Weld to weld two vertices together.

areas before they become a problem by cutting edges yourself before converting an Editable Poly to an Editable Mesh. Whenever you see a T-junction, either remove the offending edge, or create additional cuts until the T-junction no longer exists.

Make sure to convert the model back to an Editable Poly so you can continue to take advantage of the more robust tools it provides. In Figure 2.17, the model has been converted back to an Editable Poly, and the T-junctions have been removed by making cuts. You can think of this as relieving pressure, because a T-junction will otherwise be prone to creating havoc with your model if left untreated. Another

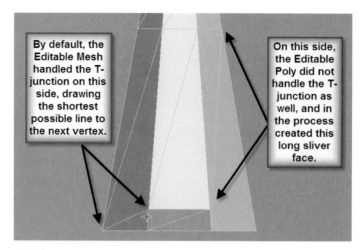

FIGURE 2.16   Note the result of leaving T-junctions in the Editable Poly.

way of looking at it is that you are tying off the vertex so that it is no longer a liability. A T-junction, when not tied off, can create five sides on the neighboring polygon. When modeling for real-time rendering, triangles are fine, as are quads, although you may have to turn the inside edge on some of the quad. But leaving five or more sides on a polygon leaves too much to chance in how the polygon will be divided into triangles.

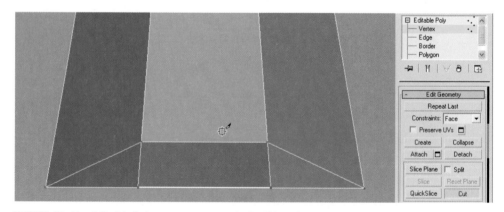

FIGURE 2.17   The Editable Poly gets cuts to repair the T-junctions.

Figure 2.18 depicts an inset being made. Select a polygon, and from the Edit Polygons rollout, click the Inset settings button to launch the dialog box. If you have more than one polygon selected, try both the Group setting and the By Polygon setting. By Polygon allows each polygon to perform its own inset.

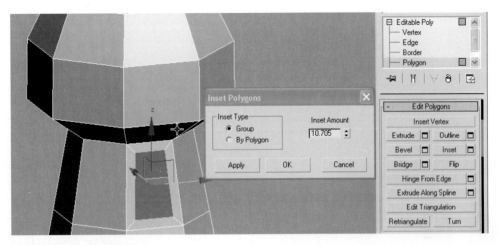

FIGURE 2.18   Creating an inset.

Once the inset is created, you may want to adjust the vertices so that they are not a simple offset from the original polygon edges. To do so, get into Vertex sub-object mode, and select any two vertices that you want to bring closer together or spread further apart. Use the Select and Uniform Scale tool to scale them along the axis they share. This method is used in Figure 2.19 to make the inset more square-shaped, rather than the rectangular shape that its parent polygon has. You can also select all four vertices and scale them along an axis.

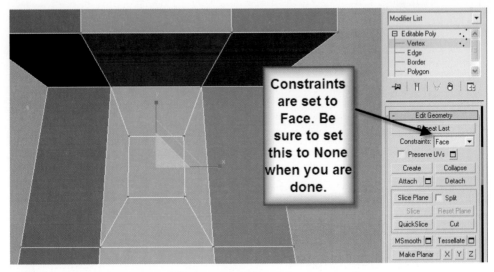

FIGURE 2.19   Scaling the vertices of the inset while Constraints are set to Face.

The Edit Geometry rollout has a Constraints setting that is usually set to None. If you set it to Face, it keeps your vertices constrained to the face of the polygon while you are scaling them, saving you repair work later. Make sure to set Constraints back to None when you have completed your task so that you can edit vertices normally again.

While working on only one face here, it is important to note that you can inset all the faces on the model at once by using the By Polygon option. Also, with Constraints set to Face, you can move the vertices to adjust the size of the inset as an entire row, quickly arriving at a model similar to Figure 2.23. However, the process of developing a model with effective use of polygons is sometimes best done one panel at a time and then cloning copies of that panel into place. This is particularly true the more complex a panel gets.

Figure 2.20 shows another useful feature of the Editable Poly menu, Hinge from Edge. This feature is good for building on to existing faces and changing the face angle at the same time. Take a moment to experiment with multiple segments and different angle values.

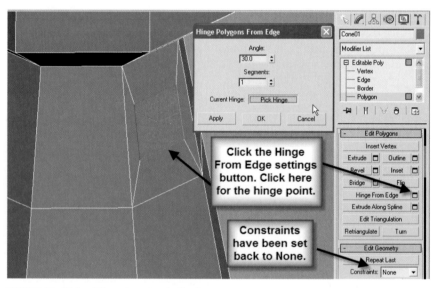

FIGURE 2.20   Using Hinge to extrude the face.

Developing this panel took some time. Rather than go through that process on every panel around the model, detach this panel and rotate copies of it into position around the original model. Make sure you are in Polygon sub-object mode, and select all the faces, as shown in Figure 2.21. From the Edit Geometry rollout, click the Detach button. Name this new object `Hinged Panel`. This effectively creates a new object, which you can replicate all the way around the model.

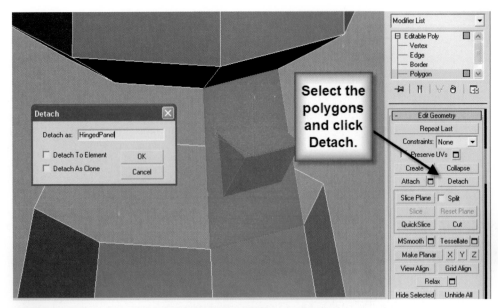

FIGURE 2.21   One section is selected, detached, and given a name.

You have to get out of sub-object mode to exit the main model and select the Hinged Panel object you just created. In Figure 2.22, you can see that the Hinged Panel object has been selected, and the Rotate gizmo is active. If you hold down the Shift key while you are rotating around the Z axis (the Z axis is highlighted yellow because it is selected here), you launch the Clone Options dialog box. Make sure your settings match those in the figure, typing in seven copies (seven new copies, + one original = eight total copies). Max divides 360 degrees into 8 and places one copy every 45 degrees. You want to copy here because you want each element created to be a separate object; soon they will be joined back together with the original model.

Clicking Attach, as shown on Figure 2.23, allows you to select any object you want to attach to the current object, one at a time. If you want to select multiple objects from a list, click the Settings button to the right of the Attach button.

At this point, the panels are attached, but their vertices have not been welded together with the main model. This is impossible to see with the naked eye, but you can prove it to yourself if you attempt to move one of the vertices where the panels meet each other. If you can move a vertex and it comes away from the model, something is wrong with that model. To weld everything together, get into Vertex sub-object mode, select all the vertices in the model, click the Weld Settings button, and manipulate the Weld Threshold value until you see a significant change in the number of vertices. If you set the Weld Threshold too high, too many vertices are welded together. To guard against this, keep a close eye on the model when you perform this operation. This type of weld only operates on *selected* vertices, so minimizing your selection set can help to control the results.

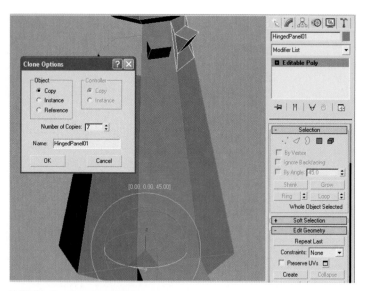

FIGURE 2.22   Rotate+Shift launches the Clone Options dialog box.

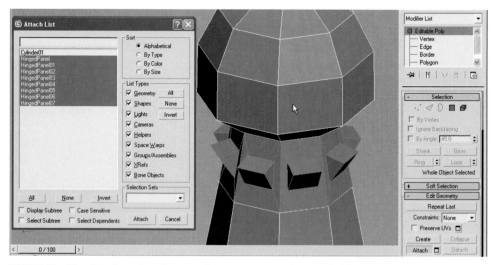

FIGURE 2.23   The Attach settings button allows you to attach several objects at once.

In Figure 2.24, an extrusion, a hinge, and another extrusion have been added to the protrusion that is on the front face of the power charger. A uniform scale is being added to the last extrusion. You can also achieve this effect by using a Bevel feature.

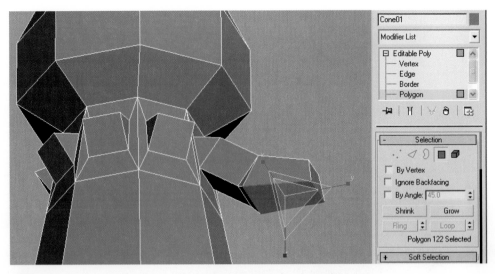

FIGURE 2.24   Scaling uniformly to add angular impact to the protrusion.

A commonly used shaping method is demonstrated in Figure 2.25, where a group of vertices has been window-selected and is going through a process of being moved and rotated to achieve a more interesting design.

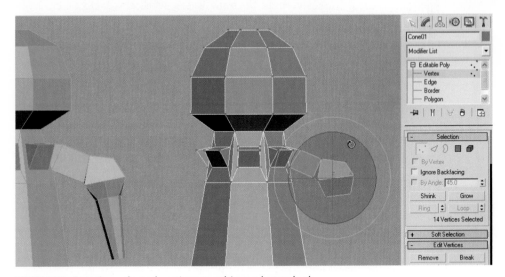

FIGURE 2.25   Rotating selected vertices to achieve a better look.

Figure 2.26 demonstrates using the uniform scale gizmo to reposition vertices. Select two, four, or more vertices and click-drag the X, Y, or Z axis to bring them closer together or farther apart.

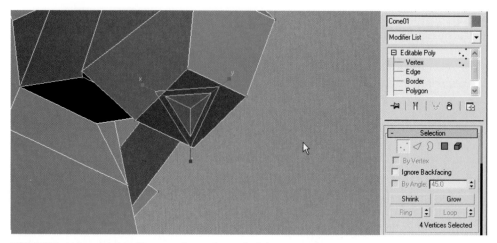

FIGURE 2.26 Using axial scaling to reshape the end of the protrusion.

If you want to snap to particular points, the 3D snap tool is useful. Set your snaps by right-clicking the Snaps toggle. Select the check boxes you want to use, and close the dialog by clicking the X in the corner. In Figure 2.27, snaps are being set to Endpoint and Midpoint.

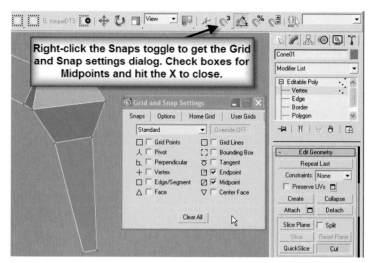

FIGURE 2.27 Snaps are being set to Endpoint and Midpoint for speed and accuracy.

If the Snaps toggle is active, your cursor should snap to whatever points you have it set to; just get into the Cut feature and feel around with the mouse for the snap, as shown in Figure 2.28. Make sure to turn the Snaps toggle off when you are finished, because this tool can make normal work difficult if it is kept on.

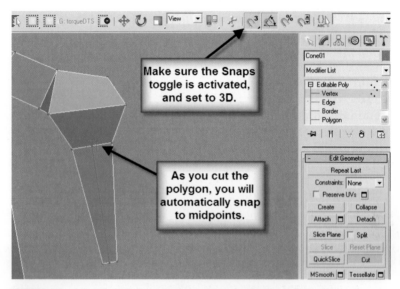

FIGURE 2.28   Using the 3D Snap tool to snap to midpoints of an edge.

In Figure 2.29, notice how the new edge created in the previous figure was terminated by connecting it to two separate vertices. This potential T-junction has been "tied off," so you should not have surprises when you convert this model to an Editable Mesh at the end of this process.

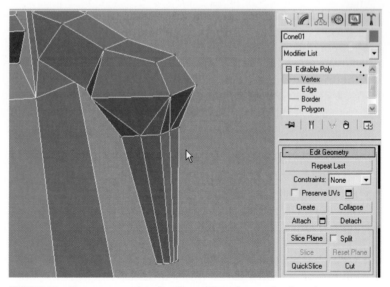

FIGURE 2.29   Cuts are completed with no T-junctions to be found.

After you have the basic edges in place, it is easy to add volume and shape to the model by moving them out a bit, as shown in Figure 2.30. This is most accurately done from an orthogonal view like front, right, left, or top.

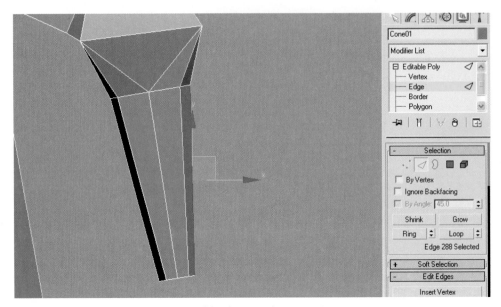

FIGURE 2.30   Moving the new edges to add volume to the protrusion.

Before this model is ready for unwrapping, it needs to be converted to an Editable Mesh. This significantly changes the look of the model, because each triangle becomes more obvious. Triangles are not obvious on an Editable Mesh while selected; you have to click on the 3ds Max background, effectively deselecting the model, to see the triangles. It is a good idea to use the Arc Rotate tool to inspect the model from all sides to check the assumptions that Editable Mesh makes about where to put triangles. In Figure 2.31, the model has been converted into an Editable Mesh, and an inside edge is being turned using the Turn button, which is available when you are in Edge sub-object mode. First activate the Turn button, and then click the edge until you like the result. For clarity, two copies of the same protrusion are shown in this image. Edge number 1 has just been turned and used to look like edge number 2.

The last step for this model is to convert it to an Editable Mesh and ensure that it still looks the way you want it to. Use the Arc Rotate tool to inspect the ways that triangles were formed, and turn any edges as necessary. In Figure 2.32, the power charger is ready to be unwrapped. Save the file as `PowerCharger.max`. A copy of this file with texturing applied is located on the companion CD-ROM. It is named `Power-ChargerTextured.max`, and it is located in `Files\PowerCharger`.

ON THE CD

FIGURE 2.31   Turning an edge to further define the shape.

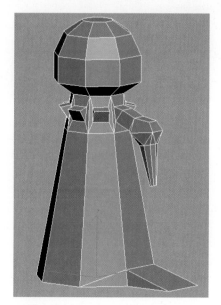

FIGURE 2.32   The model in its finished state as an Editable Mesh.

MODELING A WEAPON

To model our weapon, a plane is created in the front view and an image applied to it to use as a template. This template will serve as a guide while modeling. It's always a good idea to have references when modeling, texturing, or animating.

Creating a Template to Model By

Reset Max and set units under Customize, Units Setup to metric. Create a plane in the front view with Length equal to 200 units and Width equal to 550 units. Set Length Segments to 1 and Width Segments to 1. Use the technique discussed in Chapter 1 to apply a custom material to the object. The template material is GunTemplate.jpg, found in Files\Raygun on the companion CD-ROM.

ON THE CD

In Figure 2.33, the Material Editor is being launched in order to apply the material to the plane. From this stage in the process, you can see that GunTemplate.jpg is 550 × 200 pixels. Knowing the width and height of the template image is useful, because if you can put that template on a plane that has the same aspect, or width-to-height ratio, the image will not stretch. There are a few different ways to make a template fit well on a plane, but setting the size of the plane to the size of the image (or some multiple of the image) keeps the aspect consistent and is the most straight-forward method to explain.

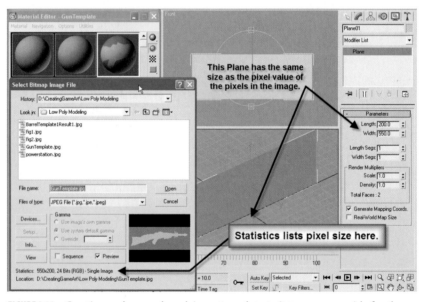

FIGURE 2.33   Creating a plane and applying a template to it to use as a guide for the model.

If the material comes in on the plane upside down or sideways, you can either rotate the plane 90 or 180 degrees and adjust the height and width values of the plane accordingly, or you can apply a UVW Map modifier and rotate the gizmo for the map as necessary. Keep Snap Angle toggle turned on at all times so your rotations are exact.

After you apply the material to the plane, freeze the plane so that you do not accidentally select it during the modeling process. Objects that are frozen cannot be selected.

What you really want here is for the plane to be frozen but the image to be visible. To do this, select the plane and right-click it. From the right-click menu, select Properties. See Figure 2.34 for a screen shot of this dialog box. Check the Freeze box and uncheck the Show Frozen in Gray box. This allows this frozen object to retain its color and material visibility. If you end up freezing the plane and the image turns gray, right-click again, select Unfreeze All, and try the procedure again.

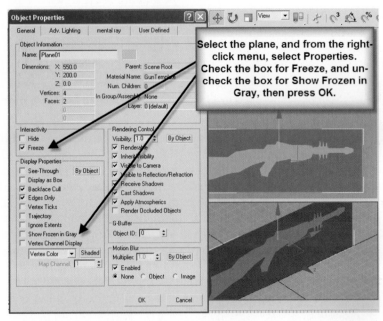

FIGURE 2.34   Turning on Freeze, and turning off Show Frozen in Gray.

Modeling with a Plane

You have modeled with 3D primitives, but you can also model with a flat plane. After your material is successfully applied to the template plane, it is time to make another plane, which can be used to build the weapon. Create a plane, and make sure it is only one segment in each direction. Position it so that it lies over the stock of the gun. Although you will be modeling in the front view, go to the top view and move the modeling plane down so that it is in front of the template. You want the modeling plane to be in front of the template plane; ultimately, you will be looking through the modeling plane at the template plane and using the template plane as a guide.

Activate and maximize the front view. Then convert the modeling plane to an Editable Poly. Right-click the Editable Poly and, from the right-click menu, select Properties to access the Properties dialog box. Click the See-Through check box to make it transparent (see Figure 2.35). You can also accomplish this using the hotkey Alt+X as a toggle for "x-ray" mode.

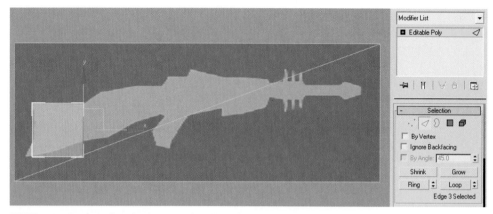

FIGURE 2.35 Convert the plane to an Editable Poly and set it to See-Through.

Move the vertices so that they fit the stock of the gun. Get into Edge sub-object mode, select the right edge of the plane and, holding down the Shift key, move the edge toward the right. Continue this Shift+Move process, following the contours of the template as well as possible along the top vertices of the plane. Figure 2.36 shows this process. Notice that the Move gizmo is visible in the image. By clicking on the yellow XY plane of the gizmo, it is easy to create each new plane. Don't worry about the lower vertices; they will be matched up later. Stop where the gun barrel starts; because the barrel is so cylindrical, you are better off using a cylinder to model it separately.

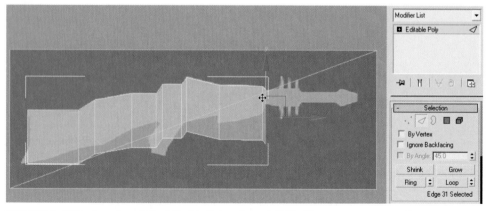

FIGURE 2.36 With the edge of the Editable Poly selected, Shift+Move creates new polygons.

In Figure 2.37, Vertex is the sub-object mode and vertices have been moved to match up with the lower points on the template. Notice that this template was designed so that the upper vertices line up with the lower vertices, and there are a planned number of segments of the gun. Having a plan makes plane-modeling go smoother. Also notice that some parts of the model are being ignored for now, and will be extruded later.

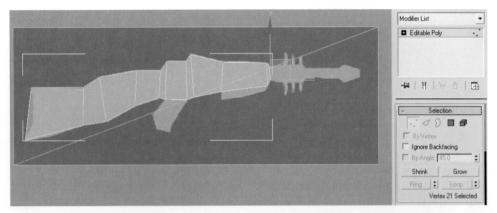

FIGURE 2.37   The vertices have been moved to conform to the template.

When you have the basic shape, add edges as necessary for the wings on the butt of the gun. (See Figure 2.38 to locate these.) Figure 2.38 also shows how to copy the edges all around the gun to add some depth to it. You will need to change your view (Arc Rotate) before you do this so that you can see the Y axis of the Move gizmo. If you need to select additional edges, hold down the Ctrl key and continue to select edges. Clicking the same edge twice deselects it. When ready, simply Shift+Move along the Y axis, as shown in the figure. Just as with the health patch, the edges are copied, in effect creating a new group of polygons.

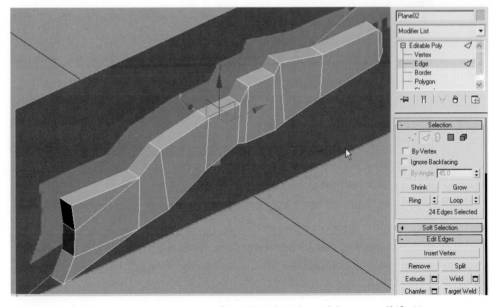

FIGURE 2.38   Select only the outside edges of the Editable Poly, and then press Shift+Move.

It is common to make a few mistakes when working with vertices and edges and end up with a mess, where the vertices and edges are no longer lying in the same plane. The next two figures demonstrate how to repair these misaligned vertices. As shown in Figure 2.39, the first step is to select all the vertices that you would like to have in a planar alignment.

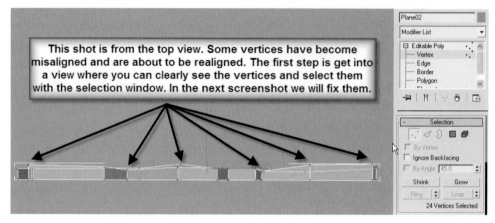

FIGURE 2.39   If you have misaligned vertices, the first step is to select them.

Figure 2.40 demonstrates what you should do with the selected vertices. Do not bother with this step unless you need to realign vertices that have somehow been moved out of alignment. The simplest way to get the selected vertices into alignment is to activate an orthogonal view that is flat to the plane you want the vertices to lie within. In Figure 2.40, this means activating the front view. Then, from the Edit Geometry rollout, click View Align. All selected vertices are then aligned with the active viewport.

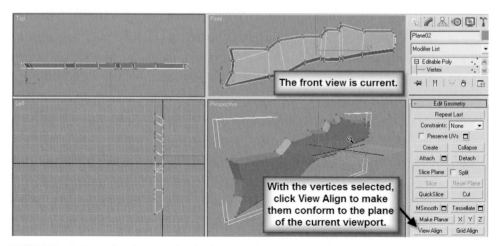

FIGURE 2.40   Activate the viewport that is planar to the vertices, and click View Align.

Move the edges and vertices as necessary to give the viewport form and volume. Try to avoid the areas that still need to be added to, where the grip is, and near the front of the gun. Figure 2.41 shows this stage of the modeling process.

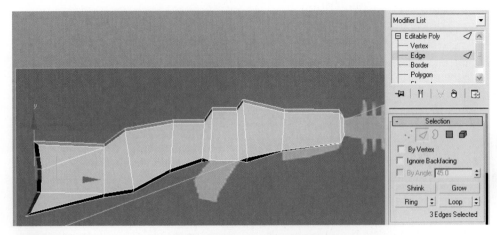

FIGURE 2.41   Adjusting the edges of the model to give it some form and volume.

Adding Symmetry to Mirror and Weld Vertices Simultaneously

Symmetry allows you to mirror a model so that it has two sides, while allowing you to weld the vertices of the two sides together. Select an edge (it doesn't matter which edge, as long as it is somewhere along the seam of the model), and add a Symmetry modifier from the Modifier drop-down list. Figure 2.42 notes a good edge to use, as well as the settings that will likely work well for you to apply symmetry correctly.

A common problem when using the symmetry feature is welding together more vertices than intended. Symmetry welds the vertices together if they are within the threshold setting. If you don't take the time to inspect your model carefully as you are adding symmetry, you may have to go back at some point and do some time-consuming rework of your mesh.

Setting the threshold too high is even more of a problem when modeling for the Torque Game Engine than otherwise; this is because for Torque, every unit is a meter. Max is unitless by default, yet most people model as though each unit were an inch. If you are designing a couch, 24 × 36 × 72 inches across, a threshold of 0.1 inch is about right; it is a small percentage of the overall size of the model. If you are designing a weapon that is 1 × 0.2 × 0.4 meters, a threshold of 0.1 meter is a large percentage of the overall size of the model. Whether you lower the threshold default on your Symmetry modifier or not, it is a good idea to inspect your model before applying symmetry and moving on.

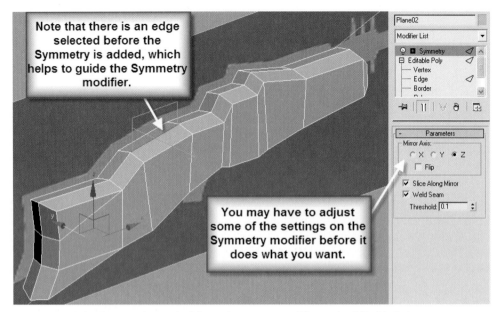

FIGURE 2.42   Selecting an edge and adding a Symmetry modifier to the Editable Poly.

Now that the model has some thickness, it's time to collapse the Symmetry modifier. It will be added again after a few more edits. To collapse a modifier in the modifier stack, right-click it and, from the resulting menu, click Collapse All (see Figure 2.43). This simplifies the model and allows you to perform necessary edits to the grip of the gun and the front area of the gun.

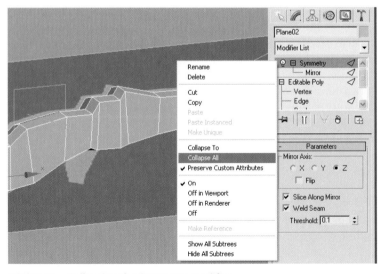

FIGURE 2.43   Collapsing the Symmetry modifier.

When you collapse a modifier, you get the warning shown in Figure 2.44. Click Yes. If you are unsure about collapsing modifiers, you can opt to click the Hold/Yes button, which saves a copy of your current modifiers. You can restore this copy by clicking Fetch from the Edit drop-down menu.

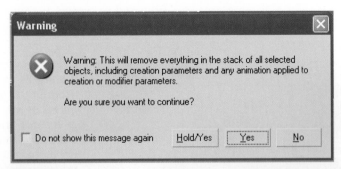

FIGURE 2.44   This warning comes up when you collapse the stack. Click Yes.

In Figure 2.45, the faces at the grip and the body of the gun are being selected and will soon be extruded a bit. The character will ultimately use these areas to grip the gun.

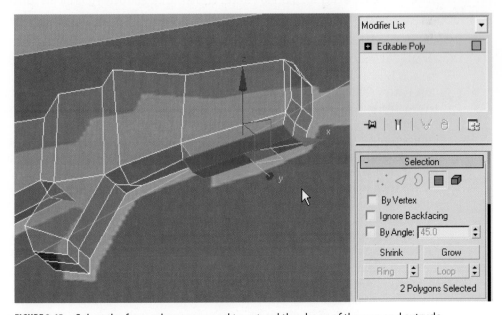

FIGURE 2.45   Select the faces where you need to extend the shape of the gun and extrude.

There is a lot going on in Figure 2.46. Two faces at the front of the gun, where the gun barrel will attach, were deleted. Two edges were added, one on each side of the gun. These edges bring the total number of edges to eight where the barrel will attach, which is perfect if you create an eight-sided barrel. Creating these edges also created a T-junction, which was dealt with by creating two edges on each side of the gun. Finally, this open area was prepared to receive the gun barrel by moving the existing eight vertices until they had a rounder shape.

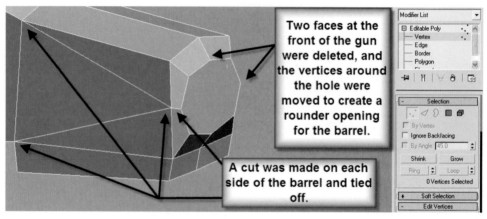

FIGURE 2.46 Adding cuts and moving vertices to prepare the end of the gun for the barrel.

In Figure 2.47, the barrel area is zoomed-in. The gun barrel could easily be created by extruding a cylinder, the same way the power charger was built. However, it is actually faster to draw a line (which creates a spline) and revolve it into a gun barrel shape. Go to the Create panel, choose Shapes, and select the Line tool. Draw this line in the front view, and make sure your settings match those in this screenshot; in the Creation Method rollout, Initial Type should be Corner, and Drag Type should be Corner. These are the best settings for low poly splines, because they minimize the number of faces created. When you get the Close Spline dialog box, click Yes. If you do not get this dialog box, delete the line and start over.

As long as the line is still selected, you can go to the modify panel, enter Vertex sub-object mode, and move the vertices around until you are satisfied with the shape of the gun barrel, as shown in Figure 2.48.

Go into Segment sub-object mode, select the axis of the line (the upper horizontal line segment) and, from the Modifier List, add a Lathe modifier. This will not come up looking proper at first; you will have to adjust some of the settings shown in Figure 2.49. Direction will probably need to be set to X, for instance. Even then, the lathed shape will look like it is inside out, which is common for lathed objects. The face normals have become flipped, meaning that they are facing the wrong way.

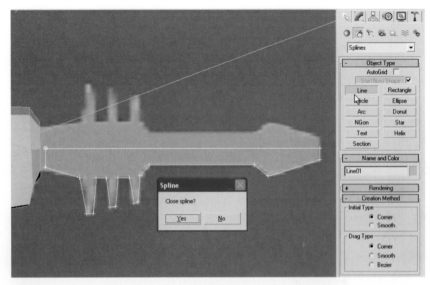

FIGURE 2.47   Drawing a spline, which we will lathe for the gun barrel.

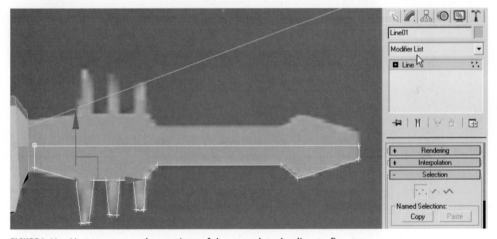

FIGURE 2.48   You can move the vertices of the completed spline to fine-tune.

Just check the Flip Normals check box, and it should look like the gun barrel in the image. Finally, set the number of segments to 8, so this gun barrel will match up to the gun body that is waiting for it.

Now that the lathe has been used to create our barrel, right-click the barrel and select Convert to Editable Poly.

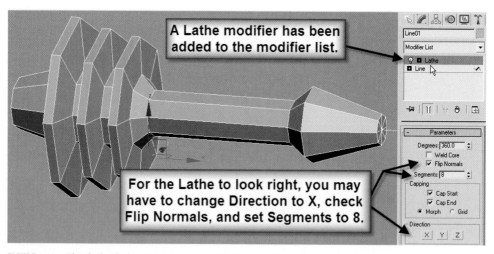

FIGURE 2.49   This lathed object took some adjusting via the menu at the right.

The first thing to deal with on this gun barrel is to delete the faces where it will attach to the gun body. This is necessary because you cannot weld the two shapes together otherwise—you need openings in both ends for the vertex welds to work.

There are two views shown in Figure 2.50: top view and front view. Use them both to make sure your gun barrel is aligned to the rest of the gun before getting into the attachment procedure.

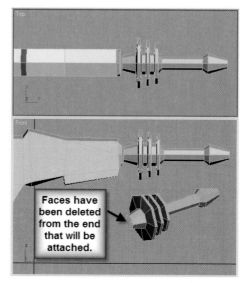

FIGURE 2.50   Both parts aligned. Polygons have been removed where they will attach.

Select either the gun body or the gun barrel, and use Attach to attach one object to the other. At that point, the two will actually be one editable body, even though you can see some space between them.

Figure 2.51 is a close-up of the vertices at the end of the gun body being welded to the gun barrel. By welding from the gun body to the gun barrel geometry, you take advantage of the more perfect cylindrical alignment of the vertices that the gun barrel has. This is because it was lathed, whereas the vertices at the end of our gun body were positioned by hand and guesswork.

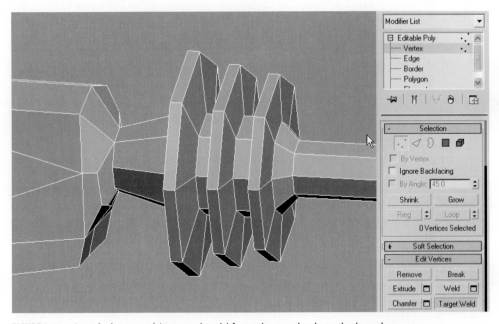

FIGURE 2.51   Attach the two objects and weld from the gun body to the barrel.

Now that you have the basic shape of the gun complete, it is time to delete half of the polygons. This sets up the model for another Symmetry modifier. This is being done so that more modeling and tweaking can be done on only one side of the gun, yet it will affect the other side of the gun simultaneously. In Figure 2.52, the top view is current for a clear shot of these polygons, which can then be selected with the selection window.

In Figure 2.53, symmetry has been added. Remember to select an edge along the seam of the model before adding symmetry; this helps 3ds Max know where the middle of the symmetry is. You can now edit one side of the gun and have the other side stay in sync. Notice in this image that the Editable Poly is the current modifier, yet the Symmetry modifier is active. This is a powerful feature—the ability to work with the foundational geometry yet see the results of a Symmetry modifier that was added later. The key to making this work is that the Show End Results On/Off toggle is toggled On.

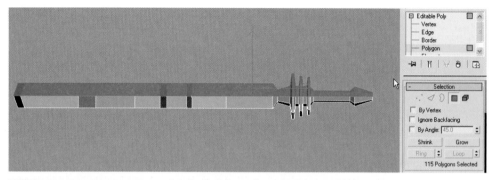

FIGURE 2.52 From the top view, select half of the polygons, delete, and resymmetry.

FIGURE 2.53 Move vertices on one side of the gun, and the other side stays in sync.

Symmetry is a great tool that can allow you to work twice as fast as usual in many circumstances. It is deceptively easy to get caught up in modeling both sides of a symmetrical object; this is a waste of your time. Symmetry can allow you to work on only one side of the object yet see the results of your efforts on the entire model dynamically. If you need to add a feature that is unique to one side of the model, add it after you have collapsed the Symmetry modifier.

At this point, the gun is pretty much ready to go. Perform a final collapse of the Symmetry modifier, convert the model to an Editable Mesh, and inspect the triangles to see that the form and flow of the edges is still satisfactory. Save the file as `Raygun.max`. A copy of this file in its completed state is named `RayGunTextured.max` and is located in `Files\Raygun` on the companion CD-ROM.

ON THE CD

Scaling Models to Fit the Torque Engine

If you imported this weapon in to the Torque Game Engine as it is, it would be as big as a skyscraper, but you can scale it down easily. Get into Vertex sub-object mode, and perform a uniform Scale on the model. Check the actual size of the model by selecting it and then right-clicking Properties. The Properties menu displays a size for X, Y, and Z dimensions of the model. Scale all the vertices of the model until the longest dimension is approximately equal to 1 meter.

If you scale a model and you are not in a sub-object mode, 3ds Max does not register the actual change in scale properly. The model appears a different size, but if you check the properties of the model, the scale has not changed. This can affect how Torque sees the model as well. For that reason, it is recommended that if you have to scale a model, you either do it at the sub-object level, or you scale it normally and use a method known as the box trick to force 3ds Max to reevaluate the scale of the model.

The box trick involves creating a box primitive, converting it to an Editable Poly or Editable Mesh, using Attach to attach your model to the box, and then, at the Polygon sub-object level, deleting the polygons that make up the box. This leaves you with a model that has in effect been reevaluated by 3ds Max and will now register the proper dimensions in Properties.

SUMMARY

We've built a simple shape, a pickup, a power charger, and a weapon. Each of these models has taught us something about 3ds Max that is essential to being a well-rounded modeler. The simple shape taught us about taking care when setting segments on primitives. The health patch gave us more practice with sub-objects, as well as showing us how to copy edges, threshold welds, scaling vertices, and deleting faces. The power station took us through clearing smoothing groups, working with Angular Snap, targeting welds, dealing with T-junctions, creating insets, using the scale gizmo axes, applying face constraints, creating a hinge, detaching faces, copying with the Clone tool, and using the 3D snap. The weapon exercise covered creating a template in the viewport, plane modeling, using view align, applying symmetry, collapsing the modifier stack, creating and editing a spline, using the Lathe modifier, and scaling a model.

In the next chapter, we will look at ways to unwrap these models so that we can effectively paint textures on them.

UNWRAPPING GAME ART

In This Chapter

- Unwrapping the Oil Drum
- Unwrapping the Weapon
- Unwrapping the Ammo Box
- Unwrapping the Power Charger
- Unwrapping the Health Patch

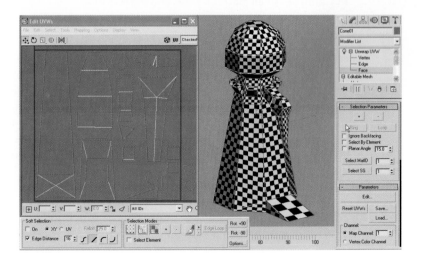

Unwrapping is by no means absolutely necessary for putting a material on a model; the example in Chapter 1, "Introduction to 3ds Max," demonstrates how to apply a custom material to a model. This may be completely adequate for some models and situations, but it almost always results in a general kind of texture that doesn't allow for details like edges of panels, rivets, eyes, wrinkles, and so forth. For more compelling and precise textures, you need to unwrap the model.

Unwrapping is a means of flattening a 3D model so that you can paint on it. It is like taking the skin off a 3D model and laying it flat like a canvas. It is of additional help if the faces you unwrap are right-side up, the way you would normally look at them, so that as you paint them they make sense. Effort and detail in this phase of the process make the texturing phase go that much more smoothly and ultimately result in better work.

UNWRAPPING THE OIL DRUM

It is good to start unwrapping with something simple like the oil drum, because unwrapping can be confusing the first several times you do it. Working through these examples will prepare you for the more challenging process of unwrapping a character, which will be addressed in Chapter 8, "Character Unwrapping."

Deciding Between Material Color and Object Color

In Figure 3.1, the Display panel is active. In the Display Color rollout on the Display panel, Shaded is set to Material Color. It is recommended that you keep Shaded set to Material Color at all times; setting Shaded to Object Color can sometimes lead to confusion when you have forgotten about this setting, and cannot figure out why your materials are not showing up on the model.

Some materials are so detailed that it can be difficult to see the polygons and their edges. If you want to create a material that is easy to work with for the unwrapping phase, select a new sample slot from the Material Editor, and click the color box next to Diffuse in the Blinn Basic Parameters rollout. Select a light color and apply it to the model. If you work with lighter colors, it is easier to see faces and edges when working in the viewports.

Also notice in this figure that you can use the Display panel to turn off helpers. (This includes dummy objects, which the Torque Exporter uses as markers.) You will want to revisit this panel when it's time to turn the display of dummy objects on or off.

Turning Off Smoothing

Unwrapping a model while smoothing is applied can distort the unwrap process. The cylinder on the left in Figure 3.2 has smoothing applied to all the polygons. 3ds Max is trying to make the facets look like they blend smoothly, which looks strange particularly when the top faces of the cylinder are 90 degrees off from the walls of

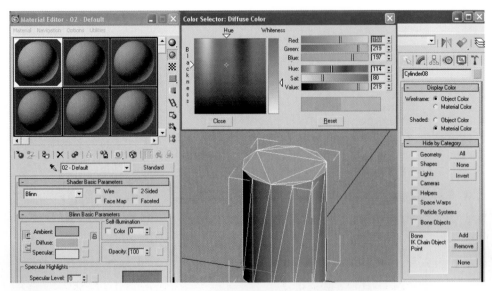

FIGURE 3.1   Ready to unwrap. Take note of the Object Color and Material Color options.

the cylinder. This was done by selecting all the polygons in the cylinder and clicking on a Smoothing Group number in the Surface Properties rollout.

A better application for smoothing groups is to select just the walls of the cylinder and assign them to a single smoothing group; then you can assign the top and bottom faces to another group, as shown on the cylinder to the right in Figure 3.2. The cylinder in the middle has all smoothing turned off, by selecting all polygons and then clicking the All Clear button. This is the way you want your cylinder set up for unwrapping. This image looks like it no longer has triangles on the top polygon. This is because it is selected; faceting lines appear only when the Editable Poly is deselected.

Applying a Cylindrical Map to the Model

By your applying a UVW map to the model, 3ds Max knows how to paint material onto the model. You can add a UVW map in 3ds Max 8 in two ways: via the UVW Map modifier, and via the Unwrap UV modifier. You may want to apply a Cylindrical map via the UVW Map modifier, as this method is also available to earlier releases of 3ds Max.

To apply the UVW Map modifier, make sure the model is selected but that you are not in sub-object mode. Go to the Modifier drop-down list and select UVW Map. From the Parameters rollout, in the Mapping group, click the Cylindrical radio button. This places a Cylindrical map around your model, as shown in Figure 3.3. If this model were not already a cylinder, you would normally have to make some adjustments in the alignment or fit of the map to your model. One of these options is to directly manipulate the UVW gizmo that is a part of the UVW Map modifier.

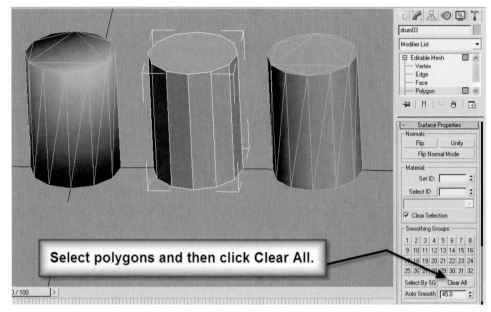

FIGURE 3.2 Turn off smoothing before you unwrap the model.

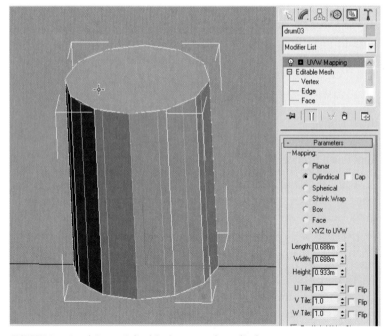

FIGURE 3.3 Applying a Cylindrical map to the cylinder.

Figure 3.4 displays alignment and fit options for the UVW map. Although the Cylindrical map will work fine, this figure is included to illustrate how you could manipulate the UVW Map Gizmo should you need to. At the upper right of this screen shot, you can see that clicking on the + (plus sign) to the right of the UVW Map modifier in the modifier stack opens the UVW Mapping modifier so you can access the gizmo. After you've selected the gizmo, you can rotate, move, or scale it as necessary if the alignment and fit controls are not giving the desired result.

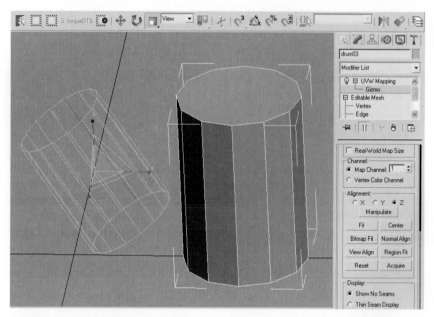

FIGURE 3.4   UVW Map Alignment options, and manipulating the UVW Map gizmo.

Applying an Unwrap UVW Modifier

You do not need to make special modifications to the gizmo at this time. Make sure you still have a cylindrical UVW map applied to the cylinder. Select the model (make sure you are not in any of the sub-object modes), and from the Modifier drop-down list, apply an Unwrap UVW modifier. Click the Edit button as shown in Figure 3.5 to open the Edit UVWs dialog box. The first thing to notice about this dialog box is that you can resize it by click-dragging the edges. This can be necessary, depending on your screen resolution, if you want to see the entire interface. Note in the screen shot the many tools at the bottom of the interface. If your tools are not completely visible, resize the window and move it around by dragging the title bar until you can see the entire dialog box from top to bottom. You will also notice that this one has been resized a bit horizontally so that you can see the model in the viewport at the same time.

The green lines you see in the dialog box are seams for the texture. Just like a clothing designer has to have seams to get a flat material to fit onto a 3D person, when you unwrap a 3D object, you are flattening it out, forming seams. The white lines are the edges between the different faces or triangles, and the checked background is a default background that will soon be turned off for clarity.

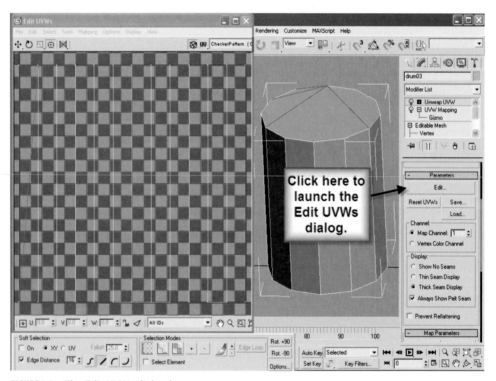

FIGURE 3.5   The Edit UVWs dialog box.

The defaults for this dialog box make it difficult to see what is really going on. Figure 3.6 shows you how to turn off the Background map and the grid. With these distractions out of the way, it is easier to recognize edges and seams. Also note in this image the check box for Constant Update in Viewports. This setting can give you real-time updates in the viewport as you adjust the UVs in the Edit UVWs dialog box, although it may be too compute intensive for some machines.

Before going any further with the Edit UVWs dialog box, look at the interface. In addition to the display tools noted in Figure 3.7, you have the same capabilities as you do with 3ds Max to spin the mouse wheel for a zoom, and press-drag the middle mouse button to pan. At the lower right are sub-object selection modes similar to those available when working with an Editable Poly. At the lower left are the Soft Selection tools. The drop-down menus are at the upper left, along with the transform tools for Move, Rotate, Scale, Freeform mode, and Mirror. Note that the Move, Scale, and Mirror buttons have flyouts that provide further functionality. Freeform mode is a tool that combines move, rotate, and scale, but this added functionality comes at a price, as the tool can take some getting used to. It is suggested for now that you stick with the basic transform tools.

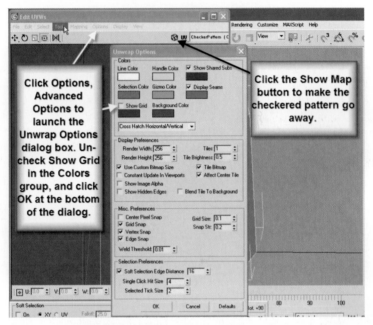

FIGURE 3.6   Making the Edit UVWs dialog box easier to look at.

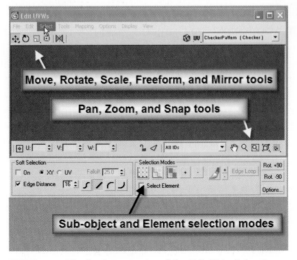

FIGURE 3.7   The basic anatomy of the Edit UVs dialog box.

If you look at Figure 3.8, you can see the cylindrical walls lie flat; they have become a little elongated, but that can be fixed. An angled seam is running across the leftmost face, but that can be repaired. One serious problem is that there is no way to account for the top and bottom of the cylinder.

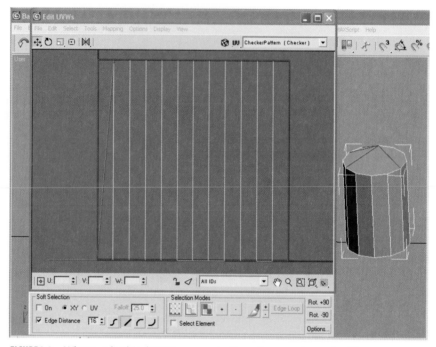

FIGURE 3.8   What a cylindrical UVW map projection gives you to work with.

When you apply the Cylindrical map to the model, it sees everything from the side, or from all sides, but it does not look from above or below. So the top and the bottom of the model appear as lines at the top and bottom of the UVs; the top and bottom faces are being seen edge-on. You can see the bottom of the cylinder best in Figure 3.8, where it appears as a line.

The standard approach for unwrapping a model is to select the faces that conform to a particular UVW map, like the cylindrical walls, and separate them from the rest of the UVs. You can select the cylindrical walls and move them away from the rest of the model, and then you can deal with the top and the bottom UVs of the cylinder. Make sure you are in Face sub-object mode, activate the Move tool, and make an implied window (press-drag-release) across the UVs for the walls of the cylinder. Take care that your implied window does not select the top and bottom of the cylinder. Now try to move the UVs.

What you should see is shown in Figure 3.9. Because the walls are still attached to the top and bottom of the cylinder, there is some stretching going on. You will have to undo this move until you can break the selection set from the rest of the UVs. The undo for the Edit UVWs dialog box is the same undo that you use for 3ds Max. It is handy to set up the Edit UVWs dialog box as shown in Figure 3.9 so that it is moved slightly to the right, and the Undo button on the Standard toolbar is visible and accessible.

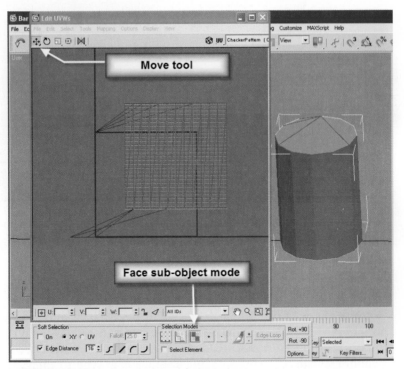

FIGURE 3.9   Attempting to move the cylindrical UVs.

Select the cylindrical walls as shown in Figure 3.10. A guideline has been drawn in for you on this screen shot (white dashed line) so it is clear where you can create your implied window to select only the UVs for the cylinder walls. Remember that for a selection window across part of an object to select that object, you must be in crossing mode, not window mode. Right-click and select Break. This breaks the selection set from anything it is attached to. Now the UVs for the cylinder walls can be moved out of the way so you can concentrate on the top and bottom of the model.

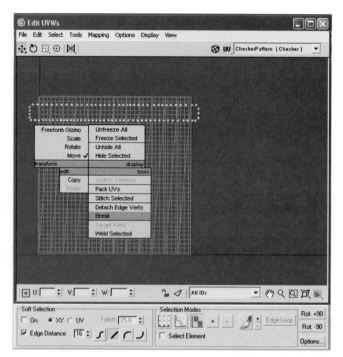

FIGURE 3.10   Using the Break command to break the walls of the cylinder free.

Applying a Normal Map

Figure 3.11 shows the cylinder walls safely placed aside and the UVs for the top and bottom of the model selected. Note that Face sub-object mode is still current. The top and bottom UVs look like lines because they are being seen edge-on by the Cylindrical map. It's time to apply another map type to them. Click the Mapping drop-down menu on the Edit UVWs dialog box, and then click Normal Mapping. Figure 3.11 shows the Normal Mapping dialog box activated. Normal mapping is an effective way to apply a map that is planar to the front, side, or top of an object.

The drop-down menu on the Normal Mapping dialog box is for Back/Front. The next option down on the drop-down is Left/Right, and then Top/Bottom. Select Top/Bottom, and click OK to close the Normal Mapping dialog box.

By applying the correct Normal map to the top and bottom UVs of the model, you end up with two Circular maps for that geometry (see Figure 3.12). Notice that the model in the viewport to the right has the corresponding geometry selected in red. This can be a useful way to track which part of the model you are working with. Now you can move the UV maps off to the side and address the problems with the Cylindrical map. Before any UV editing, apply a material to the model to see how well it is mapped.

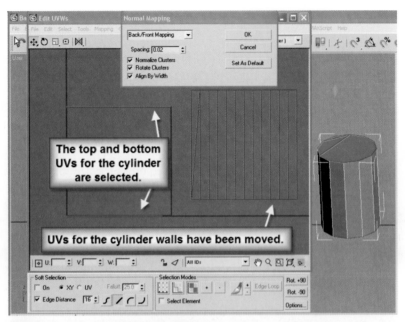

FIGURE 3.11   Selecting and remapping the top and bottom UVs of the model.

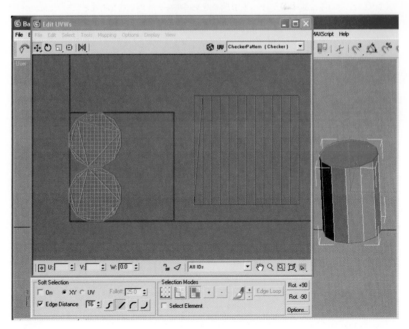

FIGURE 3.12   The top and bottom UVs of the model now have a proper map.

Applying a Utility Material

A *utility material* is a special material that helps you to accomplish a task but will not be part of the finished work. For unwrapping processes, checkered materials work well; sometimes these materials can take the form of different colored squares with numbers in the squares to help define relationships between the UVs and the model.

To see a new material on the model, go to the display panel and, on the Display Color rollout, turn on the Shaded Material Color. Select your model, and then refer to Figure 3.13 to create a checkered material. Try to get into the habit of naming your materials; any name will do, but leaving default material names invites problems later in the process, because you can end up with mixed-up materials.

Just as you created a custom material in Chapter 1, create a custom material here. If you go to the Maps rollout and click on the None button to the right of Diffuse color, the Material/Map Browser launches. Double-click on Checker, and your screen should look like Figure 3.13. The number 1 in the figure indicates where the Checker map type is in the list, 2 indicates what changes you should make to the tiling values for the checker pattern, and 3 is a reminder that you can get back to the main material editor menu by clicking the Parent button.

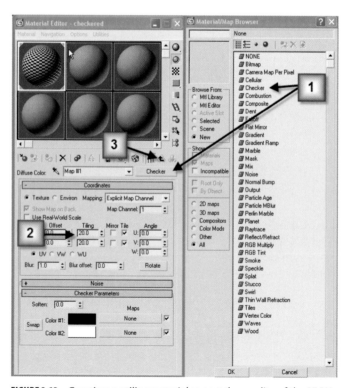

FIGURE 3.13   Creating a utility material to test the quality of the UVW mapping.

Figure 3.14 demonstrates what the Material Editor looks like when you get back to the main menu. The numbers in the figure serve as reminders to Assign Material to Selection and Show Map in Viewport. These two steps are necessary to see the checkered material on the model. There is also a reminder in this screen shot to make sure your Display Color is set to Material Color, rather than Object Color.

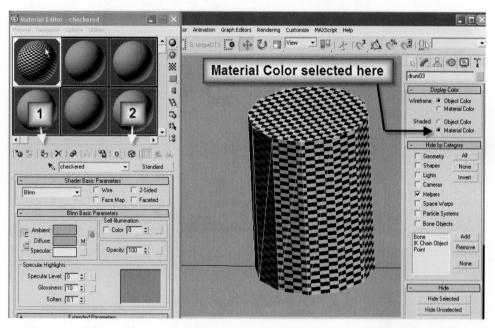

FIGURE 3.14   Assigning the material to the model, and making sure it displays correctly.

To see what was accomplished by properly mapping the top and the bottom of the cylinder with the Normal map, look at Figure 3.15. The version on the left is without the Normal map applied to the top and bottom UVs, and the version on the right is with the Normal map applied. Note the size and aspect of the checker pattern. What you want in a well-unwrapped model is a checker pattern that is as square and consistent as possible. As you can see, the version on the left is "streaking." The map applies fine to the sides of the cylinder, but it streaks across the top, because those UVs have not been properly flattened. The top of the cylinder on the right has a much more regular pattern and will lend itself well to the texturing in Chapter 4, "Texturing Game Art."

Correcting Flaws in the UVs

If you turn the cylinder around, you can spot a flaw; this same flaw is apparent in the Edit UVWs dialog box. The flaw is the presence of a seam where there shouldn't be. Inside the Edit UVWs dialog box is a right-click menu that will allow you to stitch seams

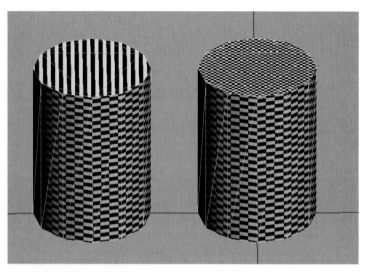

FIGURE 3.15   Before and after properly mapping the top and bottom.

or to weld vertices. In most cases, stitching seams works quite well, but in this case, welding vertices works better. Make sure you are in Vertex sub-object mode in the Edit UVWs dialog box, and from the right-click menu, select Target Weld (see Figure 3.16). This allows you to position the mouse over one vertex and drag it to the neighboring vertex to weld the two together. A big *W* appears near the cursor to indicate you are in Weld mode. If all goes well, you should see the seam in the UVs disappear.

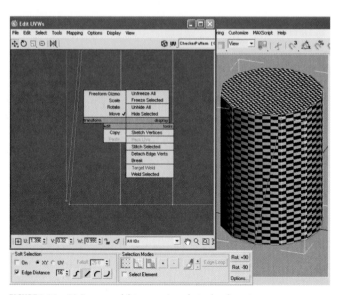

FIGURE 3.16   Using a weld to repair a detached vertex.

Moving UV Vertices to Improve the Mapping

Figure 3.17 demonstrates the process of sizing the UV maps so that the checker sizes are as square as possible. This keeps the material from stretching when you apply it to your model. In this image, all the UVs have been moved back inside the dark blue square of the Edit UVWs dialog box. The blue square is your texture space, within which all your textures must fit to be exported properly for texturing.

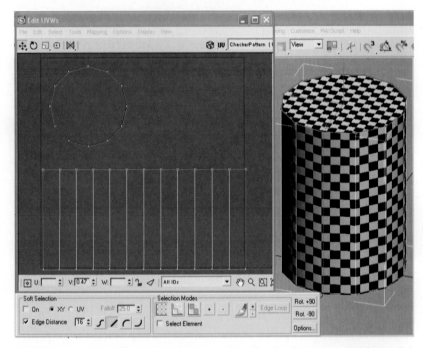

FIGURE 3.17   Moving the vertices down to adjust the checker pattern on the model.

In this shot, the model is in Vertex sub-object mode, and the top row of vertices have just been moved down, improving the aspect on the checker pattern squares. The top and bottom UVs have been placed over each other to save texture space and to make painting the texture easier. Why paint the end of the oil drum twice when you can paint it once and apply the texture to both ends at the same time? If you want a different texture on the other end of the oil drum, keep the UVs for the top and bottom separated. (You would only want to do this if the bottom of the drum will be visible in the game.) With this simple example, all that remains is to move the UVs a bit so that they are completely inside the texture space, and scale the top and bottom UVs so they fill up the texture space better.

Rendering Out the UV Template

After your UVs are properly positioned in the texture space, click Tools, Render UVW to Template to get a Render UVs dialog box so you can adjust your output settings (see Figure 3.18). If you have 3ds Max 7 or earlier, you can export a template of your UVs using Texporter. Texporter is outlined in the next section.

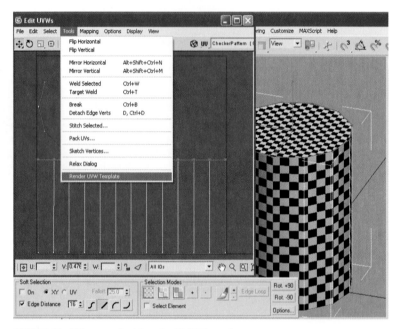

FIGURE 3.18   Where to find Render UVW Template.

Figure 3.19 shows the process after you've invoked the Render Output tool. The numbers correspond to the steps. Step 1 is to check the width and height values for the image. A simple object like this oil drum should probably get only 128 × 128 pixels because it is such a minor part of a game, but here it will be 256 × 256 just to make it more interesting to work with. You can always resize the texture later. The bigger the textures, and the more of them, the slower the game will potentially be. Step 2 is to click the Render UVW Template button at the bottom of the Render UVs dialog box. This should bring up the Render Map dialog box. Step 3 is to click the Save Bitmap button on the left side of the dialog box. This allows you to save the image in a variety of formats. TIF and TGA, with compression turned off, work best. JPGs use file compression and create a slightly fuzzy line on your templates, although the quality difference here is negligible. Later, you can use Photoshop to paint a texture over the UV template, which you can then reimport to 3ds Max and use as a material on the model; this process is discussed in Chapter 4. The completed oil drum textures and 3ds Max files are available in `Files\OilDrum` on the companion CD-ROM.

ON THE CD

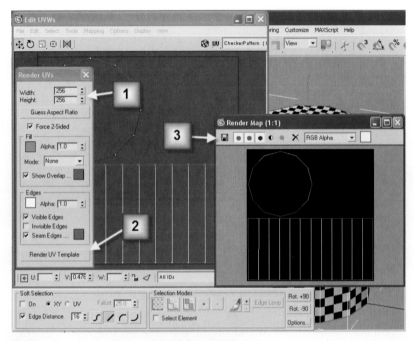

FIGURE 3.19   Rendering out the UVs for texturing.

Using Texporter: An Alternative for UV Rendering

ON THE CD

An alternative UV rendering tool is called Texporter; this is a freeware plug-in created by Cuneyt Ozdas and available on the companion CD-ROM. The CD has two versions of Texporter. The version that works for 3ds Max 4 and 5 is called `Texporter3_4.zip`, and the version that works for 3ds Max 6, 7, and 8 is called `texporter_Install_v3.4.4.6.exe`. With both versions, it is a good idea to close all other applications before installing. The `.zip` file requires you to unzip and place the `.dlu` file in your 3ds Max plug-ins directory, and the `.exe` requires you to point it to where your 3ds Max directory is located. Both look and behave the same when you are back inside of Max. Go to the Utility panel, click More, and look for Texporter in the alphabetical listing (see Figure 3.20). When you click Texporter from the list and click OK, the Texporter interface populates the lower portion of your Utilities panel.

The parameters in the Texporter interface are similar to those found in the Render UVW dialog box. Figure 3.21 displays some of these, using the unwrapped health patch as a sample model. In this image, the width and height of the texture has been changed to 256 × 256 to create a proper "powers of two" map for Torque. More parameters are available than what is captured here, but it should be noted that if you do not uncheck the box labeled Mark Overlaps, you will end up with an entirely red UV coloring, because the way the UVs on the main body of the health

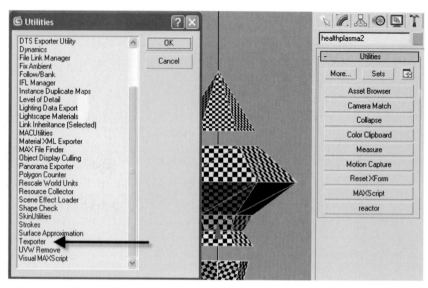

FIGURE 3.20   Where to find Texporter and other plug-ins.

patch were set up created multiple overlaps on purpose. Of course, in other situations, it can be useful to know if one UV is overlapping another. An in-depth help file for Texporter is contained within the .zip file; it applies to all versions of the tool. When you click the Pick Object button, it renders a UV template for the object you select; this rendering dialog box has a Save Bitmap button so you can export your template for texturing.

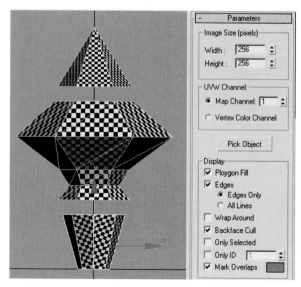

FIGURE 3.21   A look at a portion of the Texporter interface.

If you have an older version of 3ds Max and you cannot acquire or install a third-party solution for UVW rendering, you can always do a screen capture by pressing your Print Scr button on the keyboard and then pasting and cropping the image in Photoshop or another image editor. This is a last-ditch method, however, as your UV template will not be as precise as with the other two methods.

UNWRAPPING THE WEAPON

For the next example, you can unwrap the weapon built in Chapter 2, "Low Poly Modeling." Because the rifle was built using symmetry and is pretty flat on both the front and back sides (see Figure 3.22), the Normal Map unwrapping method will work well. Because of this, skip the step of adding a UVW map and go right to the Unwrap UVW modifier.

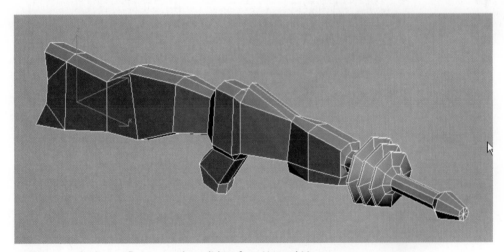

FIGURE 3.22   The laser rifle is a good candidate for a Normal Map unwrap.

In Figure 3.23, the Unwrap modifier has been added to the Editable Mesh. The Edit button was clicked, which brought up the Edit UVWs dialog box. Note that the interface window has been moved toward the left a bit so that the model can be seen at the same time. Turn off the Show Map and the Show Grid features so that you can more clearly see what is going on. Click on Face sub-object mode, window the entire group of UVs, and launch the Normal Mapping dialog box.

Mirroring and Aligning Normal-Mapped UVs

Figure 3.24 shows what the Normal Mapping dialog box settings should look like, and the result. Top/Bottom mapping is being used, although that may differ depending on the orientation of your particular model. It is a good idea to turn off the rotate

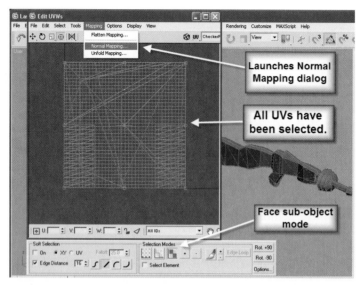

FIGURE 3.23 Selecting the UVs and preparing for a Normal map.

check box, because more than likely you will want your images to project straight so they are easy to paint later. Another thing to note about this screen shot is that the Undo button is exposed for quick access on the upper left.

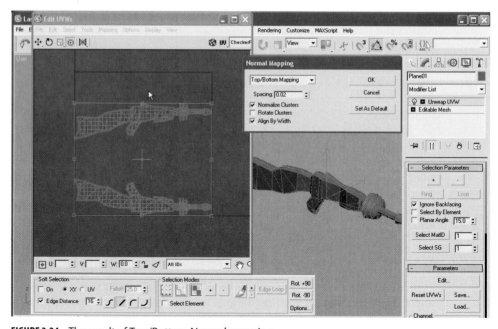

FIGURE 3.24 The result of Top/Bottom Normal mapping.

Figure 3.25 shows the solution for the upside-down UVs; select them, and click Mirror Vertical.

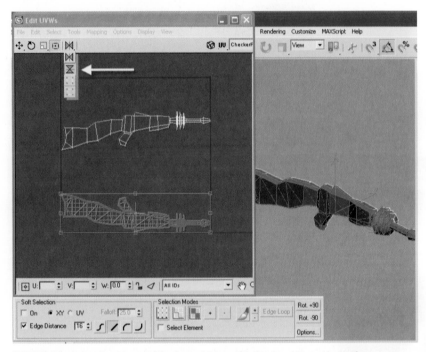

FIGURE 3.25   Selecting the upside down UVs and initiating Mirror Vertical.

Figure 3.26 shows the newly mirrored UVs being positioned directly over the UVs that were already upright. To get the lines to lie exactly on top of one another, you have to zoom in to an area with plenty of detail, like the front of the gun. Zoom in even closer than shown in this image to make the placement as precise as possible.

Once again, a utility material is helpful for judging how well the Normal mapping is working. Use the Checker map, but you may want to set the tiling of the checkers to 40 in both directions instead of 20. That makes smaller checker squares so that you can more clearly see any streaking or deformation (see Figure 3.27). Adjust tiling as necessary.

This image has good mapping on the main body of the model and a nice clean seam going along the top and bottom edge of the model. The good seam results from making sure the weapon had a consistent centerline when it was modeled. If your seam is wavy, you can blame either your model or your normal mapping technique, or both. The model has streaking along the top and bottom and along the cooling fins on the barrel. This is because those surfaces are not normal or perpendicular to the direction of the Top/Bottom Normal map.

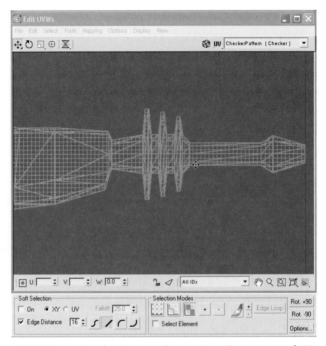

FIGURE 3.26 Using the Move tool to position the two sets of UVs over each other.

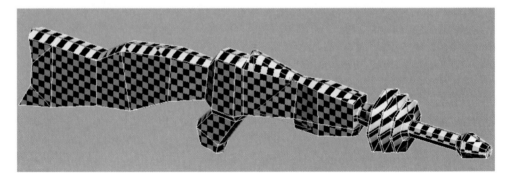

FIGURE 3.27 The checker pattern tells you how well the Normal map is working.

Normal Mapping the Cooling Fins

Next, select the flat portion of the cooling fins for remapping. This can be tricky if you are new to 3ds Max. First, make sure you are in Face sub-object mode. You will see that when you set this mode in the Edit UVWs dialog box, it also is set in the Unwrap UVW modifier to the right. The fastest way to get all the right faces is to make sure you have Ignore Backfacing turned off in the Unwrap UVW Selection Parameters rollout and that you are zoomed in tight in the Front view of the cooling fins. Use a selection window to select each set of faces that make up the main faces of the fins, avoiding small faces in the middle (see Figure 3.28). Hold down the Ctrl key so that you can continue to add window selections to the selection set. If you prefer, you can also select these faces from the Edit UVWs dialog box.

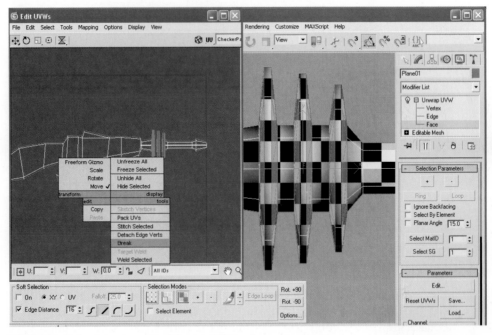

FIGURE 3.28   Selecting a portion of the cooling fins for remapping.

After you've selected the correct faces, right-click and choose Break. When the break is complete, you can use the Move tool in the Edit UVWs dialog box and move the faces to a new location. Take your time with this procedure. Sometimes you have to hunt around with your cursor before the Move symbol pops up and allows you to click and move the selected faces.

In Figure 3.29, the gun, minus the cooling fins, has been moved outside of the texture area. This is always a good practice, because all new map projections end up in the texture box, and leaving UVs in this area can create confusion. Select the fin faces, and once again apply a Normal map, this time set to Left/Right mapping. The resulting UVs flatten the fin faces for easy texturing.

Correcting the UVs at the Edges of the Weapon

Now that you've take care of the fins, you have to deal with the streaking of the texture on the top and bottom of the gun body. This is because the top and bottom

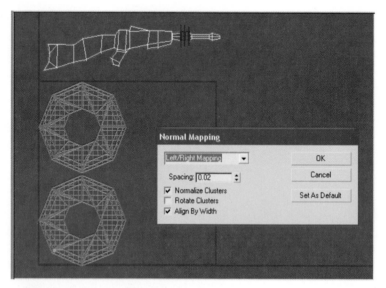

FIGURE 3.29 Applying Left/Right Normal mapping to the cooling fins.

polygons of the model are at an angle to the direction of the Normal map. You can compensate for this by moving the vertices at the top and bottom of the gun further from the gun body. This is almost like taking the gun model and starting to peel the top and bottom faces up so they face the same direction as the rest of the gun.

When you move the vertices, as shown in Figure 3.30, select them with a selection window. You are actually moving two vertices at a time, because the front and back sides of the gun UVs are sitting in the same space. Note the improvement in the image; moving the vertices in the Edit UVWs dialog box causes an immediate improvement in the viewport image of the textured model. As you move the vertices around, watch the result, and try to attain consistently sized checker squares throughout the model, from top to bottom, end to end. Look not only at sizes, but at alignment; try to keep the squares in straight rows as much as is possible.

Breaking and Scaling UVs

Just as you broke the fins off the main body of the gun, you can break the gun apart to maximize the use of the texture area. This is good practice for when you get into character texturing. Look for places that have natural seams, such as where the gun barrel meets the gun body, or where the stock of the gun meets the main body. If you make a mistake, click the Undo button on the Standard toolbar and try again. If you need to stitch two edges together, first get into Edge sub-object mode. Select the edge with the left mouse button. The selected edge will turn red, and you will see the edge that fits to it turn blue. Right-click, and select Stitch Selected. The blue edge will join your red edge. Sometimes it makes sense to move neighboring UV patches closer together before stitching or welding.

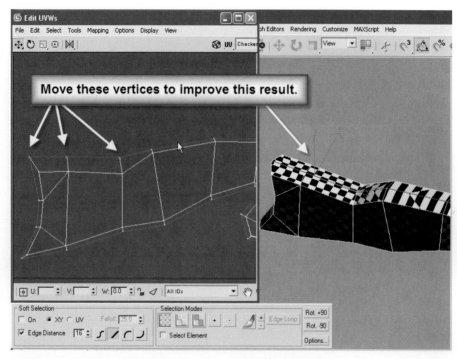

FIGURE 3.30   Moving vertices to improve the quality of the unwrap.

Note that in Figure 3.31, the entire weapon has been broken apart, but one part is missing. The end of the barrel needs mapping, too, particularly because you will want to paint the barrel opening on it. To acquire this UV, select the faces on the front of the barrel as shown in the image, and then create another Normal map as you have done before. Use Left/Right mapping, just as you did with the fins on the barrel. Place the UVs in a convenient spot.

Here it is worth noting that because you do want the stock and the body of the gun to somewhat blend together, it may help to keep their UVs the same size. Having the UVs the same size makes it easier to paint a texture that flows smoothly between the two sets of UVs. However, the barrel, fins, and barrel end are separate components and can be as big as you can make them in the remaining space.

When prioritizing how much space to allow the various UVs, think of what the visual impact will be and what you hope to achieve with your texture. In the case of the laser rifle, the bulk of the paint work will be on the sides of the stock and body, so they were given priority in the texture space.

After you have a good UV, you may want to save the UV file as a backup. Do this from the Edit UVWs dialog box by clicking File, Save UVs. Put the UVs in the same directory as the model. Render out the UVs for texturing with a 256 × 256 pixel map. The weapon textures and 3ds Max files are available in Files\Raygun on the companion CD-ROM.

ON THE CD

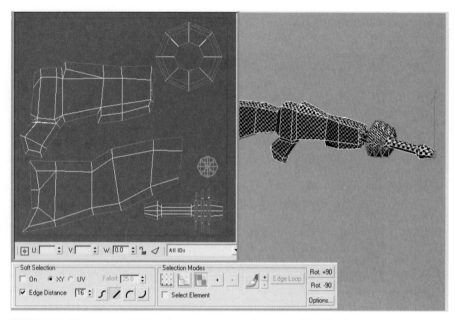

FIGURE 3.31   The weapon UVs are broken apart, and a UV is added for the barrel opening.

UNWRAPPING THE AMMO BOX

The ammo box model is nothing more than a box, converted to an Editable Mesh, with vertices moved to create a pyramid-like shape. This will be unwrapped using the Flatten Mapping dialog box, which you access through the Mapping drop-down menu. Any faces in the model that are over the Face Angle Threshold (45 degrees in this case) are broken off separately. The Normalize Clusters check box causes all the UVs to stay within the texture area. The Rotate Clusters check box allows the resulting UVs to be rotated during the flatten process. Fill Holes allows smaller UVs to inhabit any holes in other UVs to save on texture space. Figure 3.32 shows how this model is flattened. This technique is ideal for a simple model with lots of flat faces; when you use Flatten mapping with more complex or curved models, the number of faces generated is unwieldy.

In Figure 3.33, the UVs have been mirrored and arranged so that the texture space is better utilized. Depending on what texture is used for the ammo box, the upside-down UVs for the sides of the box could present a problem; however, you can rotate the entire canvas 180 degrees as necessary when it is time to texture these sides, so the orientation of the side faces should not be a problem. The bottom of the box has been scaled down because it will most likely not be visible in the game. Notice how even the checker pattern is on these faces, with no adjustment necessary.

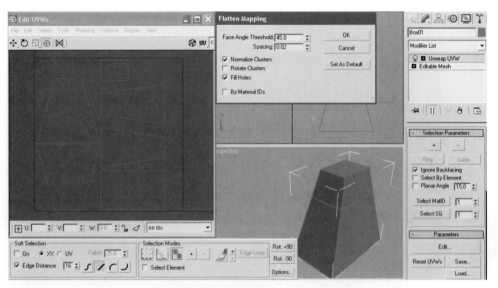

FIGURE 3.32   Flatten mapping is ideal for simple models with planar faces.

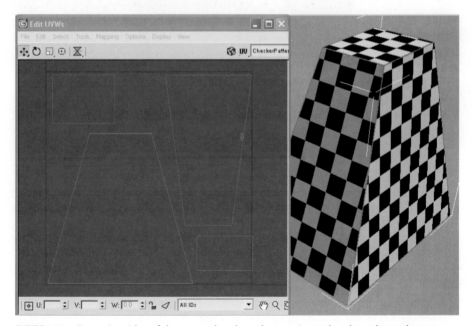

FIGURE 3.33   Opposite sides of the ammo box have been mirrored and overlapped to save texture space.

ON THE CD

The ammo box textures and 3ds Max files are available in Files\Ammo on the companion CD-ROM.

UNWRAPPING THE POWER CHARGER

For a different approach with the Unwrap UVW tool, open the power charger model. After seeing how well the Cylindrical map solved the mapping problem for the oil drum, it is tempting to try a Cylindrical map on the power charger, because it is basically cylindrical in shape. In Figure 3.34, the power charger on the left has a Cylindrical map applied, and the power station on the right has a "best align" Planar map applied to the faces that are facing the screen. The Planar map is clearly superior to the Cylindrical map for generating even, regular UVs for this model.

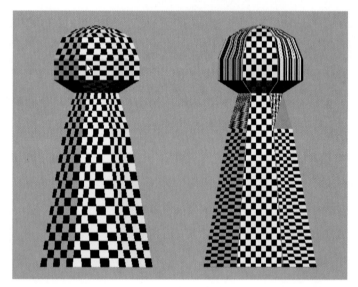

FIGURE 3.34   Wavy UVs versus ordered UVs. Which would you rather paint on?

Following is a step-by-step explanation of how to use a Planar map to create UVs for the power charger. These instructions only work for release 8 or later of 3ds Max. If you have an earlier version, you should be able to use the Planar Map button at the bottom of the Parameters rollout for the Unwrap UVW modifier. You will not have a Best Align button as is in 3ds Max 8 and beyond, but that is because your version of the Planar map does a best align as part of the basic command.

First, add the Unwrap UVW modifier to the Editable Mesh. Get into Face sub-object mode. Then select the faces you want to map on the model. Select only those that are in line vertically; even though they have different angles, they are all still roughly facing the same direction (see Figure 3.35). Click the Edit button for the Un-wrap modifier, and move the Edit UVWs dialog box window around until you can see your model in the viewport *and* the editor at the same time.

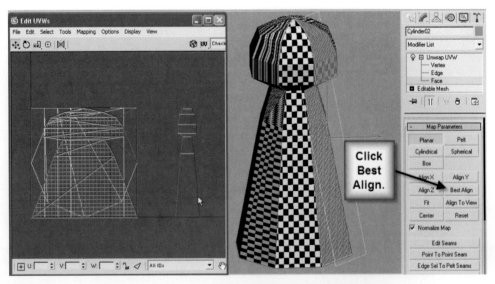

FIGURE 3.35   Select the faces and choose Planar, Best Align; then turn Planar off.

Applying a Planar Map

Next, from the Map Parameters rollout, select Planar. This puts a default Planar map on your model, but the result will not usually look very good. To get the Planar map to align to the faces you have selected, click the Best Align button. Then check your Edit UVW dialog box; the faces should be lined up better now, although they still need some work. You will *not* be able to move the selected UVs out of the texture area until you turn off the Planar button.

Notice in Figure 3.35 that Normalize map is turned on. Normalize map fills up the texture area with the selected UVs, forcing them to match the texture size and making the process of defining UVs more straightforward. If Normalize map is turned off, textures are scaled in accordance with the actual size of the model, causing the textures to tile on the model, and ultimately requiring the UVs to be scaled down.

After you have turned off the Planar button, move the selected UVs out of the texture area and into an area that is free of UVs. Next, use the Scale Horizontal tool to resize the UVs until the checker squares are actually square on the model in the viewport (see Figure 3.36).

Moving UV Vertices to Improve the Map

In this way, one vertical panel at a time, you can unwrap the entire model. But you still have to make some adjustments. If you use your Arc Rotate tool to look from underneath the model, you see a panel of the power charger that has some irregularly long checker squares. You can fix this by going to the Edit UVWs dialog box

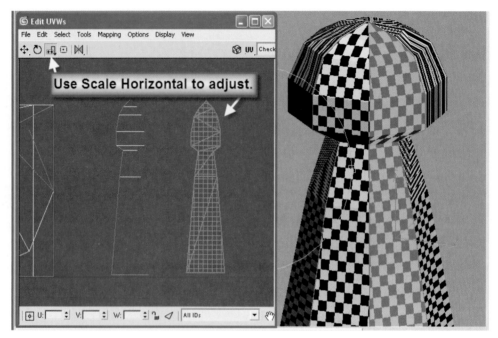

FIGURE 3.36 Adjusting the UVs with Scale Horizontal.

and moving some vertices. Looking at Figure 3.37, two sections of the power station have been mapped with the Planar tool so far. The one on the right has been adjusted by moving the vertices up, to expand the area that was streaking a little. Note the difference in the viewport.

Using a Planar Map for More Complex Models

Using this technique all the way around the power charger model, you can easily apply new UV maps by just repeating the process discussed earlier. But what if the power station has some additional features? The version shown in Figure 3.38 is more complex. In this image, only the faces that lie in the same general plane are being selected, whereas the protrusion that comes out of the middle of the face is being avoided. You can unwrap the protrusion separately. Notice that one section of the power charger has been unwrapped and laid aside already, and the next section is about to be placed exactly over the top of the first section. Just as with the top and bottom of the oil drum, laying similar sections over each other is a way to save texture space. The plan for this texture is to have it repeat on each of the eight sides of the model; by your saving on texture space in this way, the repeating texture can be higher quality, and you can paint all the panels simultaneously.

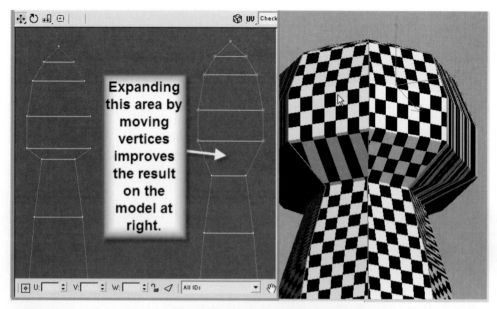

FIGURE 3.37   Moving vertices to improve the way the map lies on the model.

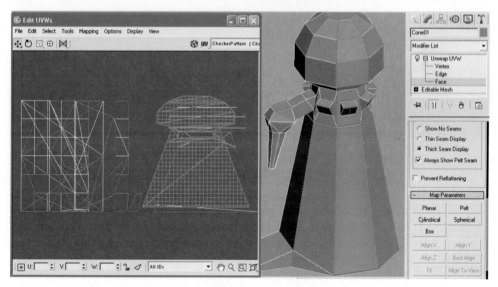

FIGURE 3.38   Laying one section of the model UVs over the next to save space and effort.

Figure 3.39 shows the cleanup involved in getting the different UV sections to lie more precisely on top of one another. This requires zooming in on specific areas and moving vertices so that the placement of the UVs has no ambiguity. A little work at this stage goes a long way when it is time to paint your texture.

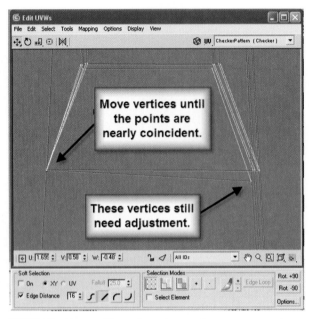

FIGURE 3.39   Zoomed in and moving vertices to create a clean, precise template.

Figure 3.40 shows one of the stages of unwrapping the protrusions that jut out along the top of the model. These resulting UVs can be laid over each other to save texture space and simplify the texturing process.

The main protrusion of the model is being unwrapped, one set of nearly planar faces at a time, in Figure 3.41. This UV set will be moved out of the texture area and rescaled so that the checker pattern is square. Step by step, all the faces in the model are accounted for until the texture area is empty. When each set of UVs has been modified so that the checker pattern looks right, they are brought once again into the texture area. The more important areas are sized larger, and less important areas are sized smaller. Then the UVs are exported as a template to a paint program for texturing.

In Figure 3.42, overlapping and positioning of the different UVs within the texture area is nearly complete. This texture will be 256 × 256 pixels, and you should try to make every one of them count. In this image, the UVs for the main walls of the structure take up the most space because the main walls are the most dominant feature in the model; the areas that are underneath the structure, which will never be seen, are not even in the texture area yet. Ultimately, they will be scaled small and placed into a corner.

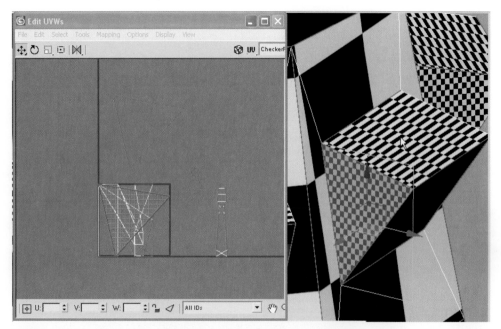

FIGURE 3.40   Using Planar, Best Align, and overlapping UVs to save on texture space.

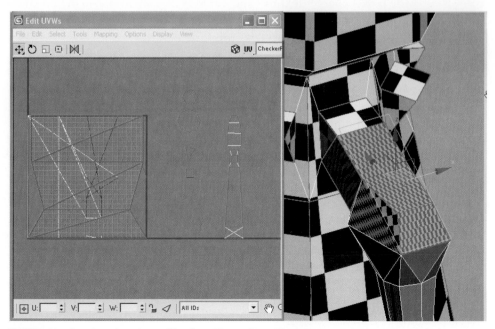

FIGURE 3.41   Another situation calling for a Planar, Best Align map.

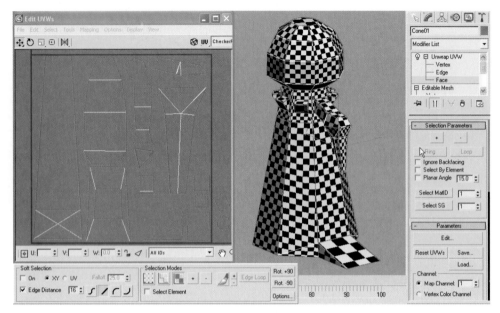

FIGURE 3.42   The UVs have been adjusted, and most are back in the texture area.

ON THE CD

The power charger textures and 3ds Max files are available in `Files\PowerCharger` on the companion CD-ROM.

UNWRAPPING THE HEALTH PATCH

In Figure 3.43, the three components to the health patch have been separated so that you can see them clearly. The top component is getting a Box map. You might expect a Cylindrical map to work better, but the Box map actually works well here. This portion of the health patch will receive a generic bitmap to suggest a blinking light. Because this texture does not need to conform to any particular position on this part of the pickup, you don't need to unwrap each face.

In Figure 3.44, a checkered material has been applied to the model, and settings are being checked in the Display panel to make sure that the material on the model is visible. As mentioned at the beginning of this chapter, you may need to switch between Display Color settings from time to time. If a material does not show up on your model, it is probably because you have set Shaded to Object Color.

The main body of the health patch is unwrapped similar to the power charger, with Planar maps on each section of the model. Each panel's UVs are being placed over one another, so that the UVs can be as large as possible in the texture space.

The lower third of the health patch is unwrapped similarly, using Planar, Best Align. But rather than laying these UVs on top of each other, they are stitched together at their edges. This takes place one edge at a time by selecting the right edge

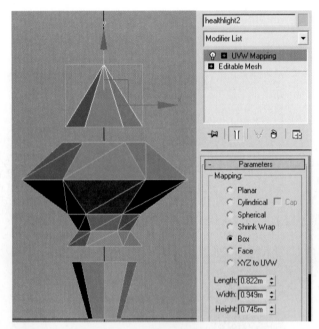

FIGURE 3.43   Three parts to the health patch. The top part gets a Box map.

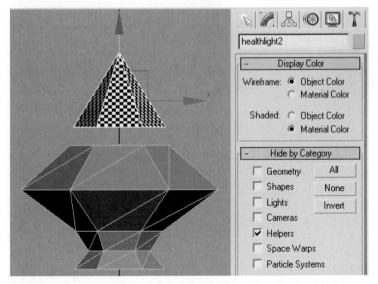

FIGURE 3.44   You may need to change shaded Display Color to Material Color to see the material.

of each UV and then using the right-click menu to select Stitch Selected, as shown in Figure 3.45. This creates a big UV map that is shaped like a fan.

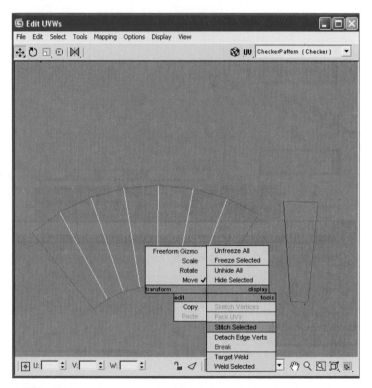

FIGURE 3.45 Selecting an edge highlights its mate; Stitch Selected joins the edges together.

Normally, a map that curves like this is a problem for texturing, but this map is going to be used to depict a flow of engine exhaust that keeps the health patch hovering above the surface. Because we are not painting panels or rivets or other specific features, the Curved map is not a problem. The main benefits that this map type gives us are a good blend between each section (because each panel is stitched together), and an accurately ordered map (as opposed to a Cylindrical map, which would be a little wavy and distort the texture).

The fan-shaped UVs don't fill up the texture area very well, so they can be broken in half by selecting half of the sections, and from the same right-click menu, selecting Break. Rotate both sections of the UVs until they are flat, and lay them on top of one another to save space. Rescale as necessary until the checker squares look good, and make sure to maximize your use of the texture area, as shown in Figure 3.44. This process gives you much better use of texture space and creates only one additional seam in the texture.

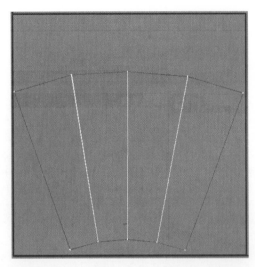

FIGURE 3.46   Break allows you to break the UVs in half and then rotate and overlap them.

Figure 3.47 shows the result of the unwrap of the main body of the health patch. This was once again done with Planar, Best Align. The top and bottom of the model will only be seen slightly, so they are not as important. Here, it is really all about the main panels, which will be more evident in the game and will therefore receive the bulk of the texturing.

FIGURE 3.47   The finished UVs for the main body of the health patch.

ON THE CD
The health patch textures and 3ds Max files are available in `Files\HealthPatch` on the companion CD-ROM.

SUMMARY

This chapter looked at several different ways to unwrap a model. The method you use depends on the geometry involved and the look of the texture. Flatten mapping works well for simple models with flat surfaces. Cylindrical maps work well for cylindrical objects. Normal mapping works well when the model has well-defined front and back sides. Planar mapping works for almost everything else. Keep in mind that smoothing should be cleared from the mesh before unwrapping it to avoid distortion. In the end, the unwrapping process is about generating and adjusting the model UVs so that the texture will lie evenly on them.

TEXTURING GAME ART

In This Chapter

- Texturing Considerations
- Texturing the Oil Drum
- Texturing the Health Patch
- Texturing the Weapon
- Texturing the Power Charger
- Texturing the Ammo Box

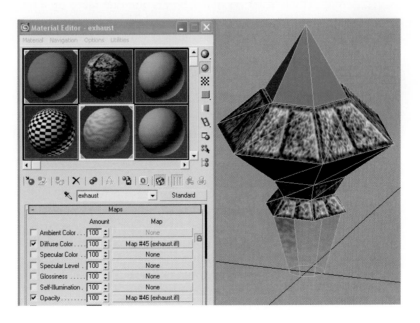

TEXTURING CONSIDERATIONS

An entire book could be written on the planning and implementation of textures; here we will focus on just a few ideas that will help to make your textures successful. Some of the items on this list are mandatory, such as using powers of two in your texture sizes. Others are merely suggestions, such as using a digitizing tablet or using layers in Photoshop.

Using the Appropriate Equipment

You can create textures with a mouse, but a three-button mouse is a clumsy input device for drawing. Your best results will be in using a digitizing tablet. Digitizing tablets come with a pressure-sensitive pen, which is sensed by the tablet and read into programs like Photoshop. Wacom makes a great 4 × 5 tablet for about $100 that plugs right into your USB port. You have much more control holding a pen than you do sliding a mouse. Also, a pressure-sensitive pen can create a thicker line with a little more pressure.

It is also preferable to have two monitors if you can afford it. A dual-screen setup allows you to stretch your viewing area over two monitors so that you can have an application like 3ds Max on one monitor and another application like Photoshop on the other. You can also use the second monitor to spread out the many menus in 3ds Max. The Edit UVWs dialog box is one that takes up a lot of space; it can be effective to devote an entire monitor to it while having another monitor to view your model. To drive two monitors, you need a video card that supports dual-monitor displays.

Using Digital Photos for Textures

A digital photo can be laid over the UV template to create a believable texture. The depth and realism of a digital photo is a valuable tool; although it is not always possible or preferable to use digital photos for textures, at minimum, they can be useful for reference. When using digital photos, first check to see if they are copyrighted or if they have a watermark on them. Carry a digital camera around and make your own texture libraries. Useful shots include larger shots like buildings, cars, and gates, as well as close-up shots like textures on walls and metallic surfaces. Aim the camera as flat to the surface you are interested in as possible. Consider bringing a tripod along for better focus. Overcast days are best for texture shots, because the scattered sunlight minimizes shadows. Shadows brand the work to a specific time of day and are hard to remove, making the texture in most cases worthless. The ideal digital texture photo is taken normal or flat to the surface, focused, and in diffuse light conditions with no clear light source.

Making the Lighting Consistent

Although you want your texture library to be relatively free of shadows and highlights, often you can add these by hand or by using some of the tools in Photoshop.

When you do this, make sure it's consistent; if the light is coming from above and to the left, try to ensure this is always the case in the model. Also take this care in the unwrapping process. It is often desirable to turn some of the mesh UVs upside-down to get them to fit onto the texture area tighter. But if there is highlight and shadow information in the texture, or if the texture has any kind of directional component, turning a portion of the UVs upside down can shatter the illusion that the texture is meant to preserve.

Creating Textures from Scratch

If you are creating a texture from scratch, you need to add some dirt or grime to the texture at some point. Without this ingredient, textures look too clean and computer generated. If you look around, the textures in your world have nicks, scratches, stains, dirt, and grime. You can often accomplish this look of dirt or grime by adding one or more layers to the texture that are actually photos of rust or grime and lowering the opacity so that the "dirty" photo only adds detail to the painted texture. There are also effects within Photoshop that can help you achieve a more realistic, detailed look.

Creating in Powers of Two

All of our textures should be created in powers of two. This means we will end up with textures that are 32×32, 64×64, 128×128, 256×256, or 512×512 pixels.

Working with Photoshop

Although you can use similar products for texture development, Photoshop has become the industry standard for image manipulation. Photoshop is a broad and deep package, but it has some specific areas that especially pertain to creating game textures.

Getting the Image Mode Right

Most of the time you will want to make sure that your Image mode is set to RGB and 8 bit. You can adjust this from Image, Mode. Depending on how you use Photoshop or what files you work with, your mode may change to Grayscale or 16 Bits/Channel, both of which severely limit your options within the software. If this happens, simply change it back to RGB and 8 Bits/Channel.

Working with Shortcut Keys

In Photoshop, you can narrow down screen clutter and make room for bigger images by using the Tab key shortcut. All you may want to see is a reference image or two and the actual texture you are painting. You do not need your toolbox or the layers pallet as often as you might think; consider working without these tools while you are painting your images and using the I key to activate the ink dropper and the B key to switch to using the brush. Use the Alt+Tab key combination to bounce between 3ds Max and Photoshop.

Using Layers for Flexibility

Layers tend to be underused in Photoshop. Just as in other software solutions, layers add power and flexibility to your design process. With layers, you can move and manipulate different aspects of your design separately. Without layers, you commit too quickly to different changes and lose the flexibility to make further changes long after the design is completed.

Using Layer Effects

There is a tremendous amount of power available in Layer Effects. Highlights, drop shadows, bevels, and other effects can be set up and saved as a Layer Style and easily applied to any other layer, in any file. Using Layer Effects, you can almost instantly create shadowed and highlighted textures that look 3D. Many of the textures in this chapter utilize Layer Effects.

Using Layer Masks for Nondestructive Editing

When we erase a portion of an image for any reason, as soon as we save, those erased pixels are gone forever. By using a Layer Mask, we preserve the entire image. If you erase too much, Layer Masking allows you to paint it back in, even a year later. This is because the Layer Mask allows you to paint-add or paint-subtract on an image, using any size, style, or opacity of brush you prefer. Layer Masking is described in more detail in the later section "Texturing the Oil Drum."

Using Actions to Save Time

We can minimize repetition in Photoshop by using actions. Actions allow you to record commands and then repeat that sequence of commands automatically as needed by clicking a button. One of the processes that takes a lot of repetition is the saving out of a PSD file so that you can check your texture in 3ds Max. Although you cannot use the native PSD file for the actual texture in the game, it is sufficient for checking how the texture is coming together on the model in 3ds Max. Usually you will find something wrong with the texture, meaning you must go back and tweak it, turn off the template layer, save the texture, take a look, turn on the template layer, tweak again, and so on. Every time you do these types of tasks, it costs you time. Making an action in Photoshop takes about one minute and pays for itself the first day you implement it. For an action to work smoothly, you need to keep your templates on a standard layer name, like `template`. Use as many layers as you need to make the texture work; the texture as you see it, but with the template layer turned off, is what you will have on your model when you are finished.

It is better to wait on actions until you are comfortable with the sequences you are trying to automate. When you are ready to automate any task, the procedure to create an action is as follows (see Figure 4.1):

1. Make sure the Actions pallet is up.
2. From the flyout on the right, select Create New Action.
3. Give the action a name (call it `SaveNoTemplate`) and assign a function key (F12).
4. Click the Record button.
5. Turn off the template layer.
6. Save the PSD file with Ctrl+S (so that you are not prompted for a name to save to).
7. Turn on the template layer.
8. Click the Stop button at the bottom of the Actions pallet to stop the recording.

Make sure Toggle Dialog On/Off is turned off so that you will not be prompted to name the exported file. You can find this toggle in the Actions pallet to the left of each listed action.

If both Photoshop and 3ds Max are open and this action is implemented, you will be able to change the texture while the template is visible and press F12 to see an updated texture on your model. You can flip between Photoshop and 3ds Max by using the Alt+Tab keys. Being able to see the results quickly and easily on the model will improve your result. If you have a dual-screen setup, you can keep both applications visible at once and work even more efficiently.

Preparing the UV Template

Figure 4.2 shows a basic template layer setup in Photoshop. The background layer has been converted to a regular layer and renamed as `template`. A new layer was created for the actual texture and thus named `texture`. The `template` layer has been dragged above the `texture` layer so that it is on top. The Blend mode of the `template` layer is set to Screen so that it shows through anything on the layers beneath it. You can paint on the `texture` layer and still see the template. In this image, notice that the `template` layer has been set to Screen mode and is positioned above the `texture` layer. When your texture is ready, save it as a JPG or PNG file, with the `template` layer turned off.

Remember that the template is like your canvas; the better the canvas, the better the final texture can potentially be. The more important faces on the model should receive the largest percentage of texture space, and the less visible or hidden faces should receive the least. Overlap similar shapes where possible to save texture space.

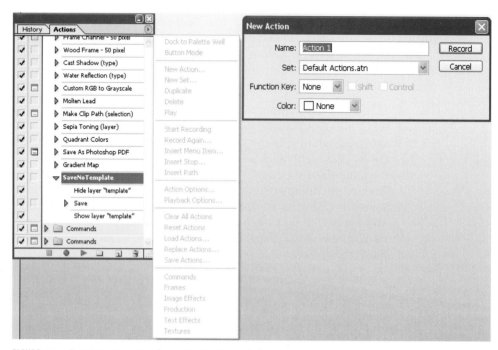

FIGURE 4.1   Creating an action from the Actions window.

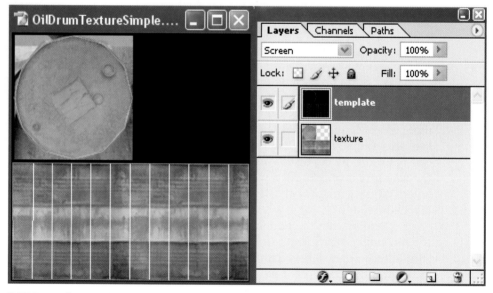

FIGURE 4.2   The template is set to Screen mode, and the texture is on the layer beneath it.

TEXTURING THE OIL DRUM

ON THE CD

The oil drum will be our first textured model. As you recall, we unwrapped the sides of this model with a Cylindrical map and separated the top and bottom faces of the model with a Planar map. Open `OilDrumTemplate.tif` (located in `Files\OilDrum` on the companion CD-ROM) and walk through the steps described in the previous section, "Preparing the UV Template in Photoshop." We will apply a digital photo to the oil drum as a Diffuse map; then we will alter a copy of the photo that we will use as a Reflection map. This will cause the oil drum to partially reflect the sky in the game.

Because we are using a digital photo for the oil drum, we need to make sure it works well flat. The oil drum presents some unique challenges in that the top, bottom, and support ribs tend to distort depending on the angle the photo is taken from. Figure 4.3 demonstrates with two inset images how much curvature there can be to deal with on a photo of an oil drum. Taking multiple shots at different heights and using only those portions of each image that have minimal curvature is one way to arrive at a decent texture. You can also minimize curvature by taking the shot with maximum zoom and then stepping back until the image is framed. In the background of this image is the finished texture, made up of multiple shots taken to minimize curvature and to collect overlapping images of the surface.

FIGURE 4.3   The curves of the oil drum must be flattened.

Pushing Pixels with the Liquify Tool

You'll need to modify many digital photos if you want to use them as suitable textures. One of the problems with the oil drum images is that the support ribs had too much curvature. The Liquify tool in Photoshop, located on the Filters drop-down menu, allows you to set a brush radius and then click-drag to push pixels in any direction. In Figure 4.4, the Forward Warp tool button is turned on. The support rib that the tool is over curves slightly downward. By carefully pushing pixels down in the middle of the drum and pushing them up at the sides of the drum, you can flatten the support rib for the texture. The Liquify tool, used with varying brush sizes, made it possible to line up the support ribs and other curving edges in the photos.

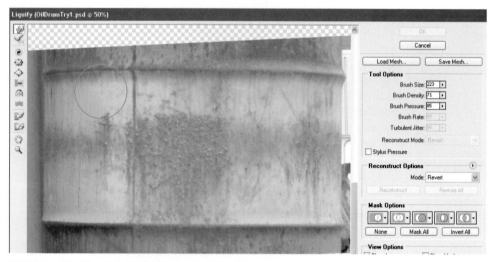

FIGURE 4.4   The Liquify tool allows us to push pixels around.

Using Offset to Make the Texture Wrap

This particular texture only goes about halfway around the oil drum. Whether your texture goes halfway around the cylindrical object or all the way around, you are going to have to deal with seams. The Offset tool, located under Filters, Other, lets you slide the texture around so you can get the seam out in the open where you can camouflage it. In Figure 4.5, the Horizontal pixels have been adjusted so that you can see the seam, which appears as a red vertical line on the left of the image. At this point, the Liquify tool was used to push the ribs at each end of the texture a bit so they would match up better. Then, by using the Clone Stamp tool, the seam was blended away so that it was no longer obvious.

Repairing Seams with the Clone Stamp Tool

In Figure 4.6, three stages of work are shown. Notice that the Clone Stamp tool is turned on in the floating toolbar at the left. In the first window at the left, two oil drum photos have been laid together and positioned, now that their ribs and other lines are nearly horizontal. At this point, the file has several layers. A seam is evident down the middle of the image.

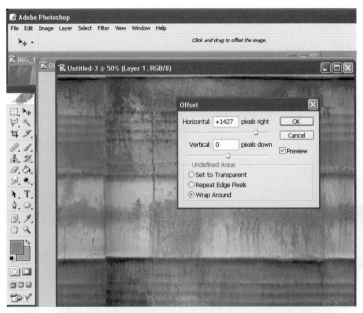

FIGURE 4.5   The Offset tool allows you to slide the seam of a texture around for easier blending.

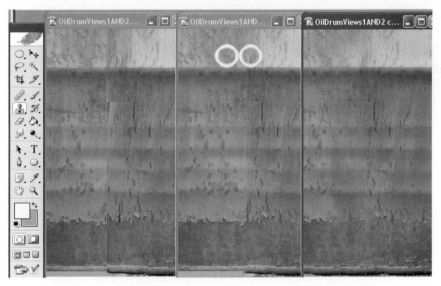

FIGURE 4.6   Three stages of using the Clone Stamp tool to camouflage a seam.

In the middle window, two white circles indicate where the Clone Stamp tool was positioned to hide the seam. The circle on the left is where the Clone Stamp tool was initialized (by holding down the Alt key and clicking), and the circle on the right is where the tool started painting (click-drag, or use a digitizing tablet and pen). This initialization and painting process copies the pixels from the initialization point to the destination point; it hides the seam well, but it also creates duplicate patterns that can detract from the believability of the texture.

In the window on the right, some of the duplicate patterns, as well as some of the differences between the two sides of the image, have been cloned away. You can do this by initializing the Clone Stamp tool in an area with consistent color and texture and then painting those pixels over an area that has a duplicate pattern. You can also do it by turning the opacity or flow down and painting different pixels over one another, although this kind of camouflage can lead to blurriness. The initial seam and the bottom ring of the drum were done at 100 percent opacity. The other work was done at varying degrees of opacity and flow, sometimes cloning pixels from one side to the other side of the image to improve overall consistency so that the two would look more like one image. This image could still be improved upon, but you need to consider how important and visible it is in the scheme of the game and keep in mind that when it is scaled down to game size, many details will be lost.

At this point, the basic texture is done. You can add this texture to your Material Editor using the same technique presented in Chapter 1, "Introduction to 3ds Max," for creating a custom material.

Reflection Mapping in Photoshop

If you want your object to map the environment in Torque, you can add reflectivity to the material. If all you are after is an overall reflection, there is no need to do anything more to your map in 3ds Max other than check the Reflection box in the Maps rollout of the Material Editor in 3ds Max and assign a value. A value of 100 percent will give you a completely reflective object, similar to placing a mirrored object in the scene. The sky of your scene will reflect in the material. This method of general reflection does not require that you assign a bitmap to the None button in the Maps rollout of 3ds Max.

You can use Layer Masking and alpha channels to build the Reflective map into a single image file. Figure 4.7 demonstrates this technique of adding reflection to a texture. First, in Photoshop, copy your main texture layer and desaturate it. In this example, the upper-left window is the start point. The image in the window to the right has been desaturated. Adjust the Brightness/Contrast until those values suit the amount of reflectivity you would like to achieve. Whiter areas reflect more, whereas darker areas reflect less. Hand-paint or dodge and burn areas if necessary. The third window, at the lower right, has had the grayscale image adjusted to fairly heavy contrast so that the black areas will not reflect at all.

Now copy the contents of this desaturated layer by using Select All, creating a Layer Mask in your primary texture layer, and selecting the Channels tab. Turn on and select the Layer Mask channel. Paste the grayscale image you recently copied onto the Layer Mask channel. At the upper right of this figure, you can see what the Channels tab should look like at this stage. Click the Layers tab and then click the

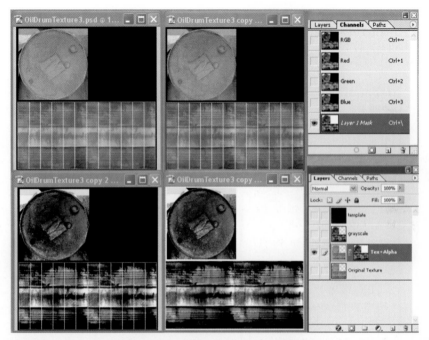

FIGURE 4.7   The stages of creating a Reflection map for the oil drum.

layer's thumbnail. (The thumbnail is the picture of the actual image for that layer.) Make sure that only this key layer is turned on when you save out a PNG file. At the lower right of the figure is a screen shot of how this should look. The `template` layer is turned off, the grayscale layer is turned off, and the original texture layer is turned off. Only the layer named `Tex + Alpha` is turned on; this layer is a copy of the original `texture` layer, with the grayscale selection pasted into its alpha channel.

Defining a Reflective Oil Drum Material in 3ds Max

After you've defined the material in Photoshop, it's time to bring it into a sample slot in 3ds Max and further define it. In the Material Editor, you can apply your texture to a Diffuse map and to a Reflective map.

Dragging a Copy of the Diffuse Map to the Reflective Map Slot

Figure 4.8 shows three stages for adding material with the alpha channel content to the Material Editor in 3ds Max. In the first stage, the material is applied to the diffuse channel as usual, but in the Maps rollout, drag a copy of the material from the Diffuse map to the Reflection map. When prompted as to whether you would like a copy or an instance of the material, choose Copy, because you want to make separate adjustments to the Reflective map here. Click on the Reflection map to change its parameters. (See the white arrow in the first image.) This takes you down a level in the Material Editor where parametric adjustments can be made to specific bitmaps.

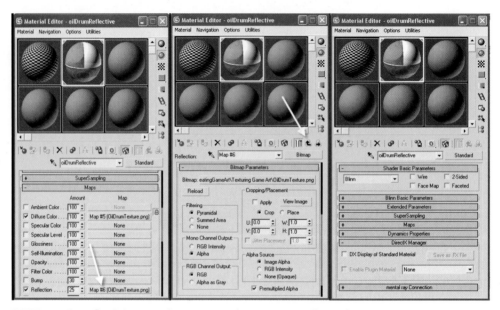

FIGURE 4.8   For reflectivity to work, you must select it in Mono Channel Output.

Changing Mono Channel Output to Alpha

In the second image, you can see that the focus is on the Bitmap Parameters rollout; in the Mono Channel Output group, click the Alpha radio button. Note here that the Alpha Source group is set to Image Alpha. You can then click the Go to Parent button (see the white arrow in the second image) to return to the main material interface.

Assigning the Material and Turning On the Show Map in Viewport Button

In the third image, you are back at the top level of the Material Editor, where you can select the object and complete the normal process of clicking Assign Material to Selection and Show Map in Viewport so that the material is assigned to your already-unwrapped and ready model. This process for defining a reflective material is the same if you want the material to be partially opaque; the main difference is that for opacity, you would drag and drop the diffuse material to the Opacity map slot instead of the Reflective map slot.

Assigning Smoothing Groups to the Oil Drum

Smoothing Group modifications for the oil drum include selecting all the cylindrical faces and, under the Polygon Properties section, assigning them to Smoothing Group 1, selecting the top of the oil drum and assigning those faces to Smoothing Group 2, and selecting the bottom of the oil drum and assigning those faces to Smoothing Group 3. After all three sets of faces are on different smoothing groups, you should have smooth cylindrical walls on the drum and realistic edges at the top and bottom where the Smoothing Groups change.

ON THE CD

All oil drum–related files are available in `Files\OilDrum` on the companion CD-ROM.

TEXTURING THE HEALTH PATCH

The main body of the health patch is a textured steel base, generated with various Photoshop filters; the raised portions of the texture were done with Layer Effects.

Creating Textured Steel

By applying four filters to a gray background, you can create an interesting texture for the main body of the health patch. The filter that makes this texture take on 3D proportions is the last one, Lighting Effects. The first three filters are there merely to give this final filter something to work with.

1. Fill the canvas with Gray using the Paint Bucket tool, with RGB values of R:123, G:123, and B:123.
2. Click the Filters drop-down menu, click Noise, Gaussian and set to 10%.
3. Click Filters, Blur, Gaussian and set blur to 3.5.
4. Click Filters, Artistic, Fresco, and set Brush Size to 2, Brush Detail to 8, and Texture to 1.
5. Reapply a Gaussian blur and set it to 3.5.
6. Click Filters, Render—Lighting Effects. Set Style to 2 o'clock Spotlight. Make sure the Spotlight covers the entire page. Set Light Type to Spotlight. Set the color to light blue (189,230,251 RGB). Set Intensity to 10, Focus to 91, Gloss to 59, Material to 82, Exposure to 26, Ambience to 24, Color RGB value to 255,254,199, and Height is set to 78. The Texture Channel is set to Blue, and White is set to High.

ON THE CD

`TexturedSteel.psd` is available in `Files\HealthPatch` on the companion CD-ROM.

Applying a Layer Style to Create Raised Steel Panels

Layer Styles are a powerful and simple way to create raised, highlighted, and shaded images. In Figure 4.9, the base material is textured steel. This base material layer can be copied by right-clicking over the layer and selecting Duplicate Layer from the right-click menu. In the figure, this layer is called `panels`. You can add a Layer Style to this layer by clicking the Add a Layer Style button at the bottom of the Layers pallet.

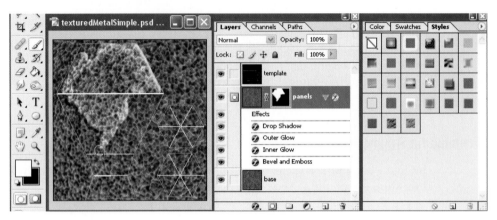

FIGURE 4.9   Using Layer Styles with Layer Masks to paint in panels.

Following are the settings for the raised panel Layer Style:

- **Drop Shadow.** Blend Mode is set to Multiply, color is black, Opacity is 25%, Angle is 30 degrees, Use Global Light is checked, Distance is 15 pixels, Spread is 0%, Size is 73 pixels, Contour is Linear, Anti-Aliased is not checked, Noise is 15%, and Layer Knocks Out Drop Shadow is checked.
- **Outer Glow.** Blend Mode is Color Burn, Opacity is 25%, Noise is 15%, RGB is 255,255,190, Technique is Softer, Spread is 0%, Size is 46 pixels, Quality is Linear, Anti-Aliased is turned off, Range is 50%, and Jitter is 0%.
- **Inner Glow.** Blend Mode is Vivid Light, Opacity is 92%, Noise is 19%, RGB is 190,190,190, Technique is Softer, Source is Edge, Choke is 0%, Size is 54 pixels, Quality is Linear, Anti-Aliased is turned off, Range is 40%, and Jitter is 0%.
- **Bevel and Emboss.** Style is Inner Bevel, Technique is Smooth, Depth is 131%, Direction is Up, Size is 6 pixels, Soften is 0 pixels, Angle is 30 degrees, Use Global Light is checked, Altitude is 30 degrees, Gloss Contour is Linear, Anti-Aliased is not checked, Highlight Mode is Screen, RGB is 255,255,255, Opacity is 75%, Shadow Mode is Multiply, RGB is 0,0,0, and Opacity is 75%.

Using Layer Masking Instead of Erase

As you can see in Figure 4.9, the Layer Style has been applied; when this happens, the Layer Style is applied to the entire layer. You can use a Layer Mask to help manage where there are pixels, and thus manage where the Layer Style is present. Adding a Layer Mask to the layer allows you to paint away the entire image and then add it back in, pixel by pixel. If you look at the Layers pallet, the `panels` layer has two thumbnails; the one on the left is for the main texture, and the one on the right is for the Layer Mask. When the Layer Mask thumbnail is active (as it is in this image), your foreground and background colors in the toolbar are set to white and black. You can paint with a white brush to add pixels to the layer, and paint with a black brush to remove pixels from the layer.

One approach to paint a template precisely with Layer Styles and Layer Masks is to make black the foreground color, paint the entire layer with the paint bucket, switch the colors so that white becomes the foreground color, and then paint with the brush. Painted pixels rise up with highlights and shadows, as shown in Figure 4.9.

To fill the template precisely, make the template layer current and use the Magic Wand tool to select the inside of a boundary. After you've selected the area, click Select, Modify, Contract to make the selection area smaller. Set the value to 1 or 2 pixels and click OK. Then make the `panels` layer current and fill the selection area using the paint bucket. You can make refinements in this filled image by using the brush. If you want to paint on the main texture, select the `layer` thumbnail first.

Animating a Pulsing Light Using an IFL Material

Creating any animated material using an Image File List (IFL) material is straight-forward. An IFL file is an ASCII text file that creates an animation by listing a series of single images that are displayed for the number of frames listed to the right of each image name. For Torque, these images must be either JPG or PNG files; usually there is a subtle transition where the images change as the sequence progresses. For example, the colors of the images may slowly transition from blue to red. The IFL file (`pulse.IFL` in this case) must have the following format:

```
pulse1.jpg 12
pulse2.jpg 2
pulse3.jpg 2
pulse4.jpg 4
```

In this example, four different JPG images will be displayed for the number of frames shown at the end of each line. If any other animations are in the 3ds Max file, you should adjust the total number of frames called out in a complete IFL cycle to match or divide evenly into the number of frames in the asset animation. The health patch is animated with 80 frames. In this IFL example, 20 frames are being used, which will cycle exactly four times during one health patch animation cycle. Each of the materials called out in the IFL should reside in the same folder as the IFL.

Animating a Transparent Exhaust Material

The exhaust for the health patch uses a gradient and ripple effect to look like gas moving out of the bottom of the model. This texture also combines Opacity mapping with animated IFL maps so that there is a moving, transparent flow coming out under the main body of the model. Opacity is achieved in a method similar to the way Reflection mapping is managed with the oil drum. The process used to make this material semitransparent is demonstrated on the video `SemiOpaqueMaterials.` `wmv` on the companion CD-ROM. This file is located in the `Videos` folder.

1. Open the 128 × 128 pixel exhaust template in Photoshop.
2. Set up the layers for a template, as discussed at the start of this chapter.
3. On your texture layer (let's call it `Layer 1`), create a gradient between a light blue foreground and a darker blue background (RGB 220,230,250 and 80,160,250). The gradient should be lighter at the top and darker at the bottom.
4. Apply a filter to make the image add wave: Filter, Distortion, Ocean Ripple. Set Ripple Size to 4 and Ripple Magnitude to 14.
5. Copy this layer and call it `Grayscale`. Desaturate it by going to Image, Adjustments, Desaturate.
6. With the Grayscale layer current, adjust Brightness/Contrast (Image, Adjustments) and adjust until the bottom of the image is completely black and the top nearly white. Select, All and then press Ctrl+C to copy the contents of the Grayscale layer. Now turn off the visibility of the Grayscale layer. You are done with it.
7. Add a Layer Mask to `Layer 1`. Go into the Channels tab, and turn on the visibility of the Layer Mask channel. Select the Layer Mask channel so that it is the active channel.
8. Use Ctrl+V to paste the grayscale image you made. Go back to layers. Click the thumbnail for `Layer 1`.
9. Select `Layer 1`, and click-drag until you are over the Create a New Layer button. This creates a duplicate layer in the position over `Layer 1`. Rename the new layer `Layer 2`. Repeat this process to create `Layer 3` and `Layer 4`.
10. Select `Layer 2` and activate the Move tool in the toolbar. Click three times on your keyboard's down arrow to move the layer contents down three pixels. Select `Layer 3` and click six times to move the layer contents down six pixels. Select and move `Layer 4` down nine pixels.
11. Turn on `Layer 1`, and make sure all other layers are turned off. Save out the file as exhaust1.png. Do the same for `Layer 2`, `Layer 3`, and `Layer 4`, creating exhaust2.png, exhaust3.png, and exhaust4.png.
12. Using a text editor like Notepad, create a text file that looks like this:

```
exhaust1.png 2
exhaust2.png 2
exhaust3.png 2
exhaust4.png 2
```

13. Save the text file as `Exhaust.IFL`.

When you are finished, your layers should look like Figure 4.10. Only `Layer 4` is visible in this image so that you can see the image has been moved down; this is the way the layers should be set up when exhaust4.png is saved out.

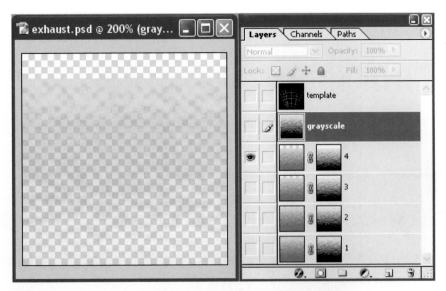

FIGURE 4.10   The transparent exhaust material is set up for animation.

Applying the Materials in 3ds Max

Figure 4.11 shows the finished health patch, with the three textures applied. The top of the health patch is a mesh named light, and it has the pulse IFL image applied. The main body of the health patch is named body2, and it has the textured metal material applied with Layer Styles to create raised paneling. The bottom of the health patch is named exhaust, and it uses IFL animation as well as an Opacity map.

Simplifying the Scene When Working with Opacity

When working with Opacity maps for Torque Game Engine assets, it is a good idea to work with just one visible object in the scene at a time. Testing and refining semi-opaque materials in 3ds Max is difficult if more than one object is visible, because you will see through one and into another, and the result will be confusing. To get rid of distracting meshes, select the object you are working with, and from the right-click menu, click Hide Unselected.

Using Mono Channel Output for the Exhaust Material Opacity Map

In Figure 4.11, the exhaust material is current in the Material Editor, and the Diffuse and Opacity maps are evident in the Maps rollout; here an IFL (text file) is calling four different PNG files in sequence. Just as with the reflective texture we used for the oil drum, the Opacity map for this material has its Mono Channel Output value set to Alpha.

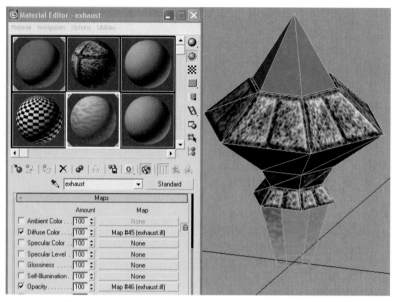

FIGURE 4.11 The finished health patch uses meshes, each with its own material.

ON THE CD

HealthPatchTextured.max and associated texture files are in the Files\HealthPatch folder on the companion CD-ROM.

TEXTURING THE WEAPON

For the weapon, you can use a metal texture for the stock of the gun and a gradient color for the fins on the barrel of the gun. In Figure 4.12, an area of the gun texture has been selected with the Polygonal Lasso tool. When the foreground color is gray and the background color is white, you can achieve a three-dimensional effect by using the Gradient tool, with the Reflected Gradient setting. The idea is to try to make the gradients blend in to one another as you work your way across the gun, so that the shape looks connected and continuous. The BlueBrushedMetal layer is turned off in this image.

To create BlueBrushedMetal, follow these steps:

1. Start with a new file that is 300 × 300 pixels.
2. Use the Paint Bucket tool to fill the canvas with gray (RGB 150,150,150).
3. Click Filters, Noise, Add Noise—15%, Gaussian, Monochromatic.
4. Click Filters, Blur, Motion Blur and set to 45 pixels.
5. Change the Canvas Size to 256 × 256.
6. Click Image, Mode, and set it to RGB Color.
7. Click Image, Adjustments, Hue/Saturation, and adjust so that Hue is 210, Saturation is 20, and Colorize is checked.

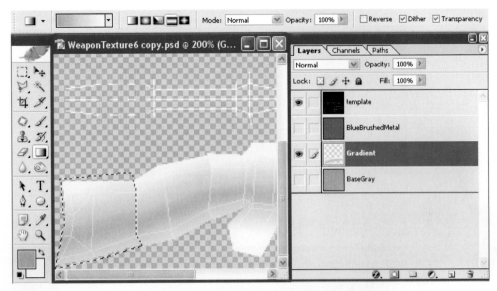

FIGURE 4.12   You can use a reflected gradient to create a 3D effect for the weapon texture.

Figure 4.13 shows this process near the end, where the canvas is being resized from 300 × 300 pixels to 256 × 256 pixels. This image is then selected, copied, and pasted into the weapon texture.

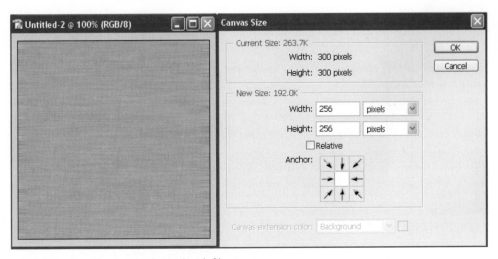

FIGURE 4.13   Creating brushed metal with filters.

Pasting the brushed metal image into this texture has created a new layer (see Figure 4.14). The layer is named and set to partial opacity over the gradients.

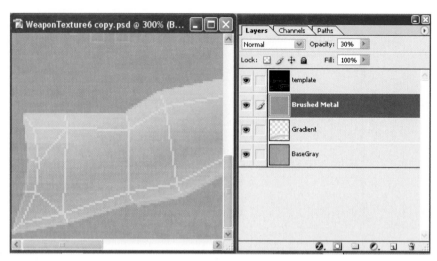

FIGURE 4.14   Adding layers with partial opacity can add depth to the material.

In Figure 4.15, the final weapon texture has been created by adding panels, an inset, text, and the steel plate material at partial opacity. A gradient colors the cooling fins on the gun. You create the panels by selecting an area within the template and adding a layer style.

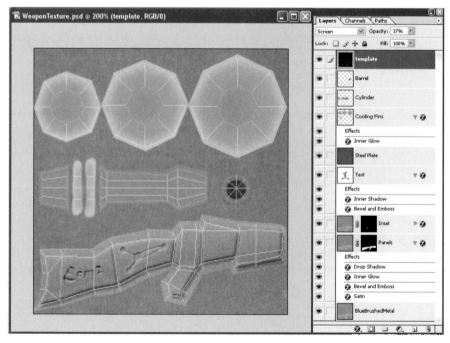

FIGURE 4.15   Multiple, editable layers make this texture flexible for future editing.

Figure 4.16 displays the finished weapon texture. After you apply the texture, you set the faces to smoothing groups so that neighboring, nearly coplanar faces are set to the same group. Where the angles between faces is pronounced, different smoothing groups accentuate edges.

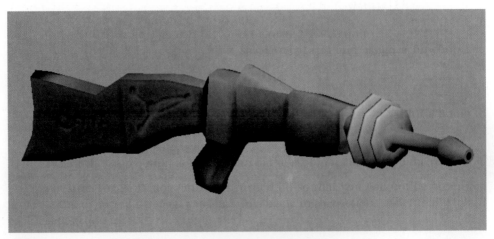

FIGURE 4.16   The textured weapon with smoothing groups applied.

ON THE CD

`RaygunTextured.max` and all associated texture files are located in `Files\Raygun` on the companion CD-ROM.

TEXTURING THE POWER CHARGER

The power charger will be a mixture of concrete and steel. The concrete will be created using filters only, and the steel will be based upon digital photos. In addition to applying materials to the faces, smoothing groups can be adjusted to help define faces and edges on the model, making the texture more believable.

Creating Concrete Using Filters

You can create concrete by starting with noise and blur. The Fibers filter creates the effect of water running down a surface for years and discoloring it, but you should use this only at partial opacity (see Figure 4.17). Dents are generated with the Sponge filter, and Bevel and Emboss Layer Effects are added to the resulting selections to give them depth.

1. Create an image that is 256 × 256 pixels.
2. Fill with RGB 150,150,150 (light gray). Name this first layer `Base`.
3. Click Filters, Noise and set to Gaussian at 5%.
4. Click Filters, Blur, Gaussian Blur and set to 1%.

5. Create a new layer, filled with RGB 150,150,150. Name this layer `Weathering`.
6. Click Filters, Render, Fibers, and set Variance to 16 and Strength to 4.
7. Change Opacity on this layer to 25%, and desaturate it to suggest weathering and streaking.
8. Create another layer, name it `Dents`, and use the Paint Bucket tool to fill it with RGB 0,0,0.
9. Click Filter, Artistic, Sponge and set Brush size to 1, Definition to 25, and Smoothness to 6.
10. Select the areas that are still black with the Magic Wand tool and delete them.
11. Change the Fill on this layer to 0%. Press Ctrl+D to deselect.
12. Add a Layer Effect—Bevel and Emboss. Set its parameters to Inner Bevel, Smooth. Depth is 1, Direction is Down, Size is 1, and Soften is 2. Shading Angle is 120 degrees, Global Light is checked, Altitude is 30 degrees, Gloss Contour is Linear, Highlight Mode is Screen, Highlight Mode color is white, Highlight Mode Opacity is 75%, Shadow Mode is Multiply, Shadow Mode color is black, and Shadow Mode Opacity is 75%.

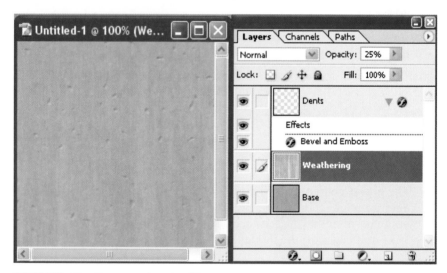

FIGURE 4.17 Creating concrete using filters.

You can paint the textured metal over the concrete texture by entirely painting out the overlay layer and then painting in the texture while Grid is turned on and Snap To is set to Grid, to keep the brush strokes straight (see Figure 4.18).

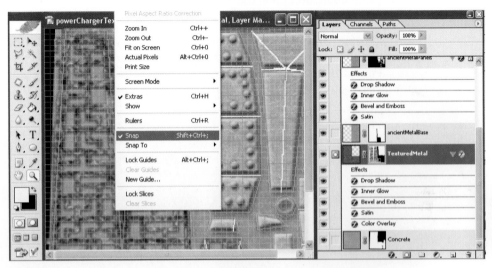

FIGURE 4.18   You can paint the textured metal over the concrete using an `Overlay` layer.

Creating Ancient Metal

Sometimes the material you are looking for comes to you in an inconvenient form. `Floordrain1.jpg` is a floor drain that seemed to have potential; unfortunately, it has slots cut throughout its surface. `Floordrain2.jpg` is a version of the same drain that has been repaired using the Clone Stamp tool.

1. Add `GrimeMR2.psd` to the image at 30% Opacity.
2. Choose Layers, Collapse Layers to merge the layers.
3. Apply the Plastic Wrap filter (Filters, Artistic) with a Highlight Strength of 4, Detail of 14, and Smoothness of 2.
4. Adjust Hue/Saturation (Image, Adjustments), increasing Hue by 25 and decreasing Saturation by 15.

This creates `AncientMetal.psd`, which is used at the top of the power charger. Layer Styles are used in the manner presented earlier to press and dent in the highlighted and shadowed material. This curves the material inward slightly so that the rivet looks as though it compressed the material slightly when it was applied. All of these materials are available on the companion CD-ROM. `AncientMetal.psd` is located in `Files\Powercharger`, and the other files are located in `Files\Misc`.

ON THE CD

Modifying Smoothing Groups for the Power Charger

You need to adjust the Smoothing Groups to complete this model. Figure 4.19 shows two copies of the power charger side by side for comparison. It is easier to see Smoothing Group issues on a nontextured model than on one that is textured. For this reason, you may want to create a basic material and apply it while you are looking for faces to put into Smoothing Groups.

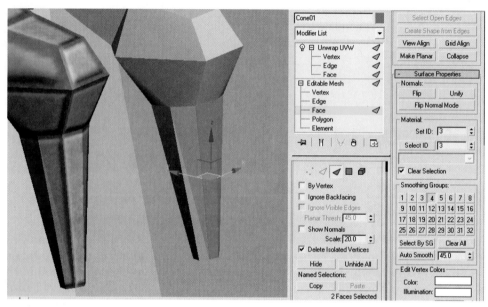

FIGURE 4.19   Setting appropriate Smoothing Groups for the nozzle of the power charger.

In this image, the right side of the nozzle of the power charger has been corrected, and the left side still needs work. Note that the left side of the nozzle has obvious faceting where two triangles form a polygon. You need to select both of these faces and assign them to a Smoothing Group. Because groups 1–3 have already been taken, these faces can be assigned to Smoothing Group 4. By going all the way around the nozzle this way, you end up with a nozzle that has clean lines. It will look much better with a texture.

When the model has good strong lines, and the edges are underlined because of Smoothing Groups use, the texture can look its best (see Figure 4.20). But the rendering you see in 3ds Max will always be slightly different from what you see in the game engine. Keep your textures layered and flexible in case you need to make changes after you've exported and analyzed your texture in the game.

ON THE CD

PowerChargerTextured.max is available in Files\Powercharger on the companion CD-ROM.

FIGURE 4.20   The power charger after smoothing and texturing.

TEXTURING THE AMMO BOX

The ammo box is a simple texture that uses a billboard to achieve an in-game glow. A *billboard* is an object that always faces toward the camera. You can create a plane as a child to the ammo box. If the plane has a glow material on it, and the plane always faces the viewer, the glow appears to be real. To tell the Torque Game Engine that your plane is a billboard object, add the prefix BB::.

The ammo mesh uses the same brushed metal technique as the weapon. A symbol has been painted over the metal on one of the faces. If you want a pickup to glow, you need to use the same method that you used for reflectivity and transparency; in addition to the basic texture layer, you need to add a Layer Mask and a grayscale image to dictate which areas are transparent and which are opaque. This Opacity map was created with the Gradient tool using the Radial Gradient setting, with white in the foreground and black in the background. Figure 4.21 shows a glow material for the ammo. Turn off all layers except the glow layer, and then save the file as a PNG.

Figure 4.22 shows what the material looks like in the Material Editor in 3ds Max. Similar to the method used for the health patch earlier in this chapter, the

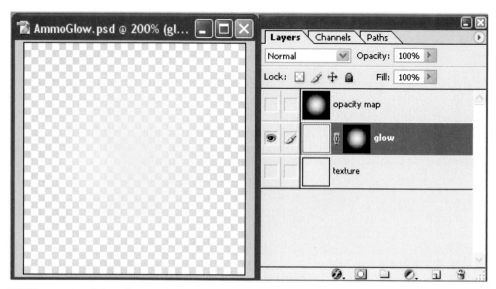

FIGURE 4.21   A radial gradient makes the ammo pickup appear to glow.

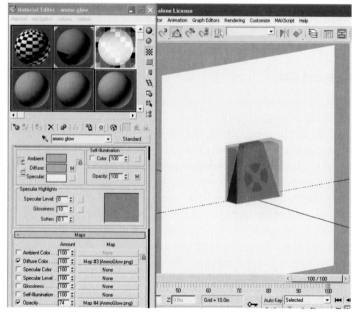

FIGURE 4.22   The glow for the ammo box uses an Opacity map and Self-Illumination.

material is first applied to the diffuse map channel and then copied to the opacity map channel, where Mono Channel Output is set to Alpha. In this figure, you can also see that Self-Illumination is set to 100 percent. Self-Illumination is located under the Blinn Basic Parameters rollout.

Figure 4.23 shows how to rotate the pivot point for the `BB::plane`. If a plane is drawn while the back viewport is current, you can adjust the pivot point so that it is oriented correctly to appear as a billboard in Torque. You do this from the Adjust Pivot rollout of the Hierarchy panel, by turning on the Affect Pivot Only button and rotating the pivot point –90 around the X axis. Notice at the top of this figure that the reference coordinate system is set to Local in the Standard toolbar. The ammo pickup with its billboard is on the left, and an unrotated plane has been placed to the right for reference.

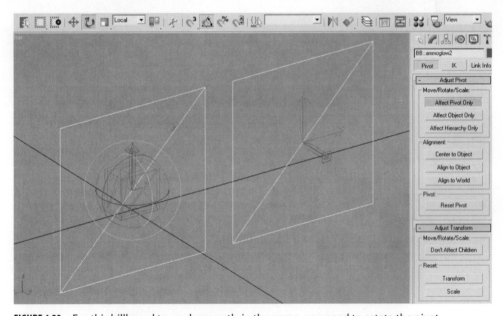

FIGURE 4.23   For this billboard to work correctly in the game, you need to rotate the pivot.

Figure 4.24 shows what this material looks like on the ammo pickup inside the game. The glow draws attention to the pickup, and the billboard effect ensures that the glow is always facing the player. If your billboard is not working, check that the name of the plane you are using for the billboard starts with `BB::`, and rotate the pivot of the plane properly.

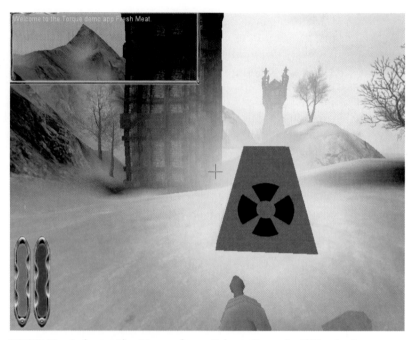

FIGURE 4.24   A plane with a BB:: prefix, partial opacity, and self-illumination seems to glow.

ON THE CD   The ammo model and all related textures are available in Files\Ammo on the companion CD-ROM.

SUMMARY

In this chapter, we discussed how to use digital photos to create your own custom textures for metal and concrete. We looked at reflective and semiopaque materials and how to create glowing materials. We explored IFL materials for making pulsing lights and jet exhaust. In the next chapter, we will cover how to animate art assets before you export them.

5

ANIMATING GAME ART

In This Chapter

- Understanding Animation Basics
- Animating a Simple Shape
- Animating the Health Patch
- Animating the Weapon

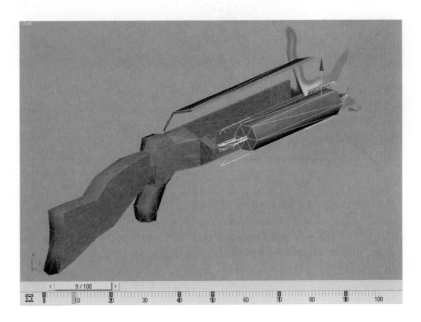

UNDERSTANDING ANIMATION BASICS

This chapter covers some of the basics of animation: keyframes, looping, and key tangencies. Animation for a game is usually *transform animation*, where something is moving or rotating. You do this by moving or rotating an object and setting keyframes. If you want to repeat an action like a ball bouncing repeatedly or a character running, you can set it up in a loop cycle that smoothly transitions from end to beginning. To make an object move believably, it is sometimes necessary to adjust key tangencies so that the object accelerates or slows down as it enters or exits the keyframe.

Creating Keyframes

Animation works by creating many frames that are shown sequentially, creating the illusion of movement. In the days of cell animation, in which every frame of the animation was drawn by hand, the master animator created keyframes and left the in-between frames to the more junior artists. A *keyframe* is a frame that gives direction to the movement; a bouncing ball might have three keyframes, where the ball is a meter high in the air, hitting the ground, and then back in the air again. If you want the health patch to be animated hovering over the ground, you might create four or five keyframes that have the patch moving up and then down and then back up to its original level. In modern days, the computer takes the place of the junior animator, creating the frames in between the keyframes for you.

To get a sense of how this works, reset 3ds Max and create a primitive in the perspective or user viewport. Turn on the Auto Key button by clicking it. It should turn red, as shown in Figure 5.1. While Auto Key is turned on, any movement or rotation you make to the selected object will create a keyframe. By default, your first keyframe is at frame 0. Slide the Time Slider to the right until you are on frame 10. Move the box in the positive X axis. You should see a keyframe created at frame 10 on the Time Slider. Move the Time Slider to frame 20. Then move the box again, this time in the positive Y axis. As soon as you move the box, another keyframe is created at whatever frame you happen to be on. Move the Time Slider to frame 30; move the box again, and rotate it this time. Finally, move the Time Slider to frame 40 and move the box again.

Note the colors of the keys that were created at frames 0, 10, 20, 30, and 40. The keys that involve movement will be red, keys that have rotations will be green, and keys with scaling will be blue. If both movement and rotation have been applied to a key, it will be red and green. Now click the Play button, and watch what happens. You created three keyframes, of which only one, frame 30, had a rotation in it. One thing to notice in this exercise is that because the rotation keyframe was not created until frame 30, that rotation you placed on the model is interpolated starting at frame 0. All the move keyframes were spaced 10 keyframes apart, so they are interpolated over 10 keyframes each. Animated movement occurs between any two given keyframes.

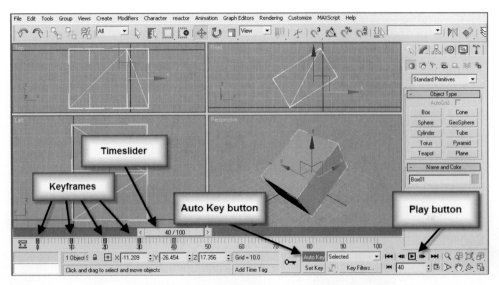

FIGURE 5.1   Auto Key automatically creates keyframes as you transform the object.

You can move keyframes by clicking and dragging to the right or the left. You can delete them by selecting them and pressing the Delete key on your keyboard. If you want to clone or copy keyframes, hold down the Shift key while you move them. You will not see the keyframes for your box or for any other object unless you've selected the object. You can't make changes to a keyframe unless you have the Auto Key button turned on. (You can create keyframes by using Set Key, which is discussed in Chapter 11, "Character Animation.")

Creating a Loop

Almost all of Torque's animations need to be looped or cycled; that is, at the end of the animation, you want the object to be ready to move back to the first frame. For example, if you want the health patch animation to suggest a wobbly, hovering type of action, you can create keyframes so that it will move a little bit. At the end of the animation, you will want to put the health patch in the same position and rotation it started in. If the object does not return to its starting position at the end of the cycle, it will appear to jump back to its start position abruptly, destroying the illusion of the animation.

An easy way to create a smooth loop is to clone the keyframe on frame 0 and copy it to the last frame of the animation. Let's suppose you want this animation to be 50 frames long. Make sure the object is selected. Then select the keyframe at frame 0; it should turn white. Hold down the Shift key and click, pressing and dragging the keyframe from frame 0 to frame 50 (see Figure 5.2). Now play the animation.

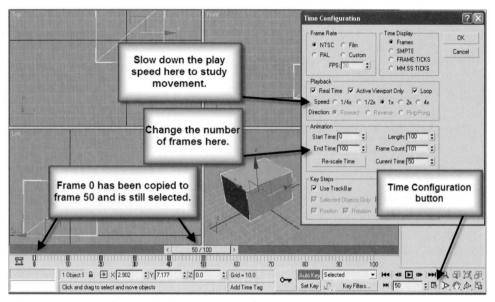

FIGURE 5.2   Creating a loop and adjusting Time Configuration.

The animation should play well, but will continue to frame 100 and then restart, making it difficult for you to know if you have a really good animation loop. Click the Time Configuration button, and set the End Time or Length to 50. Then click OK. When you play the animation again, you will get a better sense of how well this animation works as a loop. Figure 5.2 also highlights the fact that you can change the playback speed of your animation if necessary. Playback speed does not affect your animation in the game; it is only for analyzing your animation in the viewports.

Adjusting Key Tangencies

After you have keyframed an action, you may still want to make some adjustments so that the effect is more believable or interesting. The classic example of this is demonstrated with a bouncing ball. If you keyframe a bouncing ball, you normally end up with what looks like a mechanical movement. What is missing in this case is gravity. Gravity dictates that the ball should speed up as it falls and slow down as it rises. You could, of course, cause this to occur by brute force with lots of keyframing, but there is a better way. By selecting the ball and right-clicking on it, you can select the Curve Editor from the right-click menu.

Figure 5.3 depicts two stages from this editor. The first screen shot of the ball curve shows three keyframes from the ball animation; the first keyframe is the ball in the air, the second keyframe is where it contacts the ground, and the third keyframe is really a copy of the first keyframe, so that the ball ends up exactly where it started. When you select the second keyframe in this animation (frame 20), it turns white to show it is selected. Notice that in the first screen shot, the curve passing through all three keyframes is smoothly curved, whereas the screen shot at the bottom of Figure 5.3 is shaped like a big *V*. By changing the tangency type of the second keyframe to Fast with the Set Tangents to Fast button, you cause the ball to accelerate when it falls, bounce up quickly, and then gradually slow down as gravity does its work. For further work with the bouncing ball animations and related concepts, go through the Bouncing Ball tutorial that comes with 3ds Max. You can find it under Help, Tutorials, Getting Started, Animation, Animating with Auto Key, Bouncing a Ball.

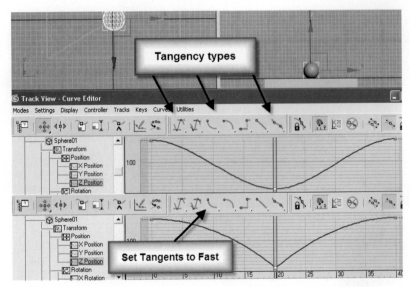

FIGURE 5.3 Changing the tangency type to Fast adds gravity to the bounce.

ANIMATING A SIMPLE SHAPE

Normally, a simple shape might have a transform animation applied to it; that is, it might move or rotate. Simple shapes can also have visibility and IFL animations applied. This example of a simple shape animation has basic movement and no texture applied. The platform is a box that was converted to an Editable Mesh and keyframed to move up and down. Both the platform mesh and the collision mesh are keyframed together; that is, while Auto Key is turned on, the meshes are moved up and down. The animation starts at frame 0, moves up at frame 80, and goes back down at frame 160. Frame 0 was copied to frame 160 to make the cycle blend together. Platform.max is available in Files\Platform on the companion CD-ROM.

ON THE CD

ANIMATING THE HEALTH PATCH

Animating the health patch is a little more involved because it consists of three components, and it uses IFL animated textures. First, you must parent the pulse and exhaust meshes to the main body of the health patch. You do this with the Select and Link tool. The location of the Select and Link button is shown in Figure 5.4. This figure also points out the location of the Affect Pivot Only button, in the Hierarchy panel. Once the meshes have been linked and pivots adjusted (if necessary), the main body of the health patch can be animated by using Auto Key.

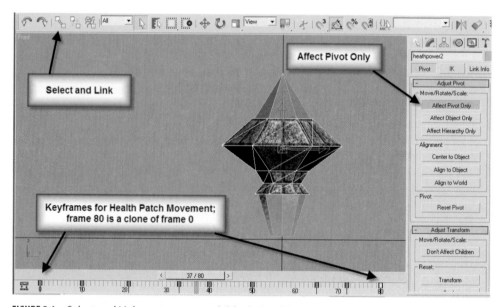

FIGURE 5.4   Select and Link creates parent-child relationships.

Adjusting Pivot Points with Affect Pivot Only

Carefully place pivot points for any object that is going to rotate. You can move the pivot point for any object by selecting the object and then turning on Affect Pivot Only from the Adjust Pivot rollout in the Hierarchy panel. Normally, you would just use the Move tool to move the pivot point until it is exactly over the area you want. Check at least two or three orthographic viewports to verify that the position is what you think it is; mesh positions can be deceptive in the user and perspective viewports. When the pivot point is in the position you want, turn off the Affect Pivot Only button.

Creating Parent-Child Relationships

The Select and Link tool in the Standard toolbar is useful for connecting two objects so that when one moves, the other does, too. The health patch you are animating in this chapter requires such a linkage so that when you animate the main body of the model, the other mesh objects come along with it. Normally, the main mesh or model is the parent, and other objects that are linked to it are the children. Using a car as an analogy, the chassis of the car is the parent, and the body, wheels, and engine are the children. If you want to attach a wheel to the chassis, you could say you are going to parent the wheel to the chassis. Then you could say that the chassis and the wheel have a parent-child relationship. The Unlink Selection breaks any linkage to the selected object. If you want to see what types of relationships are in your scene, click the Select by Name button on the Standard toolbar, and check the Display Subtree check box at the bottom left side of the dialog box. You can also use the Schematic View button in the Standard toolbar to graphically see parent-child relationships throughout the scene.

To parent the pulse and exhaust meshes to the main health patch mesh (healthpower2), press the Select and Link button, and then click-drag from the child to the parent. In the case of the health patch, drag from pulse to healthpower2, and then drag from exhaust to healthpower2.

Because all health patches are rotated by the Torque Game Engine by default, animate a slight up and down motion to give the impression that the health patch is hovering over the ground. In this figure, frame 0 has been cloned to frame 80 so that the animation ends up at the same place it started, creating an effective loop. Notice here that the time configuration settings have been adjusted so that there are only 80 total frames. Setting the total number of frames to the length of the loop will give you a better sense of how the loop will look in the game when you play the animation.

Because IFL texture animations are involved, try to coordinate the number of frames in your hovering animation so that the IFL animations divide into that number of frames. This way, the IFL animation cycle is not interrupted at the end of the hovering animation cycle. The health patch and all related files are available in Files\HealthPatch on the companion CD-ROM.

ON THE CD

ANIMATING THE WEAPON

The weapon requires no animation, but there is great potential for weapons animations. The crossbow weapon in the default starter.fps game is a good example of what is possible regarding weapons animations. The sequences available are activate, fire, reload, noammo, and deactivate. These sequences and the instructions for implementing them are discussed in more detail in Chapter 6, "Exporting Game Art."

The raygun weapon example is not animated, but the railgun is. The railgun uses three different animations: reload, fire, and noammo. Figure 5.5 shows this in process. The reload animation comprises frames 0 through 40. The cover on the railgun opens and shuts, making way for the loader, which carries a fresh slug from beneath the weapon to the barrel. The loader, which is highlighted in this screen-shot, had to have its pivot point adjusted before the rotation would look right. The loader pivot point was moved to where a physical hinge would be. This was done through the Hierarchy panel, using the Adjust Pivot Only button. The pivot point of the cover was also adjusted this way to move its hinge point to the very edge where it meets the body of the barrel. Always move a pivot point in an orthographic view-port, such as the front or right viewport, so you can be sure of positioning.

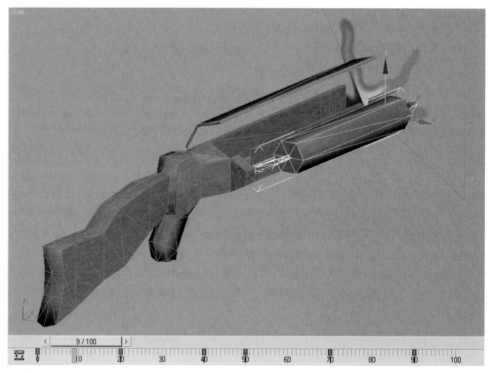

FIGURE 5.5   The loader, the cover, the projectile, and the muzzle flash are all animated for the railgun.

Initially, the projectile was parented to the loader, but this presented problems upon export where the loader and projectile were rotated 90 degrees around Z. There is likely a solution to this, but for simplicity's sake, the projectile was keyframed every two frames so that it tracked the movement of the loader and appears to fol-low it into the chamber.

The fire animation comprises frames 41 through 49 and involves a visibility animation. Figure 5.6 shows this process; the muzzleflash mesh is selected. From the right-click menu, the Curve Editor is selected. In the Curve Editor, the muzzleflash mesh is selected from the objects in the left pane. Click the Tracks drop-down menu, and select Visibility Track, Add. The new track should appear on the left side of the curve editor. Click on it to select it, and then use the Add Keys button to add keyframes to this track. In Figure 5.4, a visibility track has been added, and all the key tangents have been changed to linear with the Set Tangents to Linear button. This creates crisper transitions from visibility to invisibility. A value of 0 makes an object invisible, and a value of 1 makes it completely visible. In this figure, you can also see the keys from the movement of the plane. The visibility keyframes show up as gray on the Time Slider. If your visibility animation does not seem to be working, place the Time Slider on a frame where the object should be invisible and then render out a single frame; this will let you know if visibility is truly working or not.

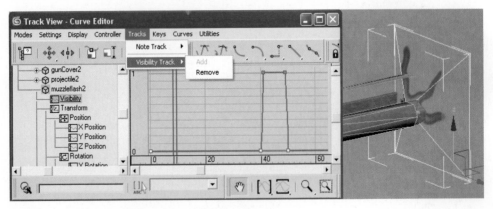

FIGURE 5.6   Adding and keyframing a visibility track.

Because this mesh is meant to show muzzle flash and it is using an IFL animated texture material, it is important that the IFL file be in sync with the visibility animation. You may need to adjust the IFL file contents so that the animated frames work with the visibility frames. The current IFL starts at frame 0 and lasts 8 total frames, repeating over and over. At frame 40, the IFL has started its loop again, just in time for the visibility animation, which starts on frame 41; the muzzle flash images are shown for two frames each.

The noammo phase of the animation comprises frames 50 through 90. This animation consists only of a partial movement of the loader mesh. The purpose of this animation is to inform the player that he is out of ammo. The projectile remains in the chamber during these keyframes, but because the player cannot see it, there is no need to move it or make it invisible.

The IFL material for this animation was created in Photoshop using a technique similar to what was used on the health patch, to generate an Opacity map so that the outside portions of the flash material are transparent. The rest of the weapon animation process is to set up Sequence objects for each animation, which is the subject of Chapter 6. The animated railgun and all related files are available in `Files\Railgun` on the companion CD-ROM.

ON THE CD

Summary

Animation is the illusion of movement. You can set keyframes that dictate what movement will take place, and you can modify tangencies to speed up that movement or slow it down. You can also animate whether a mesh is seen through visibility animation, and you can animate textures through IFL animation. After you've keyframed the animation, you need to set up Sequence objects and datablocks so that the Torque Game Engine understands how to display your animations. That's the subject of the next chapter.

CHAPTER

6

EXPORTING GAME ART

In This Chapter

- Exporting Game Art—Overview
- Setting Up for 3ds Max and Torque
- Previewing Game Art in Torque Show Tool Pro
- Setting Up and Exporting the Simple Shape
- Setting Up and Exporting the Health Patch
- Setting Up and Exporting Ammo
- Setting Up and Exporting Weapons
- Producing Simple Shape Animations
- Troubleshooting

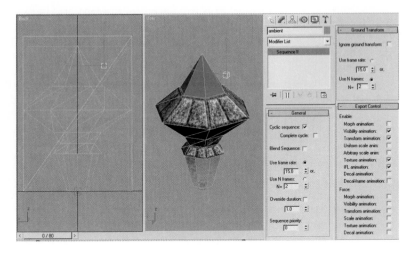

EXPORTING GAME ART—OVERVIEW

This chapter covers the setup and export for simple shapes, animated simple shapes, pickups, and weapons. Character creation, setup, and export are covered in Chapters 7 through 12.

Export Components

All art assets require some common components before you can successfully export them from 3ds Max to the Torque Game Engine. More advanced components such as level of detail markers, collision meshes, and animation Sequence objects are discussed later in this chapter, but here's the list of the basics:

- The model is an Editable Mesh.
- The model has the UVW Map modifier or an Unwrap UVWs modifier applied to it.
- There is a JPG, PNG, or ILF material applied to the model.
- The model is named and has the number 2 appended to it (that is, Health2).
- The model stands at the 0,0,0 origin in the 3ds Max file.
- The model is scaled to fit the game (1 unit = 1 meter), where a human is 2 meters high.
- Weapons and characters face toward the back.
- There is a marker (or dummy object) named Start01.
- There is a marker (or dummy object) named Base01.
- There is a marker (or dummy object) named Detail2.
- A box named bounds envelops the mesh.
- The Base01 marker is the parent of Start01 and Detail2.
- Start01 is the parent of the main mesh component, such as Health2 or Gun2.
- If other mesh subcomponents exist, they end with the number 2, and the main mesh component is their parent.

At first glance, this looks like a lot of requirements, but what it boils down to is that every model you are going to export should be an Editable Mesh that is facing back, scaled to fit the game, and properly textured. Other than that, there are some markers, which are really just dummy objects that need to be created in the file, and there are some hierarchy requirements.

Folder Structure

When you install Torque, a folder is created that can be called Torque, Torque15, or whatever you choose. The path to the files you will be most concerned about is Torque15\SDK\example\starter.fps. Starter.fps is the folder that houses the scripts (\server\scripts) and the shapes (\data\shapes). All scripts discussed in this chapter are placed in the \server\scripts folder, and all shapes are placed somewhere within the \data\shapes folder (in a subdirectory that varies with the purpose of the shape).

Static Shapes Folders

You can place static shapes in any folder you choose underneath `\data\shapes`. For example, you can group the oil drum with similar objects in the folder `\data\shapes\barrels`. If your static shape does not fit into any of the premade categories, make a folder; for example, you could have a folder called `\data\shapes\machines`, or a folder for animated simple shapes, called `\data\shapes\animated`.

Health Patches Folder

You can place health patch shape and animation files in `\data\shapes\items`. If you are simply changing the definition of the health patch, your health patches will replace the existing health patches in the mission. You can, of course, add additional health patches via the Torque Editor. Health patches have datablocks, or script definitions, that tell them how to operate.

Weapons Folder

Weapons, projectiles, and ammo files should be in `\data\shapes\crossbow` or some other weapon folder (such as `\data\shapes\raygun`). If you make changes to the folder structure for either health or weapon objects, you need to be sure that your scripts reflect those new locations. Like health patches, weapons have datablocks that tell them how to behave.

Bounds Boxes

For Torque to work properly with your files, each model needs a bounds box built around it. This is a simple box primitive that is big enough to contain the entire model. Name the bounds box `bounds`.

Markers, or "Dummy Objects"

Other considerations when exporting game art include objects that help Torque manage the models. In 3ds Max terminology, these are called *dummy objects*, but in Torque parlance, they are referred to as *markers*. If you are missing a marker or have improperly named the marker, your export will fail either partially or entirely.

Hierarchy

3ds Max can create parent-child relationships between objects, as discussed in Chapter 5, "Animating Game Art." The meshes and markers you export must have correct parent-child relationships or your export will fail.

Pickup Rotation

All pickup items including health patches and ammo rotate by default in the game. You can turn off the rotation field on any pickups including ammo and health patches, but the pickup does not stop rotating until you save the mission and relaunch Torque, entering the same mission. The rotate field is a check box that you see if you are in the Torque World Editor window and you select a health patch or other pickup item.

Animations

The primary animations you might want to export are *transform animations* (where the mesh is moving or rotating), *visibility animations* (where the visibility of an object is controlled by keyframes), and IFL animations. All animations require Sequence objects and datablocks. If you want to export a transform or IFL animation with a simple shape or a pickup, you need to create a Sequence object for it. The datablock references the Sequence object by name.

SETTING UP FOR 3DS MAX AND TORQUE

This preliminary setup prepares 3ds Max to export data by installing the DTS exporter, and it prepares the Torque Game Engine to import data by editing a script file. Entering the Torque Game Engine editor, saving missions, dealing with scripts, and working with the console window are discussed in this section.

Installing the DTS Exporter

The standard Torque DTS exporter is a plug-in for 3ds Max. There is one for 3ds Max 4 and 5, another for 3ds Max 6, 7, 8, and one for 3ds Max 9. They are all named `Max2dtsExporter.dle`. It is up to you to keep them straight on your machine; putting them into separate directories is a good idea. Place the file that is appropriate for your version of 3ds Max in the `plugins` folder of your installation of 3ds Max. Then restart 3ds Max so the software can see the plug-in. This exporter is available in the

ON THE CD

`Software\TorqueDTSExporters` folder on the companion CD-ROM.

The Dark Industries DTS exporter is a completely separate exporter. It is an EXE install that comes with a PDF guide. It is called `MaxDTSexporter_DC3.exe`. It runs an install and modifies your standard toolbar; the next time you launch 3ds Max, you will have an install. It places a DLE file called `Max2DTSExporterPlus.dle` in your `plugins` folder. This program shows up in your Add/Remove Programs list as `Max 7 DTS Exporter 1.3`. This exporter should work for 3ds Max versions 6, 7, and 8. A newer, unpackaged version of this exporter (as well source code) is available by searching the GarageGames Web site (http://www.garagegames.com). `MaxDTSexporter_DC3.exe`

ON THE CD

is available in the `Software\DarkIndustriesDTSExporter` folder on the companion CD-ROM.

You should not install both exporters simultaneously. If both exporters are installed, 3ds Max uses whichever one it wants, and you don't get consistent results. Therefore, install only one; if this is your first time, though, it is better to stick with the standard exporter until you have more experience. If you want to try the Dark Industries version, first remove the standard exporter DLE from your `plugins` folder. Remove in this case really means removing the file from the folder; renaming the file may not be enough.

Setting Up Torque for First Person Shooter

You must make one script change so that Torque launches in First Person Shooter, or FPS, mode, and you can have easy access to the Torque Editor. The `main.cs` file is located in the `SDK\example` folder. Open this file and set the `$defaultGame` variable to "`starter.fps`", as shown here:

```
$defaultGame = "starter.fps";
```

Try to back up any scripts you edit. You can edit Torque Game Engine script files with any text editor, but for the longer scripts, Codeweaver is a good solution. Codeweaver gives you colored code entries and numbered lines, as well as many other benefits. At the time of this printing, this product is available free at http://www.torquedev.com. You must register to use this product.

Deleting CS.DSO Files So That CS Files Will Be Read

The scripts you will be editing are plain ASCII, or human-readable files. All of the script files end with CS, and when they are compiled for performance, they become CS.DSO files. When you have made a change to a CS file, sometimes it will not be run unless you first delete the corresponding CS.DSO file. For example, one of the files you will be editing is called `health.cs`. After you have edited this file, delete `health.cs.dso`, because this old version may actually take precedence the next time the engine runs, which can cause you confusion and frustration. If you are editing script files, delete all of the CS.DSO files in the `server/scripts` folder to avoid this issue.

Entering the Torque Editor

You can enter the Torque Editor by launching Torque. If your installation folder is called `Torque15`, look in the `Torque15\SDK\example` folder for `torqueDemo.exe`, and double-click it to launch. Start the Stronghold mission as usual, and then press F11 to enter the Torque Editor. From here, you can access several different windows that will allow you to change the game environment. Under the Window drop-down menu, you can use the World Editor Inspector (F3) to inspect and modify existing game objects, and use the World Editor Creator (F4) to insert new objects into the game.

Saving and Renaming Missions

Most of the assets discussed in this chapter must be placed in the mission by hand. At some point, you must save the mission if you want the object to be there the next time you come into the game. To save a mission name, first make sure you are in the World Editor Inspector, as shown in Figure 6.1. Change the mission name in two places. Under SimGroup, MissionGroup, click on ScriptObject, MissionInfo. Here you can change the mission name and description. Then, from the File drop-down menu, change Save Mission As to the same name. The Script Object, MissionInfo value changes the name you see in the missions list when you start Torque; Save Mission As changes the actual name of the mission in the \data\missions folder. See Figure 6.1.

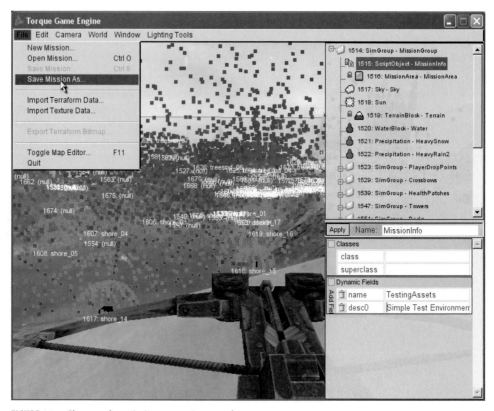

FIGURE 6.1   Change the mission name in two places.

Checking the Torque Console Window

When one of your models is not showing up, or if an animation is not running, you can often find clues to the problem by consulting the console window. You can launch this window from the Torque Editor by pressing the tilde (~) key that is located below the Esc key on your keyboard.

PREVIEWING GAME ART IN TORQUE SHOW TOOL PRO

The Torque Show Tool Pro is an incredibly useful tool for evaluating your game assets. In seconds, you can figure out if the mesh and textures are exporting properly, rather than going through the tedium of launching a game every time you need to run a test. With this tool, you can analyze animations, slow them down, study node movement, see various levels of detail, change lighting, see shaded and wireframe images, and more. Full zoom, pan, and 3D rotation is available via the mouse buttons. To use the Torque Show Tool Pro, you simply set up a project folder where you can find the DTS object and click Load DTS. To load animations for the DTS shape, click Load DSQ. In Figure 6.2, the Torque Show Tool Pro is being used to check the texture and animation of the health patch. The ambient animation is current, and the Play button is on at the bottom of the image.

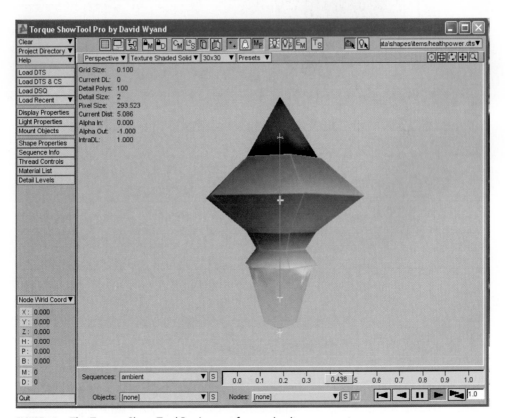

FIGURE 6.2   The Torque Show Tool Pro is great for previewing game art.

SETTING UP AND EXPORTING THE SIMPLE SHAPE

We will use the oil drum to demonstrate the setup and export of a simple shape. To keep this process as clear and simple as possible, we will export the oil drum without levels of detail or a collision mesh the first time through. Later in this section, we'll add levels of detail and collision meshes.

Accessing the DTS Export Utilities

Figure 6.3 shows that after you've placed the DTS export plug-in in the 3dsMax\ plugins folder, you can access the utility via the Utility panel by clicking on More. Select DTS Export Utility and click OK. The Utilities rollout should then appear at the bottom of your panel. This figure also shows the options available on the DTS Export menu. For any art assets other than character animations, you can simply click Whole Shape from the Utilities rollout to export the DTS shape.

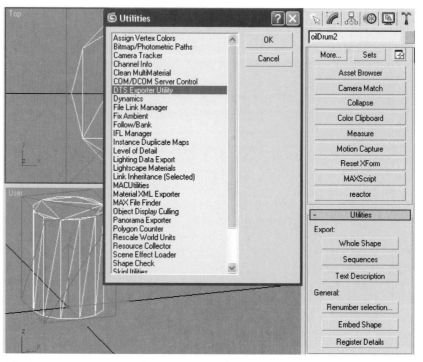

FIGURE 6.3   Accessing the DTS Exporter Utility.

Setting Up the Hierarchy of a Simple Oil Drum

Figure 6.4 shows how simple a shape can be at export time. Clicking the Schematic View button on the Standard toolbar launches the Schematic View dialog box. The view shows the three markers (or dummy objects): Base01, Start01, and Detail2.

The mesh is called `OilDrum2` and is a child of `Start01`. The `bounds` object, in green in the screen shot, is not part of the hierarchy. You can achieve this hierarchy by naming your model `OilDrum2` and clicking the Embed Shape button on the DTS Exporter menu. If you want to create the markers yourself, create three dummy objects, place them at 0,0,0, and follow the naming and parenting conventions in this figure.

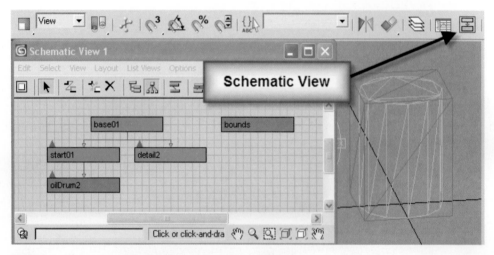

FIGURE 6.4   The components and hierarchy necessary for a super-simple export.

Exporting the Simple Shape

Export the oil drum by clicking the Whole Shape button on the DTS Export menu. When prompted, select an export path that is the same as that of the 3ds Max file you are working on, or you may have problems exporting. No matter what folder you use for exporting, ultimately you want the DTS file and any related textures to be placed in \data\shapes, in the appropriate folder. Because the oil drum is similar to a barrel, you can use \data\shapes\barrels. If your simple shape was a plant, for instance, you could create the folder \data\shapes\plants and put the DTS shape and any textures there.

Inserting the Simple Shape into the Game

In Figure 6.5, the FPS Stronghold Mission has been launched. F11 is pressed to enter the Torque Editor. By default, the current window is the World Editor Inspector. This editing window is for inspecting and modifying objects that already exist in the mission. To add a new object, you need to go to the Window drop-down menu and select World Editor Creator, as shown in Figure 6.5.

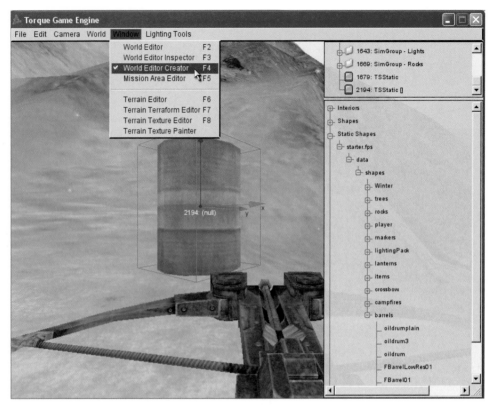

At the right are two panels. The upper panel, which has been sized down some-what, is for accessing objects already in the mission and for setting up groups to put your new objects into (which is optional). The lower panel is where you access the folder structure to insert new instances of objects. In this screen shot, you can see the Static Shapes category, under Starter.fps, Data, Shapes, Barrels, and finally the objective, OilDrum3. By clicking on OilDrum3, you automatically insert that object in the scene, roughly in front of where you are currently positioned in the game. As soon as the object lands in the game, it has positional arrows you can click-drag to move the object as necessary.

In Figure 6.6, the oil drum has been moved and scaled. Notice that the current window is the World Editor Inspector. The yellow box around the oil drum tells us that it has either just been added or it has been selected. On the right, you can see the properties that are editable for the selected object; 3 3 3 has been entered to scale the object up uniformly from the default of 1 1 1. If you find that your assets are too small compared to the rest of the game world, it is better to scale them up in sub-object mode in 3ds Max, but Torque is a good place to get a feel for what adjust-ments you need to make.

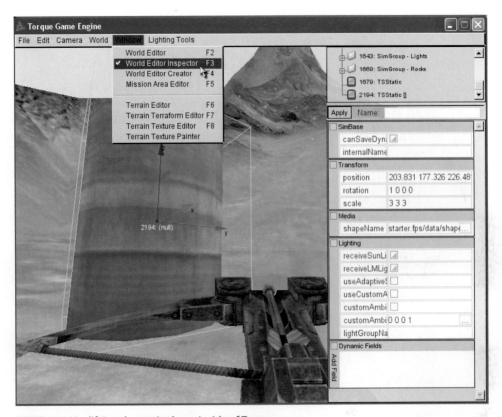

FIGURE 6.6 Modifying the static shape inside of Torque.

After you've saved the mission, the process of exporting the asset and placing it in the game environment is complete. In the next section, you apply levels of detail to the oil drum so that the engine can work more efficiently.

Applying Levels of Detail

The levels of detail, or LOD, capability in Torque allows you to set up multiple versions of any given mesh, each with different complexity, and it allows Torque to pick which version to display at any given time, based on how close the player is to the object. You can apply the Multires modifier in 3ds Max to any Editable Mesh and use it to decrease the complexity of the geometry. To use the Multires modifier, click the Generate button and then set the Vertex Percent value to a smaller number.

Here's how it works: Start with the shape the way you want it to appear when the player is pretty close to it in the game. Let's call this high-detail version shape128, because it is what the player sees if the image in question is 128 pixels or higher in the game. Now, make a cloned copy of this same shape, but decrease the number of polygons by about half, and call it `shape64`. This is the version of the shape the player sees if the image in the game is between 64 and 128 pixels high. The final mesh is called `shape2`; you can simplify it further, because it appears to the player only when the player is far away from it, and it takes up between 2 and 64 pixels in the game. For each of these meshes—`shape128`, `shape64`, and `shape2`—a detail marker is required: `detail128`, `detail64`, and `detail2`.

All of these detail dummies should be children of `base01`. Of all the shape files, only `shape128` (the highest resolution one) should be a child of `start01`. `Shape64` and `shape2` have no parents or children.

If you want to convert the oil drum model to one that uses different levels of detail, start by deleting all the markers we have now. All that should be in the scene is `OilDrum2` and a box named `bounds`. Apply a Multires modifier to `OilDrum2`. Use Edit, Clone to clone two copies of `OilDrum2`. Call them `OilDrum64` and `OilDrum128`. Use the Select by Name tool on the Standard toolbar to select `OilDrum64`; turn on the Generate button at the bottom of the Multires Parameters rollout, and change the Vertex Percent value to 50%. Select `OilDrum2` the same way, and set its Vertex Percent to 25%. Then select `OilDrum128`, and click the Embed Shape button on the DTS Export Utility menu. This process creates the hierarchy and markers shown in Figure 6.7.

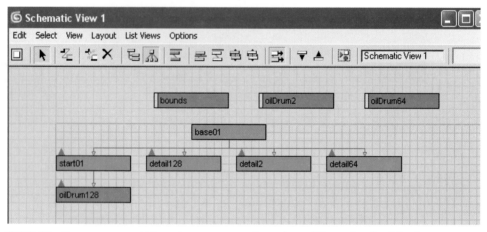

FIGURE 6.7   Components and hierarchy necessary to have three different levels of detail.

Because a game engine must render objects dynamically in real-time, game speed is greatly affected if too many polygons are being rendered at any given time. By setting up LOD for all shapes that have any complexity, you can improve the performance of the game and only render the complex geometry when necessary. When the player is looking at a complex object, other objects in the far distance are at their simplest detail setting.

Causing Collisions

If you want this object to be capable of causing a collision if a player bumps into it, you must create an additional shape that encloses the object as tightly as possible without becoming concave. In other words, you must use a box or an Editable Mesh that as closely as possible matches the geometry of the shape, yet is completely convex. A simple sphere or box is a good example of a convex shape. A star is another example of a convex shape, because at least a portion of its geometry self-intersects. A further requirement is that the collision mesh should not exceed the perimeter of the bounds box. The collision mesh must be called Col-1, and you must have a marker called Collision-1. The hierarchy in a file utilizing collisions is that the collision marker (Collision-1) is a child of base01, and the actual collision mesh (Col-1) is a child of start01. You can clone one of the detail markers and name the new copy Collision-1, or you can create a dummy object and parent it to the base01 marker. Figure 6.8 shows the updated hierarchy for the oil drum with collision objects. This file (OilDrumTexturedcol.max) is available in Files\OilDrum on the companion CD-ROM.

ON THE CD

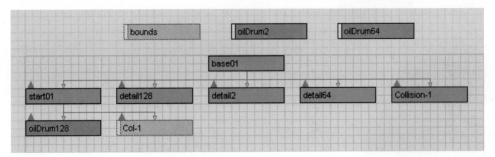

FIGURE 6.8   Components necessary for levels of detail and collisions.

With all these meshes for LOD and collision residing in the same space, take care when you apply materials—particularly materials that have transparency. With so many meshes in one place, it is easy to apply a material to the wrong mesh. Hiding any meshes you are not actually working on helps keep things clear. When in doubt, use the Select by Name tool in 3ds Max to select objects.

SETTING UP AND EXPORTING THE HEALTH PATCH

The health patch has multiple LOD meshes and a collision mesh and utilizes both transform animation and IFL animation. The hierarchy necessary for this shape is shown in Figure 6.9. The health patch is similar to the oil drum in respect to the base and start markers, the bounds box, and a detail marker. Where the health patch differs is in the linked meshes and the animation Sequence object (which will be discussed shortly). As is evident from this figure, the two meshes (pulse and exhaust) are parented to `healthpower2`. This linkage is enough to cause them to be included in the export process. They do not require their own detail markers.

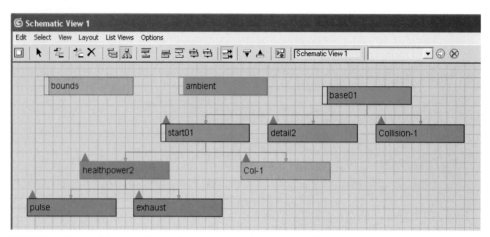

FIGURE 6.9   The health patch hierarchy; `exhaust` and `pulse` are children of `healthpower2`.

Colliding with Health Objects

Health patches need a collision mesh, because it is only when the player collides with a health patch that the patch can be activated. Do not expect health patches to stop your player the way a tree or a regular static object does when you collide with it. The collision property of a health item engages only if a player who hits it is low on health. Otherwise, you can run right through them. Even when your player is low on health and runs into a health patch, the collision only triggers an increase in health, at which time the health patch deletes itself from the game.

Embedding Sequence Objects

If the art has any animation, even if it is just IFL material animation, your DTS file needs to have a Sequence object embedded within it. The Sequence object, applied in 3ds Max, tells the Torque engine what frame the animation starts on and where it ends, and it passes along other settings. The Sequence object must be referenced in your Curve Editor for the start and end frames. This means you have to add keys to the Sequence object in the Curve Editor. Also, you need to select the Sequence object and go to the Modify panel and adjust advanced export settings, to include IFL or any other animation data you want to export.

Don't worry about exporting a sequence file separately unless you are doing a character run cycle animation or something similar and you want to keep your different sequences separate. Otherwise, the DTS shape has the animation sequence bundled into it. You can find the Sequence object in 3ds Max in the Create panel under Helpers, General DTS Objects (see Figure 6.10). Sequence is the only option available in this menu; the Sequence object is drawn similar to the way a dummy object is drawn, by doing a click-drag. By selecting and right-clicking on the Sequence object, you can choose Curve Editor from the right-click menu and locate the Sequence object Start and End Track.

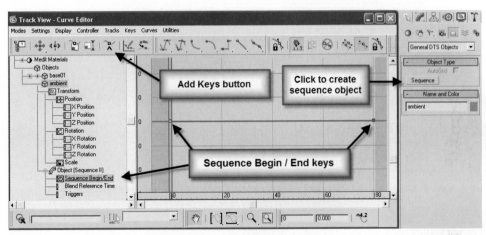

FIGURE 6.10   Creating the Sequence object, and adding the Begin/End keys in the Curve Editor.

If your Sequence object is not showing up in the Curve Editor, you may need to adjust the Curve Editor Filters; click Display, Filters, Show Group, Objects. Some of the sample files that come with the Torque Game Engine use an On/Off controller for the Begin/End of the Sequence object; at least in release 8, the default controller type for the Sequence object is Boolean. Either type of controller should work, because they behave the same. Boolean is probably easier to use; if you decide to use the On/Off controller, add your keyframes from the Dope Sheet (Modes, Dope Sheet), because you cannot add keyframes to an On/Off controller from the Curve Editor.

When a Sequence object is being used for any kind of animation, check its parameters before exporting the DTS. In Figure 6.11, the Sequence object has been selected and the Modify panel reflects the options available in the General, Ground Transform, and Export Control rollouts. Normally, you use a cyclic sequence (a repeating loop), and Ground Transform is unchecked. In Export Control, check any boxes that apply. Some boxes, such as the Decal Animation check boxes, are based on earlier engine requirements and are no longer used.

On the left side of this prepared image, you can see a wireframe image of what is being exported; the various markers are in green at the bottom of the health patch, and the Sequence object is the white box at the upper right (white because it is selected). The blue box around the health patch is the collision mesh, and the

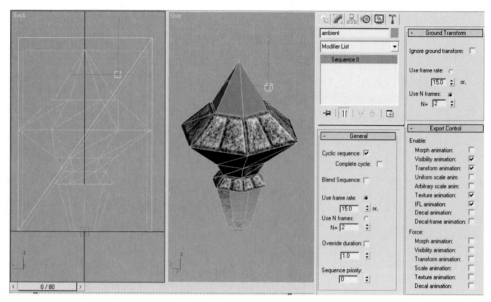

FIGURE 6.11 The export settings for the Sequence object in the Modify panel.

yellow box is the bounds box. When working with shaded images, you usually need to select any boxes that are in the way and use the right-click menu to hide selected objects. Hiding the bounds box or collision meshes does not prevent them from being exported.

Inserting the Health Patch into the Mission

You can insert the health patch into a mission the same way you inserted the simple object, except that health patches and ammo are found under the \data\shapes folder. Make sure you are in the World Editor Creator window when inserting shapes, and then select the World Editor Inspector window if you want to edit the size or some other characteristics of the shape (see Figure 6.12).

Scripting Health Patch Animation

A health patch performs no special animations, other than the standard pickup rotations, without activating its Sequence object. The following code is placed in the file health.cs, which is located in the \server\scripts folder. Health.cs already has a function called onCollision; in the code that follows, we are adding a function called onAdd, which is executed when the health patch is added to the world. Using this code assumes that you have a Sequence object named ambient in the 3ds Max file, and that the beginning and end keys are set for the start and end of the animation in

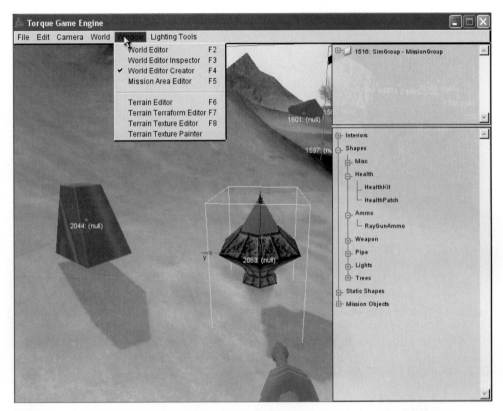

FIGURE 6.12   Inserting the health patch via the World Editor Creator window.

the Curve Editor. Be sure to delete `health.cs.dso` from the same folder to ensure that `health.cs` is read and compiled the next time you start Torque.

```
function HealthPatch::onAdd(%this,%obj)
{
    %obj.playThread(0,"ambient");
}
```

Analyzing the Characteristics of a Health Patch

Health patches have the same requirements as simple shapes, but they also need a datablock that tells Torque they are a health patch and you have to place them in the correct folder. Fortunately, the datablock is already created for you in the standard `starter.fps` install. Because pickups use a datablock, you can animate them. The health patch datablock is called `health.cs`, which is located in `starter.fps\server\scripts`. The following code shows an excerpt from `health.cs`, which describes what to name the health patch and where to put it.

```
datablock ItemData(HealthPatch)
{
    // Mission editor category, this datablock will show up in the
    // specified category under the "shapes" root category.
    category = "Health";

    // Basic Item properties
    shapeFile = "~/data/shapes/items/healthPatch.dts";
```

The tilde in the last line is a way of saying that the `shapeFile` is located in the `starter.fps` folder, under `\data\shapes\items`. If you move the original `healthpatch.dts` to a storage folder (or if you rename it), you can replace it with your own design. Using the name `healthpatch.dts` saves you script editing.

The health patch data files are available in `Scripts\Data\Shapes\Items`, on the companion CD-ROM. `Health.cs` is available in `Scripts\Server\Scripts` on the companion CD-ROM.

ON THE CD

SETTING UP AND EXPORTING AMMO

The hierarchy for ammo is shown in Figure 6.13. At a minimum, you need the same markers and meshes as you would for a simple shape. The collision mesh and markers are mandatory because that is how the engine tells that you have reached this pickup. You have to place this object inside the game the same way you placed the health patch inside the game, except that ammo will have its own folder. The ammo, like the health patch, automatically rotates when it is inside the game. Place the `ammo.dts` shape and the texture associated with this file in whatever folder you have designated for the weapon. For example, the crossbow `ammo.dts` is kept in `data\shapes\crossbow`. The ammo for the raygun is kept in the new folder `\data\shapes\raygun`, along with the actual weapon and associated files. To place the ammo in the mission, use the same technique that has been described for simple shapes and pickups. As long as the `ammo.dts` file is in the right folder, and the ammo-related scripts have been properly edited, the ammo should appear under `shapes\ammo`.

The ammo shape has a plane that is designated as a billboard object. The way the billboard is used in this shape is to create a glow effect. For any shape that has a billboard, you need a mesh that has `BB::` in the prefix, as in Figure 6.14. All billboard objects must start with `BB::`. Other requirements necessary for the billboard to appear in the game are covered in Chapter 4, "Texturing Game Art." The ammo shape and its associated files are available on the companion CD-ROM.

ON THE CD

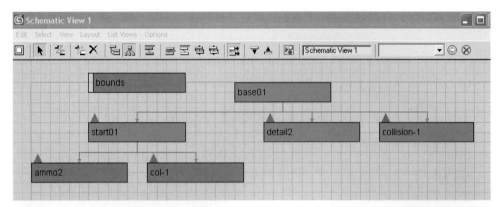

FIGURE 6.13   The simple ammo hierarchy.

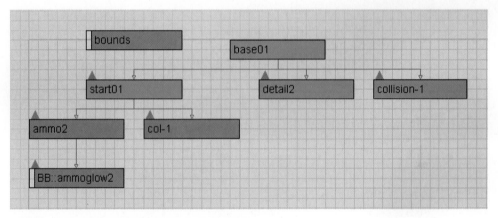

FIGURE 6.14   The hierarchy for ammo with a billboard.

SETTING UP AND EXPORTING WEAPONS

Setup and export of weapons is similar to that of health patches, except some additional files work with weapons. The best way to develop your own weapon is to start with an established weapon like the crossbow and copy the contents of that folder to your own folder, replacing the shapes as you go. That way you have all the basic files you need in one place. If your weapon shape is going to have animations, you need Sequence objects for each animation. Finally, you need to alter the scripts to ensure that Torque understands where to find the weapon files.

Weapons Components

The typical weapon is similar to the typical health patch; it requires markers, a bounds box, a datablock, and a particular location. A weapon also has a `MountPoint` marker that tells the weapon where to mount to the character and a `MuzzlePoint` marker that tells the projectile where to launch from. A weapon also needs a `projectile.dts` shape; this projectile is what is fired from the weapon.

The Projectile

ON THE CD

Figure 6.15 shows the simple hierarchy necessary to create a projectile, along with a wireframe image. This projectile shape is a cylinder, although your projectile can be any shape you want. The projectile shape is available on the companion CD-ROM.

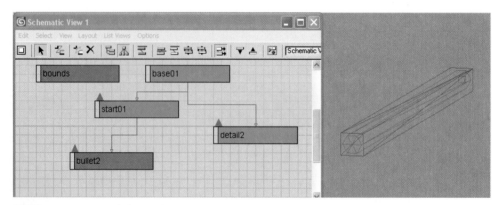

FIGURE 6.15   A projectile hierarchy.

A Simple Weapon Hierarchy

Figure 6.16 shows the hierarchy of a weapon with no animations. This example is taken from the raygun.

Preparing and Exporting Weapon Animations

For every weapon animation, including any IFL texture animations, you need a Sequence object. Figure 6.17 shows the relatively complex hierarchy necessary to support animations. `Reload`, `fire`, and `noammo` are Sequence objects that define the start and end points of animations.

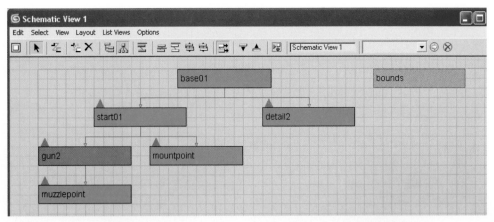

FIGURE 6.16   A simple weapon hierarchy with no animations.

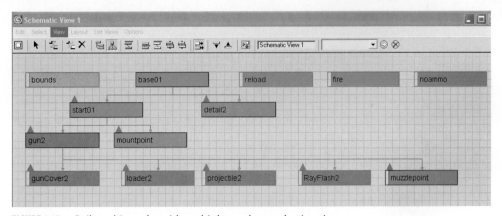

FIGURE 6.17   Railgun hierarchy with multiple meshes and animations.

Figure 6.18 shows the settings necessary for the `fire` Sequence object. In this screen shot, the `fire` Sequence object is selected, and the Modify panel is active. Because this animation uses an IFL texture animation, as well as visibility animation, you need to check both of these boxes before clicking the Whole Shape button in the DTS exporter menu.

The weapon should snap right into the player's hands based on your `Mount0` marker location in the character file and the `MountPoint` marker in the weapon file.

Scripting for Weapons and Ammo

Your custom weapon or ammo works in Torque only if the proper scripts are in place. The following is a basic set of edits that should allow your weapon and ammo

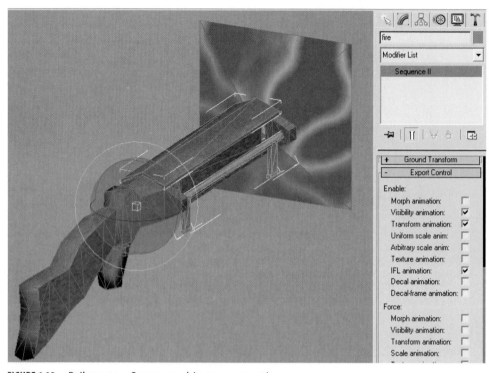

FIGURE 6.18   Railgun `fire` Sequence object export settings.

to work in the FPS game. If you are interested only in adding your own weapon and do not want to use your own ammo shape, simply ignore any references to ammo.

Make a folder for your weapon in `\data\shapes`. There is already a `crossbow` folder; use this folder as an example. You can call your weapon folder `rifle`, `raygun`, `railgun`, or anything else you want to name it. Your weapon folder needs the following files, all of which can be borrowed from the `crossbow` folder or from the `raygun` folder.

- `debris.dts`
- `splash.png`
- `projectile.dts`
- `ammo.dts`
- `weapon.dts` (`crossbow.dts`, `raygun.dts`, or whatever you have named it)

Copy an existing weapon datablock and rename it. That is, you can copy `crossbow.cs`, rename it `raygun.cs` or `railgun.cs`, and change the references in the code to reference your own DTS shape in your own folder.

Editing Raygun.cs

It is generally okay to search and replace all references to crossbow with raygun in this file, but you have to be careful that you also change any paths (for example, \data\shapes\crossbow becomes \data\shapes\raygun) and that you do not repath the sounds for loading and other actions to sounds that do not exist. If you are not sure what to edit to add your own custom weapon, study the raygun.cs file and replace references to raygun with references to your own weapon name.

In the code that follows, the path to the actual sound file for a weapon firing sound has been changed because, in this case, you have been provided with a raygun firing sound (rayblast.ogg, on the companion CD-ROM). When you put this OGG file in your \data\sound folder, raygun.cs should be able to find it. If you want to use a custom projectile for your weapon, you can reference it in the Projectile-Data datablock. The rest of this listing has some of the more critical replacements shown, but the best reference is the raygun.cs example.

Find:

```
datablock AudioProfile(RayGunFireSound)
```

Edit:

```
filename = "~/data/sound/relbow_mono_01.ogg";
```

To read:

```
filename = "~/data/sound/rayblast.ogg";
```

Find:

```
// Projectile object
```

Edit:

```
datablock ProjectileData(CrossbowProjectile)
projectileShapeName = "~/data/shapes/crossbow/projectile.dts";
```

To read:

```
datablock ProjectileData(RayGunProjectile)
projectileShapeName = "~/data/shapes/raygun/projectile.dts";
```

Find:

```
// Ammo item
```

Edit:

```
datablock ItemData(CrossbowAmmo)
```

To read:

```
datablock ItemData(RayGunAmmo)
```

Edit:

```
shapeFile = "~/data/shapes/crossbow/ammo.dts";
```

To read:

```
shapeFile = "~/data/shapes/raygun/ammo.dts";
```

Edit:

```
pickUpName = "crossbow bolts";
```

To read:

```
pickUpName = "raygun bolts";
```

Find:

```
// Weapon item
```

Edit:

```
datablock ItemData(Crossbow)
```

To read:

```
datablock ItemData(RayGun)
```

Edit:

```
shapeFile = "~/data/shapes/crossbow/crossbow.dts";
```

To read:

```
shapeFile = "~/data/shapes/raygun/raygun.dts";
```

Edit:

```
pickUpName = "a crossbow";
```

To read:

```
pickUpName = "a raygun";
```

Find:

```
// RayGun image
```

Edit:

```
datablock ShapeBaseImageData(CrossbowImage)
```

To read:

```
datablock ShapeBaseImageData(RayGunImage)
```

Edit:

```
shapeFile = "~/data/shapes/crossbow/crossbow.dts";
```

To read:

```
shapeFile = "~/data/shapes/raygun/raygun.dts";
```

Find:

```
// Projectile && Ammo.
```

Change the item, ammo, and projectile references from crossbow to raygun.
Find:

```
//Images have a state system
```

Change any crossbow references below this line to raygun.

Editing Game.cs

`Game.cs` is where different datablocks are loaded when the game starts. Comment out the crossbow datablock so that it doesn't load, or you may have problems loading the game. `Raygun.cs` is loaded in its place, and inventory references are changed from `crossbow` to `raygun`.

Find:

```
function onServerCreated()
```

Edit:

```
exec("./crossbow.cs");
```

To read:

```
exec("./raygun.cs");
```

Find:

```
// Starting equipment
```

Edit:

```
%player.setInventory(Crossbow,1);
%player.setInventory(CrossbowAmmo,100);
%player.mountImage(CrossbowImage,0);
```

To read:

```
%player.setInventory(RayGun,1);
%player.setInventory(RayGunAmmo,100);
%player.mountImage(RayGunImage,0);
```

Editing Player.cs

Player.cs is the script file that sets many of the parameters that the main character in the game uses. Here, two inventory lines are being added.

Find:

```
//Allowable Inventory Items
```

Then add these lines:

```
maxInv[RayGunAmmo] = 50;
maxInv[RayGun] = 1;
```

Editing AiPlayer.cs

The example given here applies if you want to assign the raygun to both the player and the AI player (the character that the computer controls). In Chapter 12, "Character Exporting," another scenario is presented, in which a new player definition is created for the AI player. This scenario uses a robot character mesh and a blaster instead of a raygun.

Find:

```
function AIManager::spawn
```

Edit:

```
%player.mountImage(CrossbowImage,0);
%player.setInventory(CrossbowAmmo,1000);
```

To read:

```
%player.mountImage(RayGunImage,0);
%player.setInventory(RayGunAmmo,1000);
```

ON THE CD

The raygun data files are located in `Scripts\Data\Shapes\Raygun` on the companion CD-ROM. The associated scripts for the raygun are located in `Scripts\Server\Scripts` on the companion CD-ROM.

PRODUCING SIMPLE SHAPE ANIMATIONS

If you want to animate a simple shape, such as getting a flag to wave, a tree to move, or a door to slide open and closed continuously, the first thing you need is an animation that works. You also need a Sequence object that defines the frames of the animation and the correct export settings. In addition, you need a datablock that defines the DTS file as well as the name of the animation sequence, and a reference in the `game.cs` file that points to the datablock. Finally, you need to place your DTS object in the proper folder and add the DTS object to your Torque mission via the Torque Editor. Figure 6.19 depicts the hierarchy for a simple shape animation; the components look the same as for a simple shape like the oil drum, except that the mesh and the collision mesh are animated, and we have added a Sequence object.

Creating the Simple Shape Datablock

The following file excerpt comes from `platform.cs`. This script references a simple box with no texture that has been animated to move up and down. The first part of

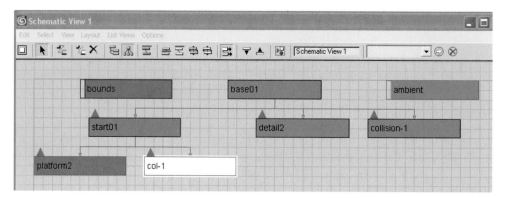

FIGURE 6.19   The hierarchy of an animated simple shape.

this file is the definition of the datablock. The category variable describes where to find the DTS object in the Mission Editor's creator tree (see Figure 6.20). `Platform.dts` is the shape file. In this case, we created the folder `animated` to have a place for all static shape animations. The next part of the file is the function `Platform`. This runs an animation called `ambient`. `Ambient` is the name of the Sequence object in the 3ds Max file. The last part of the file is the function `StaticShapeData`. This method creates the `StaticShape` datablock type.

```
datablock StaticShapeData(platform)
{
   category = "Misc";
   shapeFile = "~/data/shapes/animated/platform.dts";
};

function platform::onAdd(%this,%obj)
{
   %obj.playThread(0,"ambient");
}
function StaticShapeData::create(%block)
{
   %obj = new StaticShape()
   {
      dataBlock = %block;
   };
   return(%obj);
}
```

You can use this code for any static shape animation by replacing the word `platform` with the name of your own DTS shape, making any changes necessary to the `shapeFile` path, and replacing the word `ambient` with the name of your own animation Sequence object. Make sure to match the case and spelling of your Sequence object exactly.

Editing Game.cs to Call Your Script

The following code shows an excerpt from game.cs. Game.cs calls various scripts that will be used in the game. In this case, you have to add a call to platform.cs. Place your CS file at the end of the list for function onServerCreated(). All of the data-blocks listed in this function are loaded as the Torque simulated server is created. Platform.cs is not loaded unless it is added to Game.cs.

```
exec("./player.cs");
exec("./chimneyfire.cs");
exec("./aiPlayer.cs");
exec("./sgExamples.cs");
exec("./platform.cs")
```

Figure 6.20 shows the process of adding the animated platform to the mission. In the World Editor Inspector (F3), select animated shapes from the Shapes list, not from the Static Shapes list. The Misc category within the Shapes list is defined in the script file platform.cs. Platform.cs is available in Scripts\Server\Scripts on the companion CD-ROM.

ON THE CD

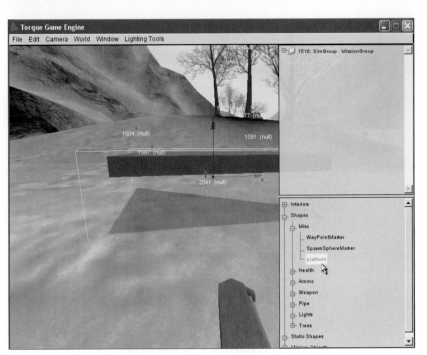

FIGURE 6.20   Inserting the animated simple shape via the Shapes list.

TROUBLESHOOTING

Plenty of issues can come up when you are exporting shapes and sequences from 3ds Max to Torque. The following sections can help, but note that the information is not exhaustive. The site http://www.GarageGames.com is the home of the Torque Game Engine. It has a range of resources in the form of Frequently Asked Questions, user forums, and technical documents. One of the best methods to use when looking for more information about a subject on this site is the Search button.

The Shape Does Not Appear in the Game

If the simple shape or pickup is not visible in the game, you might have a detail marker that does not have a mesh. For example, if your shape has markers for `detail128`, `detail64`, and `detail2` in the hierarchy, yet you have only a single mesh named `shape2`, the only time you will see anything in the game is when your shape is so far away that it is only between 2 and 63 pixels high. The solution is to make sure that every detail marker has an equivalent shape mesh with the same identifying number.

The Texture Does Not Show Up in the Game

The first thing to check if a texture is not showing up in the game is that the texture is in the proper folder. Wherever the DTS shape is, a copy of the texture should be also. If you are using an IFL material, you need to ensure that the IFL file and the JPG or PNG textures that are being called by the IFL file are in the right folder.

Weapon View in First Person Mode Is Incorrectly Offset

If you have set up your weapon's `MountPoint` and the character `Mount0` markers as best you can and the image of the weapon still looks off in the game, you may want to try adjusting the placement offset for the weapon, which is specified in the `raygun.cs` or `weaponname.cs` file. Look for the commented line:

```
// Specify mount point & offset for 3rd person, and eye offset
```

Edit the Offset line. Increasing positive X values should move the weapon to the player character's right, increasing the positive Y value should move the weapon in front of the player, and increasing the positive Z value should move the weapon higher. Decreasing these values does the opposite.

SUMMARY

Exporting game art from 3ds Max to the Torque Game Engine requires that the meshes, markers, details, and bounds boxes be positioned properly and in the proper hierarchical relationship to one another. If an IFL or transform animation of any kind is associated with the file, you need a Sequence object specifying the beginning and the end frames of the animation and an appropriate datablock calling the Sequence object by name. You need to save any shape files to the proper folders. For exporting character meshes and animations, see Chapter 12.

CHARACTER MODELING

In This Chapter

- Modeling a Character—Overview
- Setting Up Templates in Photoshop
- Setting Up the Template Planes in 3ds Max
- Modeling the Astronaut Character Mesh
- Adding Accessory Meshes
- Modeling a Robot with Multiple Meshes

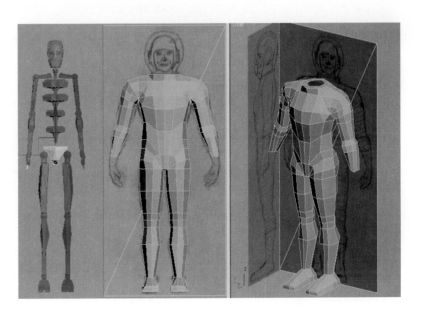

Modeling a Character—Overview

This chapter covers low-polygon character modeling. You can develop a low-poly model of a character in many ways; here the focus will be on box modeling, with some plane modeling thrown in for the face. Other methods include building a converted, surfaced spline cage or volumetrically building up a character's body with combined primitives. Box modeling is the most straightforward method, and it allows for the character body to be built so that it has a clear seam along the side and thus can be easily unwrapped and textured. If you are not already familiar with both box and plane modeling, make sure you work through the examples in Chapter 2, "Low Poly Modeling," before you begin this chapter.

Planning for Unwrapping the Model

How will you unwrap the model? Does the modeling technique you used lend itself well to unwrapping? Is the model posed in a way to make skinning and unwrapping straightforward? When you model, you are creating your own canvas that you will ultimately paint on. If you can model in such a way as to make the unwrapping process cleaner, you will spend less time wrestling with the UV map and more time texturing. Not only that, but some things are nearly impossible without a good clean UV map to work with. If you have not unwrapped a model before, you will probably have to go through the modeling/unwrapping cycle a few times to appreciate how the two are related.

Acknowledging Character Polygon Limitations

Think it through. How many polygons do you really need for this project? The Kork player body in the sample Torque file has about 1,900 faces. The fewer faces you use on any particular piece of geometry, the more you can expend on other items in your game. If you can keep the polycount low, there is a better chance that more people can play your game on slower machines. You can set your polygon budget by using the Polygon Counter, located in the Utilities panel by clicking the More button.

Setting Up Templates in Photoshop

You can, of course, model freehand, but in the majority of cases, it is best to start with a template of some kind. As you remember from Chapter 2, the template for the weapon was a single image of a gun, which was applied to a plane. For a character, you need at least two views: a front view and a right-side view.

Posing the Character

The Vitruvian Man, shown in Figure 7.1, is a sketch made by Leonardo da Vinci according to the proportions dictated by the Roman architect Vitruvius. This pose, with arms out and legs apart, is often used by character modelers. One reason for this is that when the mesh is tied to the skeleton, you can assign vertices to different bones with no risk of assigning a vertex to the wrong bone. Because the pose is so spread out, the skinning process goes quickly. A pose like this also makes more sense if the player will have a full range of movement, because the arms are about halfway up.

Contrast the Vitruvian man with the Kork character, which is the default character mesh that comes with Torque (see Figure 7.1). By modeling the character in a more relaxed pose, with arms near the sides and legs straight down, you minimize problems with deformation of the mesh when joints expand and contract. The positions for shoulder and hip are closer to actual positions you will use in animating the model, and because you have so few polygons to deal with, skinning the mesh to a bones or biped system should be fairly straightforward.

FIGURE 7.1   The Vitruvian Man pose versus the Kork pose.

Sketching a Front and Right-Side View of the Character

Start with a sketch of the front and side views of your character. A rear view is optional. Draw these darkly enough so that they will provide clear templates for your modeling when you scan them and bring them into 3ds Max. Make sure the two views are lined up, so that the eye on one view is in the same position as the eye in the other view, and the shoulder axis lines up. The hips, the knees, and the bottom of the feet are all key points that should align in your sketch prior to scanning the drawing.

Scanning and Creating Two Matching Images in Photoshop

Scan the drawing and bring it into your photo editor (Photoshop or a similar product). Using cut, paste, copy, and the Marquee tool, create two images as separate files. One can be called `BodyFront`, and one can be called `BodySide`. If you turn on the Grid in Photoshop so that the Marquee tool snaps to it, you can be precise about the way you cut out the front and side views of your character. In Figure 7.2, the front and side views were drawn so that they line up; using a grid to cut them generated two new images that are the same height. After you've cut or copied an image, you can create a new file and make sure that Preset is set to Clipboard. Then simply paste the image into the new file; it will fit perfectly. On the right side of Figure 7.2, you can see the result of pasting the images. You make the two images the same height to keep them in sync, so that you have a consistent reference while you are modeling. Two drawings of the astronaut character are available if you would like to use them. They are named `BodyFront.jpg` and `BodySide.jpg`, and they reside in the `Files\Astronaut` folder of the companion CD-ROM.

ON THE CD

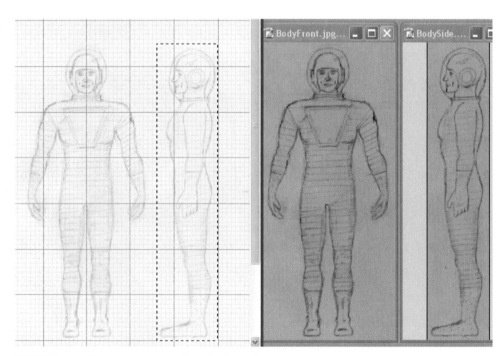

FIGURE 7.2   Creating character templates in Photoshop.

Turning Down the Brightness and Saving the Images

Change the Brightness of each image so that it is relatively dark by going to Image, Adjustments, Brightness/Contrast. Drag the Brightness slider to the left until the image is fairly dark, yet discernable. In Figure 7.2, you can see the adjusted images on the right. This makes working with the templates in 3ds Max more pleasant and productive. Save the images as JPGs.

SETTING UP THE TEMPLATE PLANES IN 3DS MAX

Setting up the units and creating proper templates for the creation of the character involves a few steps. Make sure the planes have the same proportions as the templates, apply the images to the planes, and snap each template plane to the grid. Ultimately, you can use whatever method you want to get both images into 3ds Max and lined up with one another. This process, as well as the first stages of modeling the character from a box, are on the video `CharacterModeling.wmv`, in the `Videos` folder of the companion CD-ROM.

ON THE CD

Setting Up Units

You have the option of modeling the character at any size and scaling it down later, or modeling it at the precise size initially. It is easier for most people to model at a size they are comfortable with and then scale down the model later; a downside to this approach is that your templates will no longer match the scaled model, although you can also rescale templates if necessary. To set your units to metric, go to Customize, Units Setup, select Metric, and make sure that 1 unit is set equal to 1 meter. This puts you in the right scale for Torque.

Creating Template Planes

Create two planes in 3ds Max. One should be flat to the front view, and one should be flat to the right view. Make the planes the same approximate proportions as the images in your photo editor. For example, the `BodyFront.jpg` file is 423 × 780 pixels, so make the front plane with the same ratio. That way, the image fits on the plane perfectly and allows you to line up front and side templates easily. You can create a plane that is 423 wide by 780 high, 42.3 wide and 78 high, or 4.23 high and 7.8 wide. If you prefer, you may also create planes of any size, apply a UVW Map modifier to them, and use the Bitmap Fit option to force the bitmap into the correct aspect to avoid bitmap stretching.

Orienting the Template Planes

Make sure the two planes are oriented correctly. Keep in mind that a plane has one visible side, so if you suddenly cannot see a plane, it is probably facing the wrong way. It is easy to mix up the two planes and put the front where the side should be, or vice versa; or to plug in a height value where you should have plugged in a width value. If this happens, rotate the planes (with the Rotation Snap tool turned on) 90 degrees or as necessary until you have the front plane oriented so that it is flat in the front view, and the right plane oriented so that it is flat in the right view. Please note that, by default, 3ds Max has a left view; for our purposes, we want to change the left viewport to be the right viewport. Right-click on the viewport's name to change the view to a right view.

Snapping the Template Planes to the Origin

Use the Move tool with 3D Snap turned on to move the planes so that the corner of each sits on the origin point in 3ds Max. You must have your grid turned on to see the origin. The G hotkey turns on the grid. Set the Snap toggle to snap to vertices and to grid. The method of doing this takes some practice if you've never done it before; you select the plane, get your mouse near the corner of the plane you want to snap, and drag the plane to the point on the grid that is at 0,0. In Figure 7.3, the front plane is in position, and the side plane is being snapped into position by moving it from the vertex to the gridpoint at 0,0.

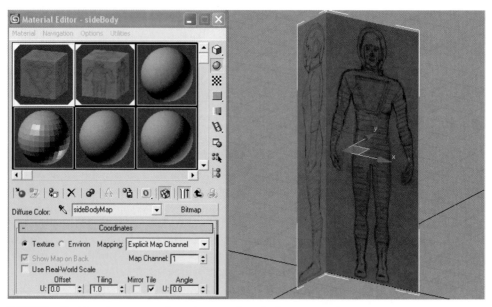

FIGURE 7.3 Position the two template planes and apply the template images.

Applying the Templates to the Planes

With both planes oriented, sized, and snapped into position, it is time to place the front and side templates on them. Open the Material Editor (press M) and create a new custom material, as described in Chapter 1, "Introduction to 3ds Max." Your first material will be called `BodyFront`, and the second material will be called `BodySide`. Apply each of these materials to the respective planes of front and right side. Remember to check the Show Map in Viewport box in the Material Editor so that you can see the templates in each viewport. Adjust the template positions so that the tops of the head, chin, hips, knees, and feet on both templates match up.

Freezing the Templates

Freezing the template planes keeps them from being accidentally selected while we are modeling. To freeze the template planes, select them, right-click and select Properties, and then check the box next to Freeze. Make sure to uncheck Show Frozen in Gray, and then click OK. If you leave Show Frozen in Gray checked, all frozen objects turn gray, and we will not be able to see the actual template, which is the whole point of this procedure.

MODELING THE ASTRONAUT CHARACTER MESH

Start the modeling process by creating a box and converting it to an Editable Poly. Change the properties of the box and the viewport so that the box is transparent but the edges are visible. Early in the process, invoke the Symmetry modifier so that you can work more quickly, modeling just one side of the character while being able to see the complete model take shape. Extrude legs and arms from the torso of the character, and add edges to suggest a rounder body and limbs. You'll create the head and hands separately and add them to the model.

Starting with a Box

Place the first piece of modeling geometry at a key spot in the model. Look for an area in the model that is central, from which you can build out. In most characters, that area is the torso. Create a box standard primitive that has only one segment for length, width, and height, and adjust these values until the box is the same size as the lower part of the torso. You need to use your Move tool to get this looking right. Don't worry about making the box look right for the upper torso yet. Check the side view to see that the box lines up well.

Making the Modeling Process Easier by Adjusting Properties

Now make the box transparent so you can see the template through it. To make the box transparent, select it, right-click and go to Properties, See-Through, and click OK. Convert the box to an Editable Poly. (Select it, right-click, and select Convert to Editable Poly.) Here it would be nice to see the edges of the box. Make sure Edges are enabled for selected objects by right-clicking on a viewport name and then clicking Configuration; check Display Selected with Edged Faces. Note on this screen another useful option called Use Selection Brackets. Turning off this option gets rid of the white brackets around selected objects, which can improve clarity in the viewports. Note in Figure 7.4 that the torso has begun to take shape, and Selection Brackets are turned off to make seeing the real edges of the model easier.

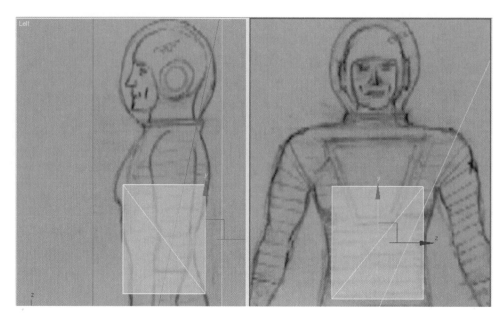

FIGURE 7.4 Starting with a box.

Adding Symmetry to Speed the Modeling Process

After you have the basic shape of the torso, you can use a Planar Slice to cut the model into a left and right half. Then delete the left half of the model, select an edge along the midline, and apply a Symmetry modifier. If you then turn on the Show End Result toggle, you can continue to work on the Editable Poly while both sides of the model stay in sync with any changes. For a review of how to use the Symmetry modifier, see Chapter 2.

Extruding the Arms and Legs

You can extrude and bevel arms and legs from the main torso. Select a face, Extrude or Bevel, click OK, make an adjustment by scaling or rotating the selected end of the limb, and repeat. As you go through this cycle, attempt to match the lines of the template with your model. Work primarily in the front view, but periodically go to your perspective view and right side view to make sure you are on track with the template. Figure 7.5 shows this process.

Moving and Adding Vertices as Necessary

Every time you add an extrusion or bevel, double-check your work and adjust vertices as needed to keep the simple form as accurate as possible. You can see in Figure 7.6 that the shape of the shoulder has undergone some modification already; the

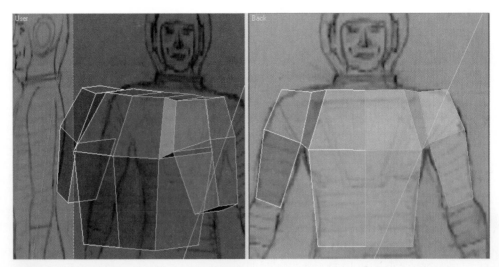

FIGURE 7.5   Build the body with a series of bevels.

rather simple polygons have been adjusted by moving vertices, sometimes one at a time. It is easier to manage a few vertices at this stage than to wait until there are more edges and vertices to contend with.

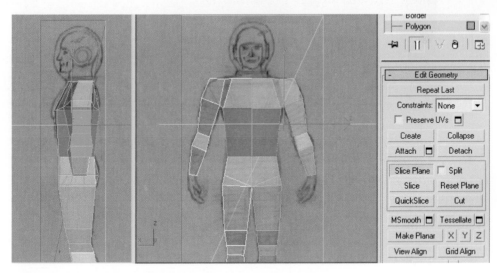

FIGURE 7.6   This Slice Plane will be applied only to the selected faces.

This figure also demonstrates that you can cause a slice plane to cut through only those polygons that are selected. While in Polygon sub-object mode, select the polygons you want to slice, turn on the Slice Plane button, and click the Slice button.

This slice helps to create a line defining the lower part of the chest without generating additional cuts on the arms.

Adding Edges with Row, Loop, and Connect

After you have the basic idea of the torso, arms, legs, and feet, it is time to select an edge on the front of the torso and use Ring to select a ring of edges parallel to your selected edge. You then click the Connect button to connect the selected edges with an edge that passes through the middle of all of them. In Figure 7.7, two models are shown and the menus expanded to illustrate how to prepare the model for the next phase. In the model at the left, horizontal edges are being selected, which happen to be lined up in a row on the mesh. You can select one such edge and then click the Ring button to capture all edges that are similarly ringed around the mesh. You need to select some of these edges by hand by holding down the Ctrl key and clicking on them.

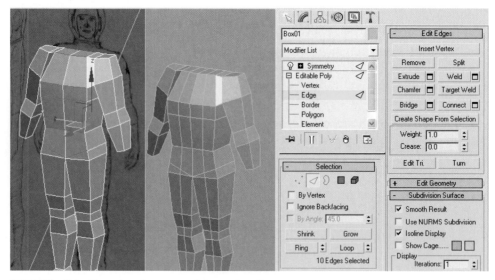

FIGURE 7.7   Selecting edges by row, and then using Connect.

After you've selected all the edges, use the Connect button from the Edit Edges rollout to cause a connecting edge to pass through the middle of all the selected edges. Once you've done this on the front and back of the model, you also must do it to the sides of the model, from the groin to the neck. In addition, you need to connect the front and back edges of the arms. This doubles the number of polygons on the model, but because of the way you built the model, each polygon is effectively used.

Adding Volume and Shape to the Mesh

By selecting the newly created edges and moving them slightly away from the model, you add volume and shape. The idea is to move away from the "box man" and more toward naturally shaped limbs. The body and limbs that had four edges each now have eight. In Figure 7.8, the new edges on the front of the legs are selected and moved slightly forward to suggest roundness.

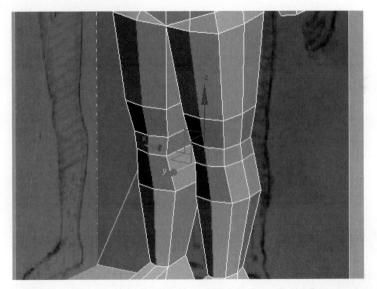

FIGURE 7.8   Moving edges to add shape and volume to the body.

Using Edge Loops

Edge Loops allow the character mesh to move more believably than standard modeling techniques. In Figure 7.9, six steps take us from our extruded shoulder to a flow of edges that will look and move more naturally. The upper-left image is the original starting mesh. The upper-middle mesh has had the vertices at the armpit area welded together. At the upper right, edges have been cut, connecting the edge at the top of the bicep to the edge that runs under the armpit. The mesh at the lower left has had the vertical edges above the bicep removed. A quick way to remove an edge and any associated vertices is to select the edge and hold down the Ctrl key while you press the Backspace key. The lower-middle mesh has had an edge added near the chest to eliminate the five-sided polygon that was formed. At the lower right, the vertices have been spread out more evenly to create a more uniform and rounder shoulder shape. Complete this same procedure on the back of the shoulder. Edge Loops allow you to model more in accordance with how actual musculature is set up.

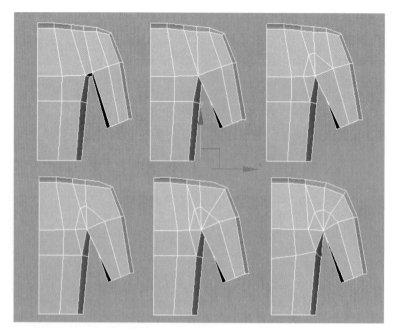

FIGURE 7.9   Six steps to creating an Edge Loop.

Planning for Movement

As the body is going together, what's going to move? The typical FPS character doesn't have facial animations, and it usually doesn't even have working hands. There are only upper and lower arm and leg bones, one bone for each hand, one for each foot, two spine bones, a pelvic bone, a head bone, and possibly a neck bone and both clavicle bones. These bones have to move in at least a root animation, a run cycle, a backward run cycle, a sideways run cycle, a jump-fall-land cycle, and a death sequence. Because you will be putting bones inside this mesh, which will be responsible for a set of vertices, it is useful even at this early design stage to consider where the hinge points are for each joint.

If you are going to be using a biped for your skeletal structure, you can create a test biped next to your character mesh to help you in the planning process. You can create a biped from the Create panel, under Systems, Biped. Press and drag to create a biped. Manipulating the biped skeleton is discussed in detail in Chapter 10, "Character Rigging." Simply select and hide it when you are not using it, or delete it when you are through with it. Figure 7.10 shows the nearly complete character mesh alongside a biped as bone assignments are being considered. A collar has been built into the neck area of the mesh to hold the head and provide a platform for the helmet, which you'll apply as a separate mesh.

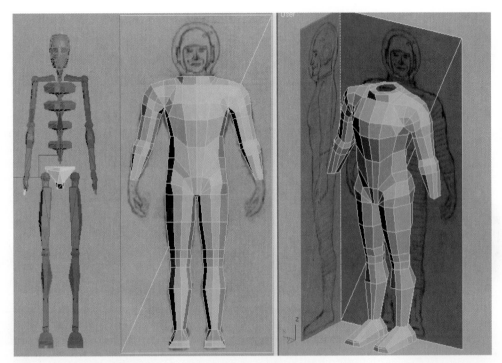

FIGURE 7.10   Building the character mesh with the biped bones in mind.

Modeling the Hands

One of the best references for modeling a hand is to look at your own hand. You can pose one hand in position while the other is free to drive 3ds Max. You can model the hands as a kind of mitten, where you apply the fingers via the texture, or you can model the fingers separately. If you model the fingers separately, you should decide at this stage whether you will use separate finger bones to move them or just model the hands ahead of time so that they are ready to receive the weapon. For the astronaut, the hands were modeled with the fingers in the proper position for holding the weapon; finger bones were not used to change their position.

It can be a good idea to model the hands separately from the body of the character so that they can receive undivided attention. Often when modeling hands while the body is attached, you will find yourself constrained by the body mesh being so close and always in the way or in the background. When the hand is complete, you can attach it to the rest of the character mesh. A little forethought makes this process go more smoothly. Try to model the hand so that the number of vertices in the wrist matches the number of vertices in the wrist of the character body. That way, you can easily attach the two and weld them together.

Figure 7.11 shows five stages to creating a hand. To start modeling a hand, create a box that is 4 × 3 × 1 segments, as shown. In the next stage, you convert the box to an Editable Poly, and extrude a thumb area. Welding two vertices of this extrusion gives you the triangular shape. In the third stage, the Editable Poly has been adjusted a bit so that where the fingers start, the polygons are already rotated into position. Following that, 2D splines are drawn for each finger. The fingers of the hands need to be precurved, with thumbs somewhat opposing them, in a loose-holding position. Similar to the way we created the 2D profile for the barrel of the weapon, our simple lines serve as a tool to help extrude each finger. If you create your own finger splines, you have to draw them, one by one, most likely in the right or left viewport. Then you have to make adjustments, vertex by vertex, in the other viewports. When the fingers are ready to extrude, select the polygon you want to extrude, and from the Edit Polygons rollout, click the Setup button for Extrude Along Spline. In the Extrude Polygons Along Spline dialog box, select the spline you want the selected polygon to follow, and click OK. See the figure for settings. The last two stages of the hand are cleanup stages, where vertices are welded and edges removed to minimize the polygon count. This file is called `HandSetup.max`, and it's available in the `Files\Astronaut` folder on the companion CD-ROM.

ON THE CD

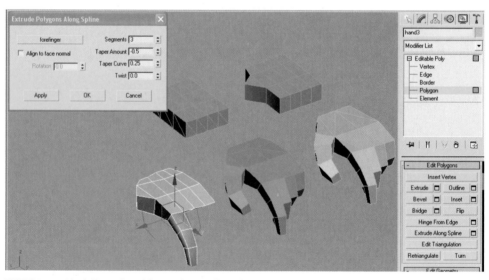

FIGURE 7.11　Modeling a hand from a box in five steps.

Merging and Scaling the Hand to Fit the Body

In this example, a hand was made without concern for units or scaling to demonstrate how you might scale and use an oversized mesh. When you're finished with the hand, name the mesh and save the file. Open your main character file, select File, File Merge, and locate your own hand file. Alternatively, you can use

ON THE CD

HandSetup.max (again, available on the companion CD-ROM under `Files\Astronaut`). You will see a dialog box that allows you to select various elements from the file for merging. Select `Hand5`, or whatever your mesh was named, and click OK.

If you merge or import a file that is too big or too small, you can get into Vertex sub-object mode and scale down the hand with a Uniform Scale until it looks like it will fit the model of the body. Often when a file is merged, imported, or scaled, moving the mesh can be tricky, because the Move gizmo is now situated far away from the model. To correct this, while the hand is selected, activate the Hierarchy panel, and in the Adjust Pivot rollout, turn on Affect Pivot Only (see Figure 7.12). Move the pivot for the mesh closer to where the mesh is. A quick way to do this is to click the Center to Object button while the Affect Pivot Only button is turned on. Make sure to turn off Affect Pivot Only before proceeding further. In this screen shot, the hand mesh is about the right size but still needs to be rotated and placed next to the wrist.

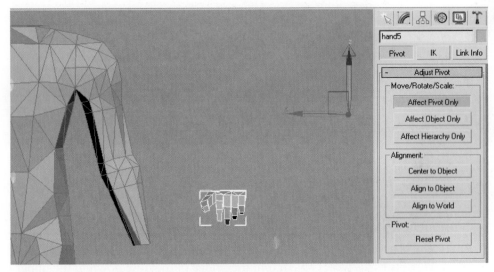

FIGURE 7.12   Affect Pivot Only allows you to move any object's pivot point.

In Figure 7.13, the hand mesh is being attached to the rest of the body. Usually it's a good idea to leave a little gap between objects, as when you attached the barrel of the weapon to the main weapon body in Chapter 2. If you have a different number of vertices on the wrist of the body and on the wrist of the hand, you have to weld or make additional cuts as necessary so that no vertices are left stray. After you've attached the hand, select its vertices and move it back up where it belongs, so that the arms are not too long.

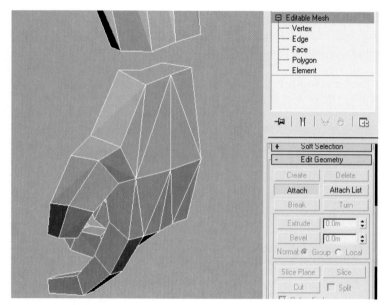

FIGURE 7.13   The hand is being attached with a gap to make welding easier.

Modeling the Head and Face

As with the hands, you can model the head and face separately and then attach them to the body of the character. You can model the head from a sphere, a box, or a plane. This example uses plane modeling to create the facial features and then creates the rest of the head with a geosphere primitive. The face is mostly planar; for a low-polygon character, you merely need to establish the nose, lips, and eye sockets.

Figure 7.14 shows six stages to modeling the astronaut's face. In stage 1 at the upper left, the nose is a 1 × 1 segment plane that has been converted to an Editable Poly; its edges were copied from the bridge of the nose down to the upper lip. This is readily accomplished in the side view. The lips are at this stage separate; the upper lip started as a plane and was converted to an editable poly, and the edges were copied to the corner of the lip. This is essentially just two quads and one triangle at this point. The lower lip is similar—just one quad and one triangle. Creating a triangle from a plane is as easy as welding two vertices together. The eye at this stage is just a 1 × 1 segment plane. When all of these components look good from the front, check the side view and move them as necessary to conform with the template.

In stage 2, at the upper middle of the screen, the edges of the nose mesh have been copied down the side of the nose where it meets the plane of the face. The eye has been cut into eight segments. Although it is impossible to see from the front view, the corners of the lips have been moved back to reflect the curve of the mouth.

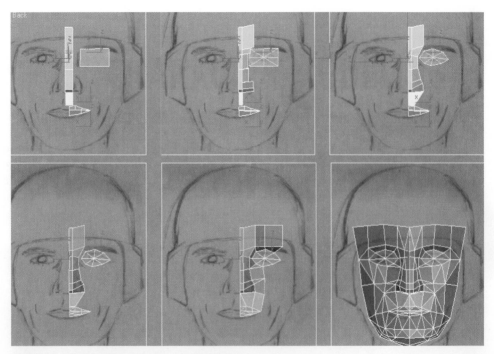

FIGURE 7.14   Six stages to creating a low poly face.

In stage 3, at the upper right, the nose polygons have been welded together, and the eye vertices have been moved to follow the shape of the eye. In this stage, the eye was also rotated a bit to reflect the curve of the face.

Stage 4, at the lower left, has all the meshes attached to form one mesh. An edge has been cut in the lower lip to connect with the first vertical edge in the upper lip. Both upper and lower lip vertices should be moved to give a slightly outward protrusion.

Stages 5 and 6 are made up of connections between polygons. You can select two edges, and the Bridge feature will connect them. You can also weld together vertices. You can copy edges to create polygons, or you can create polygons by using the Create button and clicking three or four vertices in a row. If you do this, always end on the first vertex you started on; this tells 3ds Max that you are finished selecting vertices.

Finishing Off the Head with a Geosphere

To finish the head, you can use a geosphere primitive. The geosphere is superior to the standard sphere for two reasons. First, the geosphere is more efficient in that it can cover the same facet detail with fewer overall faces. Second, the regular sphere (or the lat-long sphere) sacrifices efficiency at the poles, and these poles are difficult to texture properly with any kind of unwrapping scheme. When you look at these two factors combined, it makes sense to go with the geosphere every time. The type of geosphere being used in Figure 7.15 has an Octa Geodesic Base Type, and it has Smoothing turned off. Use the template to scale and position the geosphere. Attach the geosphere to the existing facial features mesh, and fill in any holes in the mesh with copied and welded faces. At the top of Figure 7.15, you see the geosphere being positioned. At the bottom, the geosphere has been converted to an Editable Poly, and the lower half of the polygons have been deleted. In the front and side views, adjust vertices to conform with the template. This character wears headphones inside of his helmet; a plane, with two segments in each direction, provides a good start for these. You can adjust vertices and scale and move the entire outer edge to give the headphones depth.

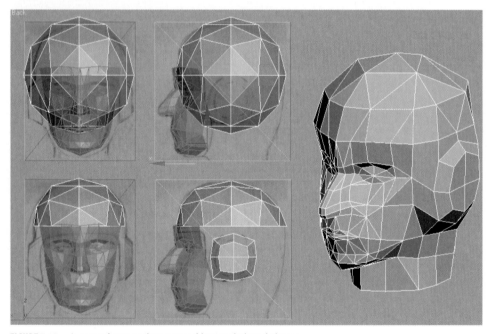

FIGURE 7.15   A geosphere makes a good low poly head shape.

At the far right of Figure 7.15, the finished head has had the geosphere mesh extended by copying edges. Attach the geosphere mesh, the facial features, and the headphones, and fill in any gaps by copying edges or creating polygons.

Converting to Editable Mesh and Turning Edges

If your model is still an Editable Poly, convert it to an Editable Mesh. The Editable Mesh uses triangles, and you will see edges bisecting your four-sided polygons.

Sometimes these go the wrong way, so you have to turn them. You may want to keep using symmetry so that you can just turn the edges of one side. When turning edges, look for areas that are deep in shadow, that create a crease where you don't want one, or that otherwise disturb the flow of the model. Figure 7.16 has two models. The green one on the left has markers for three edges that need to be turned, and these three edges have been turned in the blue mesh on the right. To turn an edge, get into Edge sub-object mode, activate the Turn button, and click where the edge divides the polygon. This step concludes the basic character model. The character model is available on the companion CD-ROM. It is named `AstronautMesh.max`, and it is in the `Files\Astronaut` folder.

ON THE CD

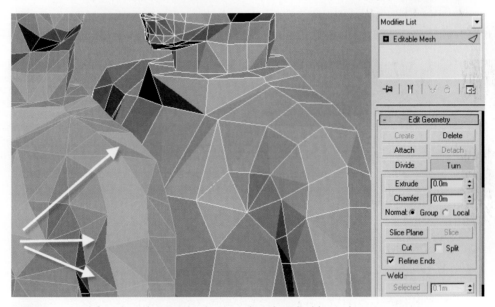

FIGURE 7.16   Look for edges that need to be turned on the Editable Mesh.

ADDING ACCESSORY MESHES

You can create additional meshes to add to the visual impact of the character by making sure the mesh is an Editable Mesh, that it has a valid material (JPG or PNG), that it has a valid UVW Map modifier or an Unwrap UVW modifier, and that it is parented to the proper bone on the character. If you want to create eyes, teeth, or other accessories for your character, you can add them the same way. The astronaut's helmet is an Editable Mesh that was built around the character model to demonstrate how you can add an accessory mesh to a character. This mesh is parented to the head bone of the character.

Creating a Helmet with Detached Polygons

Figure 7.17 shows an effective way to build geometry off an existing character mesh. Detaching polygons as a cloned object will leave the original polygons in place and generate the foundation of a well-fitting helmet for the character at the same time.

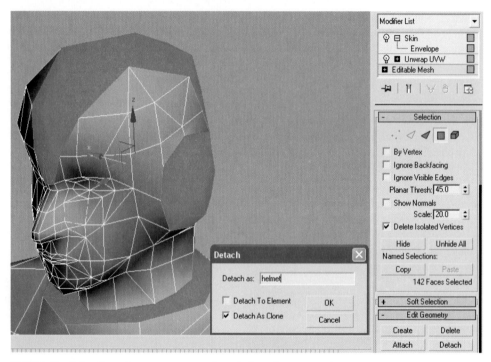

FIGURE 7.17   Using Detach to generate the foundation of a new mesh.

The helmet needs a mouthpiece. Just like the gun barrel in Chapter 2, this added extrusion begins as a line with a few segments. In Figure 7.18, vertices are moved in the top and front views until the spline starts off perpendicular to the originating face and the last segment lines up with the mouth area. Even after this mouthpiece is extruded, the vertices still need some adjustment for the mesh to look right.

Adding a Shell Modifier

In Figure 7.19, the mesh has been converted to an Editable Poly to take advantage of the Extrude Along Spline feature. (This is the same technique that was used for creating the hand earlier in this chapter.) A Shell modifier is added to the mesh to add thickness. This image at the left is the mesh in its preshell state; all unnecessary faces have been deleted in an attempt to keep the polygon count low. The point at the

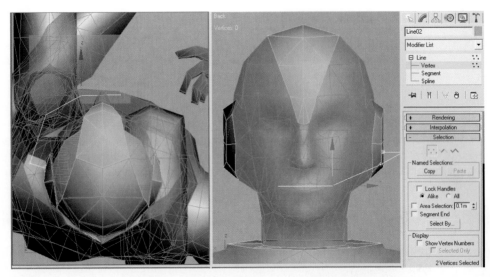

FIGURE 7.18   Vertices on this spline are adjusted to prepare for an Extrude Along Spline.

forehead was simplified by removing edges, and all of the nonvisible faces on the inside of the helmet were deleted. The inside faces of the extruded mouthpiece were deleted so that they would shell properly and not self-intersect. The image at the right shows the mesh after the shell has been applied. A shell can go to the inside or to the outside; in this case, the shell went to the outside because the helmet was already tightly fit to the character's head. After the shell, this helmet came in at 273 faces. The next step for this helmet model is to convert it back to an Editable Mesh. The helmet model is part of `AstronautMesh.max`, in the `Files\Astronaut` folder of the companion CD-ROM.

ON THE CD

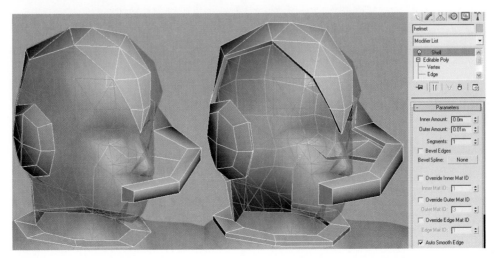

FIGURE 7.19   Unnecessary polygons are deleted, and a Shell modifier is applied to the helmet.

MODELING A ROBOT WITH MULTIPLE MESHES

A classical robot's parts are hard surfaces that will move almost as though they are all part of an exoskeleton, without a need for a skin stretching between joints. Each component is modeled separately, and then all are attached into one big Editable Mesh. In the rigging process, the mesh is assigned to the skeletal system; each component, such as the upper arm, is assigned to its own bone. When the bone moves, it moves 100% of the vertices that make up the upper arm of the robot; there is no blending or partial vertex assignments. If you model the different components as separate Editable Meshes or Editable Polys, when you attach them, the different components form different elements. The parts are attached, even though you may be able to see space between them. See Figure 7.20 for an example of this; the robot at the left is being built using a template and separate editable poly models for each component. The robot on the right was created by modeling 16 separate components, attaching them into one Editable Poly, and then converting to an Editable Mesh. The upper arm is being selected while in Element sub-object mode. This makes it easy to select components when you get to the unwrapping and rigging stages.

FIGURE 7.20 Modeling a robot from separate components.

If each of these components is going to be rigid in the rig, whether you are using a bones or biped skeleton, you have to think about what bone is going to be attached to what element. If you are using a biped and you have only one big torso for the robot, you have to assign the lower vertices of the torso to the pelvis and the upper vertices of the torso to the spine(s). The selection process can get tricky with so many vertices in the same general area. Another approach is to have two components for the torso so that you have a pelvic unit and an upper torso unit.

There is one anomaly to consider with a robotic character: if the robot is going to be holding a rifle in the traditional way, it may have a hard time making the support hand reach around without creating a big gap between the upper arm and the back. One way to minimize this is to prerotate the biped upper arm and hand, as described in Chapter 10. Another technique that may help is to design the shoulders of your robot so that they overlap the spine or torso a bit, and thus maintain a relatively normal appearance when in "ready" position. A final workaround is to arm your robot with a handgun or guns that are situated in the chest area, so that there is no extreme arm/shoulder positioning necessary. You can access the robot mesh in the file RobotRootPose.max, in the Files\Robot folder of the companion CD-ROM.

ON THE CD

SUMMARY

Starting with at least a front and side template of the character, you prepare templates in Photoshop so that both views are the same height and you darken the templates. You apply these templates as materials to planes in 3ds Max, and you set up the planes so that you can build the model using them as a guide. You can use a box to model the torso of the character, extrude the limbs, and use connections to create additional edges. Facial features can be created by sculpting a box as we did the body or by copying edges from a plane; for the general skull shape, the geosphere works well and is particularly efficient with its use of polygons. You can create additional meshes by detaching existing polygons from your character. If your character is a robot, model the components with separate meshes, and then attach them when you are done. As you will see in the following chapters, component models have selection advantages when it comes to unwrapping and rigging.

CHARACTER UNWRAPPING

In This Chapter

- Unwrapping a Character—Overview
- Unwrapping the Hands with a Planar Map and Adding Them to the Body
- Unwrapping the Body with a Normal Map
- Unwrapping the Character's Face
- Creating a Character UV Template
- Unwrapping the Helmet
- Unwrapping a Component Mesh
- Unwrapping with Multiple Materials IDs
- Saving, Loading, and Combining UVs
- Baking the Texture into the Mesh

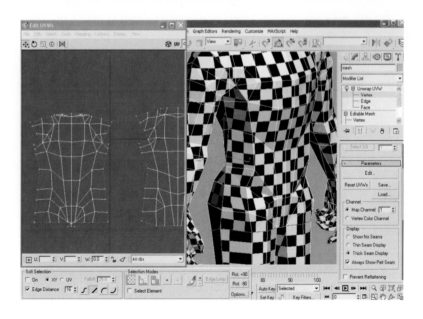

UNWRAPPING A CHARACTER—OVERVIEW

Unwrapping a character is more difficult than unwrapping weapons and pickups because the mesh is more organic. Setting up the UVs properly in the Edit UVWs dialog box can be like putting together a complex 3D puzzle where the shapes keep changing. If you have worked through Chapter 3, "Unwrapping Game Art," and you are patient, you should see promising results with a few hours' work. If you are using your own mesh, try to keep it simple the first time through.

Unwrapping Before You Rig the Model

Unwrapping is best done before rigging your model. You can do it later, but if you are using a biped skeleton, and the Skin modifier is already added, make sure that the biped is in Figure mode; otherwise, when you select faces on the model, they may be slightly offset due to minor adjustments in bone position when you switch out of Figure mode. You can also make a copy of the entire character mesh from the rigged character (again, while the biped is in Figure mode) and delete the Skin modifier from the copy. You can then unwrap this copied version of the mesh; its UVs are saved and applied to the actual character. As long as the number of vertices stays the same, the UVs should transfer from mesh to mesh without difficulty. If you see green lines in any of your UVs that come from an overhang or from polygons that face the wrong direction, it's likely you have found some stray vertices in your mesh.

Understanding the Impact of Stray Vertices

Any stray vertices in your model at this stage of the game cause issues in your unwrapping process. You don't want to get nearly finished with the unwrap and find that you have to weld some vertices together. Changing the vertex count on your Editable Mesh can cost you some of the work you have done in the Edit UVWs dialog box unless you detach the problem area before fixing it and then reattach to the main body. Figure 8.1 shows a before and after image; the image on the left is the completely unwrapped character with carefully placed UVs in the texture area, and the image on the right is what the texture and UVs can look like after any vertices are welded, or if any parts of the mesh are detached. Depending on how much your model is changed, you can lose all of the UV work you have done. Clicking the Undo button does not fix this problem. Hold off on positioning your UVs in the texture area until you are sure the model is what you want. In most cases, you can rescale and reposition these UVs by bringing in the finished texture as the new background and adjusting the UVs until they fit the saved texture file.

Removing Stray Vertices

If you are not sure whether you have stray vertices or not, one technique is to select all the vertices in the Editable Mesh, and from the Edit Geometry rollout, in the Weld group, click the Selected button. This operation is easier to do with an Editable

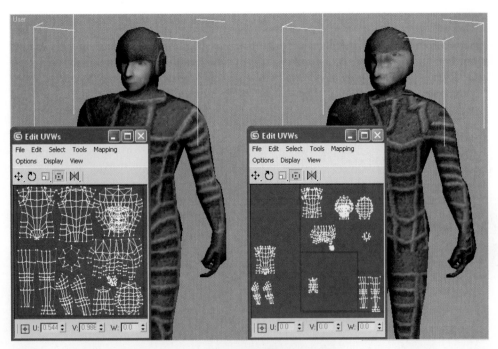

FIGURE 8.1   Changing the vertex count on the mesh affects your UVs.

Poly, because the Threshold Weld dialog box gives vertex count feedback. As long as you set the threshold value correctly, this process should weld any stray vertices. For a hand on a 2.5-meter character, a weld threshold of 0.01 meters should work well. You can also try rotating the model and moving vertices to see if they are not properly welded; in addition, visually inspect the model after any threshold weld process to make sure you did not weld too many vertices together. The smallest areas of the mesh are most prone to being welded inadvertently. If you perform a threshold weld while zoomed in on small detail areas like the lips or fingers, when you see these smaller features begin to weld together, you know it's time to increase the weld threshold value.

UNWRAPPING THE HANDS WITH A PLANAR MAP AND ADDING THEM TO THE BODY

Hands can be difficult to unwrap, particularly if they are already in a bent position. Of course, you can do this while the hands are attached to the body, but here we want to demonstrate how you can detach parts of your character mesh during the unwrap process. One reason for doing this is that it is time consuming to unwrap a hand, and it's not necessary to do it twice; by unwrapping one hand, you can then mirror it to the other side and reattach it to the body. Another reason for detaching the hand might be that you need to make some modeling changes, and you want to work on it without being tied to the entire body; again, if you fix one hand, you may want to just mirror it to generate the other hand. If the hands need to have different finger positions, it might still make sense to develop one good core hand and then adjust the fingers on the other hand as necessary.

In Figure 8.2, both hands were detached from the body, and the right hand was deleted. The left hand had the Unwrap UVW modifier applied, and Planar maps were used to capture the back of the hand, which was then moved out of the texturing area. This process is similar to what we used to unwrap the power charger in Chapter 3. Select the faces, turn on the Planar button, select Best Align, and then turn off the Planar button so that you can move the newly created UVs out of the texture area and go to the next set of faces.

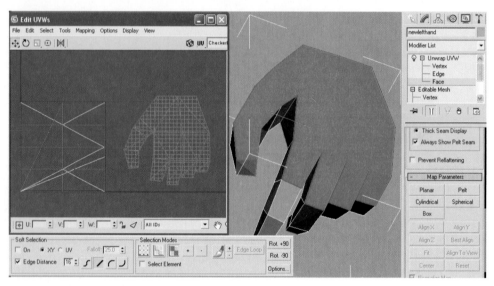

FIGURE 8.2   The back of the hand is planar mapped and moved aside.

When you're done with the back of the hand, you can unwrap the back of the fingers, the palm, and the sides of the hand (see Figure 8.3). Select as many faces as you can that are roughly in the same plane, repeating the process you used for the back of the hand until you've unwrapped all of the high-visibility areas. The different portions of the hand can be broken off and oriented to create one big hand, laid out flat, and centered on the area of the little finger. Some scaling and mirroring are necessary during this process. The areas between the fingers can be overlapped to save texture space; they will receive a generic texture.

All possible edges were stitched together to give as much continuity as possible to the texture. Figure 8.4 shows a screen shot of the finished UVs for the hand and the texture on the character. Remember that if you cannot stitch an edge, you may be able to weld a vertex. Both options are available from the right-click menu as long as you are in the correct sub-object mode. You should be in Edge sub-object

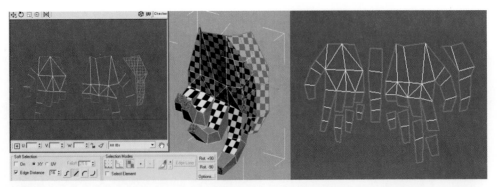

FIGURE 8.3   The parts of the hand are unwrapped and placed in position for stitching.

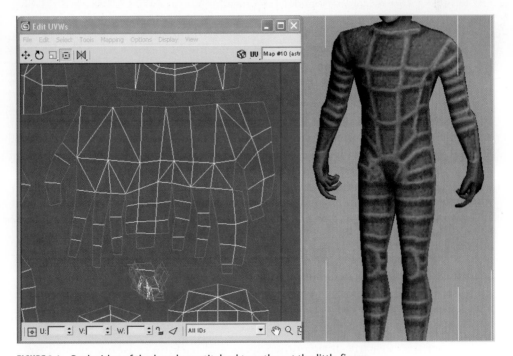

FIGURE 8.4   Both sides of the hand are stitched together at the little finger.

mode to stitch edges together, and you should be in Vertex sub-object mode to weld vertices. Review Chapter 3 if you are not sure how to perform planar unwraps and stitch/weld UVs.

When you've unwrapped this hand, use the Mirror tool (located in the Standard toolbar) to mirror the hand around X to make the right hand (see Figure 8.5). If you have not moved the right hand from its position, you only have to worry about the positioning of the mirrored hand. This figure shows the Mirror tool in action; you are looking at the back viewport, at the front side of the character, and mirroring a copy of

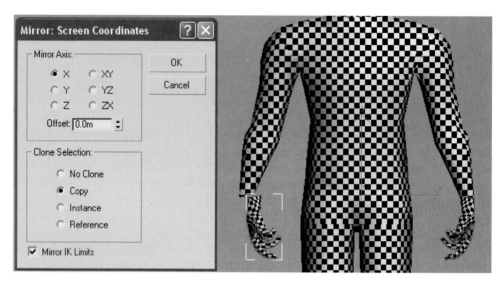

FIGURE 8.5   The mirror tool allows you to mirror around any axis or plane.

the left hand around the X axis. If you cannot get the hand positioned well enough with the Offset value on this dialog box, you can always move the hand after clicking OK.

Now that you've unwrapped the hands, how do you reattach them to the body? First make sure to save the UVs. Select the body mesh, and attach both hands to the body. Then weld the vertices in the wrist area together using an implied window and the Threshold Weld tool. Add an Unwrap UVW modifier to the body mesh, click the Edit button, and you should see the UVs for the left hand exactly where you placed them, with those of the right hand perfectly overlaying them. The rest of the body mesh UVs should be in the texture area.

UNWRAPPING THE BODY WITH A NORMAL MAP

This example involves unwrapping the astronaut using the Normal map method. This is the same method we used to unwrap the weapon, and it is by far the most straightforward way to get a character ready for texturing, particularly if the character has a clearly distinguished front and back. Because we created the astronaut mesh by starting with a box and using the Symmetry modifier, we ended up with a pretty good seam that divides the front and the back faces of the body of the mesh. See Figure 8.6 to note the seam and the front/back faces.

Make sure your character mesh is an Editable Mesh and that Symmetry and any other modifiers are collapsed. Just as in Chapter 3, add the Unwrap UVW modifier to the mesh and click the Edit button. This opens the Edit UVWs dialog box. Resize and move the dialog box until you can see the tools at the bottom. Turn off the map display as well as the grid markers to simplify the display. Get into Face sub-object mode, and if there are any body parts (such as hands) that have already been unwrapped, move them aside. Next, select all the remaining faces, and go to Mapping,

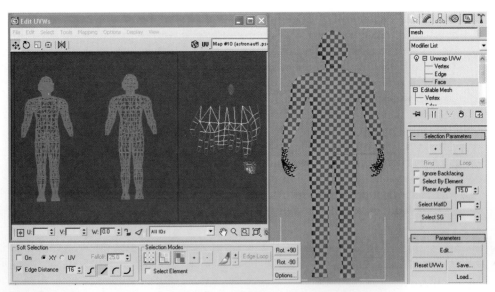

FIGURE 8.6   A Normal map is applied to the front and back of the character.

Normal Mapping. Select Front/Back, and uncheck the Rotate option. This should give you a front and back view of the character mesh.

Breaking and Overlapping UVs

Select the head in the front set of UVs and right-click Break. Move the head away from the rest of the body. Do the same with the back set of UVs. If the hands have not already been set aside, do this now by breaking them off the front and back UVs and moving them out of the texture area. Now your astronaut body should be without a head or hands. The challenge now is to find places where you can overlap UVs to save on texture space. Overlapping also simplifies your texturing work. Some areas are obvious candidates for overlapping, such as the front of both legs and the back of both legs. A trickier area is the front and back of the torso. Because the geometry and edge flow differs significantly from front to back, overlapping does not work as well here; however, you can still do it, depending on the texture. When you are overlaying UVs, make sure to zoom in to place them as precisely as possible.

Breaking and Reorganizing UVs

Depending on your model, some of your UVs may end up in the wrong place. This can happen if the seam along the sides of the mesh is not consistent; if some of the faces on the front side of the mesh actually face the back of the mesh, they will end up with the backside UVs. If there are overhangs, such as at the character's chin, these faces may end up with the backside UVs. You can select these faces from the Edit UVWs dialog box or from the viewport, and you can break them off and re-attach them where they belong by stitching edges or welding vertices.

In Figure 8.7, two triangles on the back of the character's neck have been as-signed to the front of the body because they were actually facing the front. You can select these, break them off, move them to the backside UVs, and stitch/weld them into place. The green lines in this image underneath the eyes indicate a detached vertex in the model. To fix this, you can detach the head mesh, repair it by welding the vertex, and reattach it to the main body of the character.

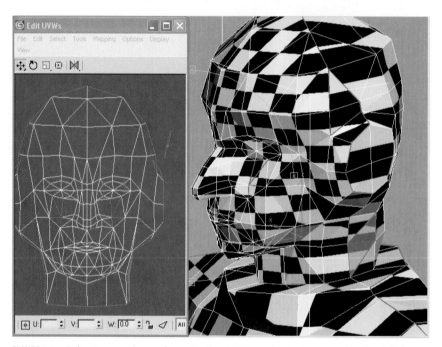

FIGURE 8.7   Selecting a polygon from the front UVs, which belongs on the back UVs.

Adjusting the UVs on the Body

You can now adjust the vertices of the astronaut UVs so that the streaking on the sides of the body is corrected. First, create a checker material and apply it to the mesh. Adjust your viewport view and the Edit UVWs dialog box so that you can see both at the same time. Because the front and back UVs of the mesh have been over-laid, make sure that you window the vertices as you select them, or you will not be selecting both of them. If your computer can handle it, make sure Options, Advanced Options, Constant Update in Viewports is checked on; that way you can see the effect each vertex move has on the texture in the viewport.

Figure 8.8 shows the process of selecting the vertices on the right side of the torso front and moving them to the left to widen the UVs and cause a more ordered checker pattern on the model. When you are using Planar or Normal mapping, every face on the model that is not very nearly flat to the plane needs some kind of adjustment; the more skewed faces need the most adjustment.

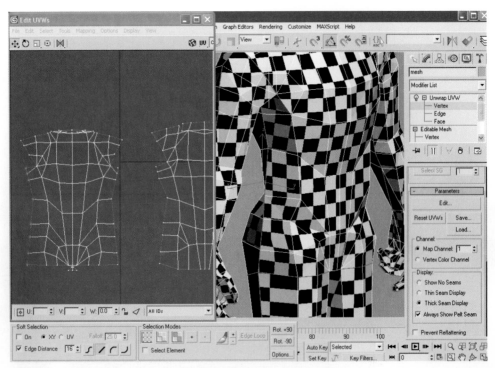

FIGURE 8.8   Selecting and moving a column of vertices to fix the side streaking.

UNWRAPPING THE CHARACTER'S FACE

You can unwrap the head with a Normal map, a Planar map, or a Cylindrical map. Each of these options has its pros and cons. The Planar map behaves pretty much the same as a Normal map, depending on which way the head is tilted; because the Normal map projects to the existing orthographic views, if the character is looking straight on, you usually get a pretty good approximation of the character's features. Planar mapping has the additional ability to do a Best Align for the selected faces, which could generate more accurate UVs than a stock Normal map. What is useful with a Planar map is the idea that the face you are UV mapping will look recognizable from the front. A Cylindrical map, on the other hand, tends to distort the facial features and might make it harder to texture, even though the cylindrical shape might be more suitable for the shape of the head overall.

Adjusting the UVs on the Face

After you've applied the facial texture to the model, obvious problems become apparent; Figure 8.9 gives an example of this. Notice in the upper-left image that the area near the tear duct is distorted. Now look at the image at the upper right and you can see the problem; the checkered test pattern is wavering heavily in that area. The two images in the lower half of Figure 8.9 show how moving a few vertices so that the checkered pattern is more ordered also makes for a better, more finished texture.

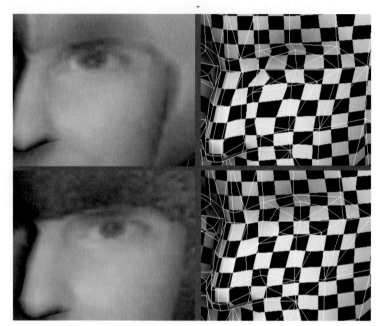

FIGURE 8.9   You can improve the UVs around the eye by moving a few UV vertices.

Unwrapping with the Pelt Map

The Pelt map is a feature that is available to those who have version 7 or later of 3ds Max. This feature automates much of what is normally done by hand; if you unwrap the front side of a 3D object, there are generally points along the edges where you have to pull out the vertices so that the UVs can "catch" the texture and avoid streaking along the sides. The Pelt map looks like a device used to stretch out the pelts of skinned animals. Each vertex on the "stretcher" pulls with a spring tension on the outermost vertices and is dampened toward the inside. In a sense, this acts like a soft select.

To use the Pelt map, launch the Unwrap UVWs modifier. Start by clicking the Edit button and selecting the faces you want to unwrap. Then click Pelt from the Map Parameters rollout, and select an alignment option from the buttons immediately below (such as Best Align). Finally, click the Edit Pelt Map button to get to the point shown in Figure 8.10.

Figure 8.11 shows what happens to the vertices as well as the textured model when you click the Relax (Light) button a few times. The vertices at the borders of the map are pulled on and expanded; this generally improves the overall UVs, although it may still be necessary to move some of the vertices by hand.

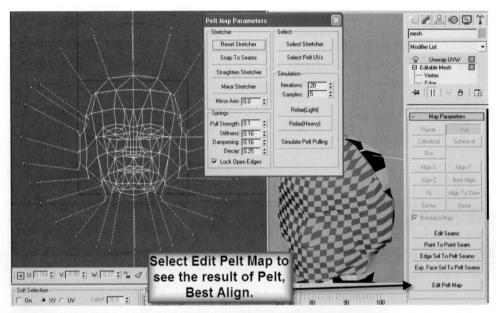

FIGURE 8.10   After you've selected the UVs, click Pelt, Best Align, Edit Pelt Map.

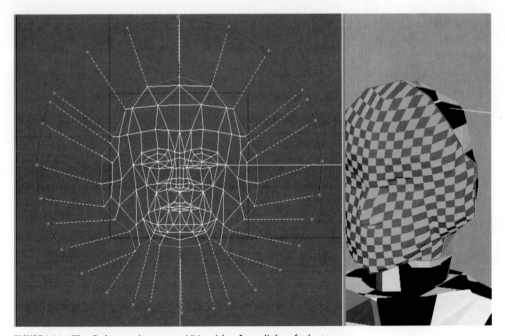

FIGURE 8.11   The Pelt map improves UVs with a few clicks of a button.

CREATING A CHARACTER UV TEMPLATE

After you've created the UVs, you need to scale and position them for maximum effect in the game. Prioritize what is most important visually and scale those UVs bigger; for instance, the face and hands of the character demand more detail than the legs and arms (see Figure 8.12). In some cases, it helps to have certain UVs next to each other to make the texturing task easier; because our character will be wearing a ribbed spacesuit, it will be helpful for the leg UVs to be next to each other so the ribs can stay lined up. An option here is to create a vertical seam along the edges so that the horizontal ribs do not have to blend perfectly. The circular UVs in the center of the texture area are for the neck area, which the helmet rests upon; these UVs were generated from the top view. All UVs should be right-side up if possible so that they are in the orientation you are used to looking at them in; this makes texturing them more natural. It can also be helpful if you scale those UVs that are receiving the same texture the same amount, so that less adjustment is necessary in the texturing process. Try to leave as little blank space in the texture area as possible.

Just as you did in Chapter 3, in the Edit UVWs dialog box, select Tools, UVW Template to generate a UV template and export it as a bitmap. Because this is a character, you can set the size to 512 × 512, the biggest possible texture size allowable by the Torque Game Engine. The unwrapped astronaut mesh is named `AstronautMesh.max` and is available in `Files\Astronaut` on the companion CD-ROM.

ON THE CD

FIGURE 8.12 The finished UV template.

UNWRAPPING THE HELMET

Figure 8.13 shows the helmet unwrapped; this was done with Planar, Best Align, selecting nearly coplanar sections of the helmet one at a time and then stitching them together for continuity in the texturing process. The ear and mouthpiece areas were separated, but all outside-facing UVs were given as much texture space as possible. The UVs for the edges and inside faces were scaled down and overlapped, reflecting their lower priority in regard to visibility and impact on the texture. The unwrapped helmet texture is included in the file `AstronautMesh.max` and is available on the companion CD-ROM under `Files\Astronaut`.

ON THE CD

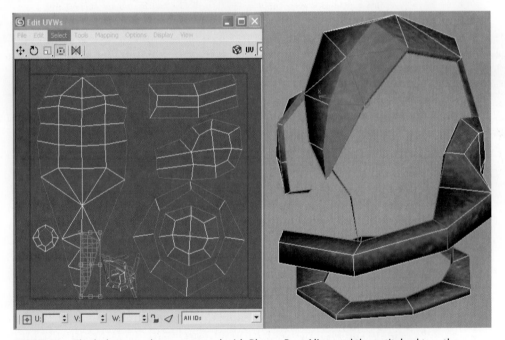

FIGURE 8.13   The helmet can be unwrapped with Planar, Best Align and then stitched together.

UNWRAPPING A COMPONENT MESH

The robot in Figure 8.14 is unique in that it was built from components that were attached at the end. This process automatically created a different element for each of the components within the Editable Mesh. Each portion of the mesh can be added to the Edit UVWs texture area by using the Select by Element option of the Unwrap UVWs modifier. In this case, the element was then broken into planar sections using Planar mapping. A Planar map is particularly important for the faces of this model because there are round elements such as rivets and rivet patterns that would become oblong with anything less than a perfectly flat Planar map.

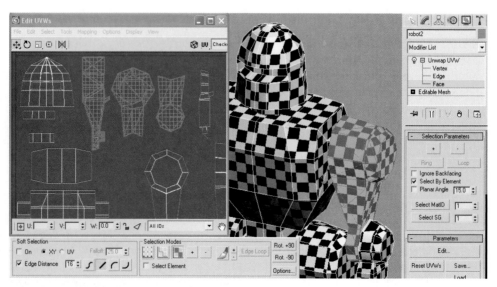

FIGURE 8.14   When a mesh is created from components, use Select by Element.

UNWRAPPING WITH MULTIPLE MATERIAL IDS

You can apply this method to your pickups or to characters; you set up a Multi/Sub-Object material that allows you to change the color and material ID of selected faces so that you can easily manipulate different selection sets from within the Edit UVs dialog box.

Creating a Multi/Sub-Object Material

The first step in this process is to create a Multi/Sub-Object material. You do this by clicking on a new material sample slot and then clicking the Standard button, which takes you to the Material/Map Browser (see Figure 8.15). Set Browse From to New. In the list, double-click the Multi/Sub-Object selection; this should change your Material Editor interface so that you can set the number of materials you want and assign colors to them. (Names are not necessary but can be helpful in keeping track of your polygons.) Assign this material to your model, and make sure Show Map in Viewport is turned on.

Assigning Mesh IDs to Polygons

Next, assign each relatively flat portion of the model to a Mesh ID. In this example, the front and back of the head, torso, legs, arms, and collar area are assigned separate IDs, names, and colors. The arms and feet of this model have been left off for

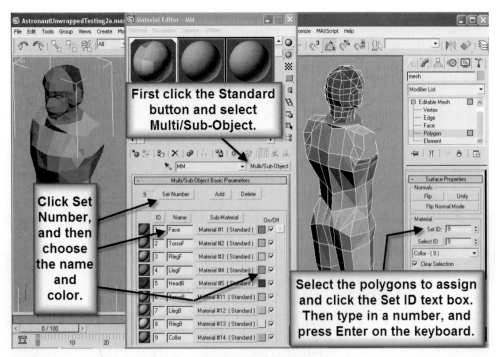

First click the Standard button and select Multi/Sub-Object.

Click Set Number, and then choose the name and color.

Select the polygons to assign and click the Set ID text box. Then type in a number, and press Enter on the keyboard.

FIGURE 8.15   A Multi/Sub-Object material and setting Mesh IDs.

brevity. From the back view, it is easy to select the polygons on the face of the model with a selection window if Ignore Backfacing has been turned on. After you've selected these polygons from the Editable Mesh modifier, locate the Material group in the Surface Properties rollout. Click the text box next to Set ID and type in the number 1; then press Enter on your keyboard. This is how you assign Material IDs. Repeat this process for all the polygons in your model until no more gray polygons remain. If you are not sure what has already been assigned, use the Select ID button to show you which polygons have been assigned to any given number. You do this by entering the number of the ID in the text box and then clicking Select ID. Even if you take this system no further than this, it is a helpful tool to manage your different polygon selection sets and make sure you have not forgotten any polygons.

Accessing the Selection Sets in the Edit UVWs Dialog Box

In the Unwrap UVW modifier, within the Edit UVWs dialog box, you can display UVs by Mesh ID by selecting from the drop-down list shown in Figure 8.16. You can also choose to show All IDs. This process makes selecting UV sets simple for applying maps and making other adjustments.

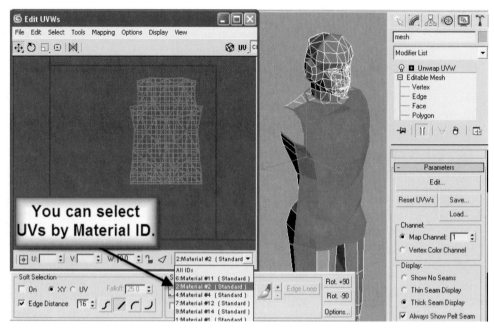

FIGURE 8.16   Viewing materials by Mesh ID from the Edit UVWs dialog box.

SAVING, LOADING, AND COMBINING UVS

You can detach sets of polygons from the mesh and copy and then rotate them to make portions of the mesh easier to unwrap. You can unwrap these copies and save and apply the UVs to the original detached mesh portions; when the original mesh is reattached, it retains the UVs. We are not actually using this method for our characters; nonetheless, you should be aware of this technique. You can use this method, for example, to unwrap a character that was modeled in a "ready" stance, rather than in a more traditional da Vinci pose.

Figure 8.17 gives an example of this procedure. A checker material has been applied to the torso so that you can see the UV mapping. The arm on the left has been detached and moved slightly so you can see that it is no longer a part of the original torso. (Normally, you would not move the original arm; you would just detach it.) To the right, a copy of the arm has been rotated so that it is vertical. In the next version, the arm has been rotated 90 degrees, so we are looking at the side of it. In the next view, the arm has had a Planar map applied to it via the Unwrap UVW modifier. You can save the UVWs from the Parameters rollout of the Unwrap UVW modifier or from the File menu of the Edit UVWs dialog box. After you have the UVWs, you can delete the mesh that has been rotated. Then select the original arm that was detached, add an Unwrap UVW modifier to it, and load the UVs you just saved. Each time you load saved UVs to a portion of the mesh, move the UVs to a new location in the mapping area so that each set of UVs has its own place. Then you can attach Editable Meshes that have been mapped in this way; after you've attached them, they should retain their UV maps, giving you one complete mesh with all the necessary UVs.

FIGURE 8.17   A copied arm is rotated, unwrapped, and has UVs saved.

BAKING THE TEXTURE INTO THE MESH

As long as you keep a copy of the actual UVs, or even a copy of the entire 3ds Max file that was used for the final texture, you can collapse the Unwrap modifier into the Editable Mesh. You can do this by right-clicking on the Unwrap modifier in the modifier stack and selecting Collapse All, or by right-clicking on the model and selecting Convert to Editable Poly. This simplifies the modifier stack and makes dealing with the complexities of rigging and animation a little more straightforward. You can reacquire the UVs if you add another Unwrap UVW modifier to the mesh. Remember that it is always a good idea to save a backup copy of your files before the various modifiers have been collapsed; it is equally important to save your UVs at various stages of completion in case you need to retrieve them for some reason.

SUMMARY

The intent of this chapter was to provide an overview of the unwrap process and demonstrate some of the more useful techniques. In general, it is best to arrange your UVs so that they are right-side up and recognizable for the texturing process. Planar maps tend to work best for characters due to their ability to provide ordered UVs and clean seams, as long as your selection and alignment work is done well.

Going through the unwrap process on a model as complex as a character usually makes artists rethink the way they modeled their character; some models lend themselves more to unwrapping than others. Likewise, the texturing process makes you rethink the way you unwrapped your character. The process of modeling, unwrapping, texturing, rigging, and animating becomes a cycle; by the time you reach the end, you've already determined changes to make the process easier and the results better the next time around.

CHARACTER TEXTURING

In This Chapter

- Texturing the Astronaut
- Texturing the Robot
- Modeling Textures in 3ds Max
- Troubleshooting

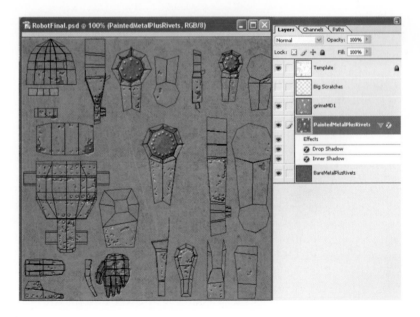

TEXTURING THE ASTRONAUT

Texturing the astronaut involves setting up a proper template, making sure all faces are on the same Smoothing Group, and creating an overall texture using Layer Masks, Layer Effects, Filters, and digital images as necessary.

Setting Up in Photoshop

Set up the astronaut UV template on the first layer in Photoshop, and make sure this layer is named `template` so you can use the Action created in Chapter 4, "Texturing Game Art." Set this layer to Screen Blend Mode. This layer will be visible from any layers you create beneath it.

Using the Same Smoothing Group

Make sure that all the polygons on your character are on the same Smoothing Group. Skinned meshes (which is what the character mesh will ultimately be) can have only one Smoothing Group. If you do want the faceted look, for example if your character is a robot and you want more obvious edges on the mesh, click Clear All in the Smoothing Groups rollout.

Creating the Astronaut's Spacesuit Texture

ON THE CD

`TexturedSteel.psd`, which was created in Chapter 4, will be used as the foundation for the ribbed spacesuit. This file, along with `GrimeMD1.jpg` and `GrimeMR1.jpg`, is located on the companion CD-ROM under `Files\Astronaut`. Open a copy of `TexturedSteel.psd`, and make the following edits:

1. Click Filter, Distortion, Glass. Then set Distortion to 9, Smoothness to 3, and Frosted Scaling to 150.
2. Click Image, Adjustments, Brightness/Contrast, and raise both up to 14 percent.
3. Click Filter, Blur, Gaussian Blur, and set to 0.8 percent.
4. Add `GrimeMD1.jpg` as the new top layer. Call the layer `Grime`.
5. Use the Magic Wand tool to capture the darkest areas of the `GrimeMD1` image, and make a new layer selection for the dents. Call the new layer `Dents`.
6. Take the `Grime` layer down to 20 percent Opacity.
7. Make the `Dents` layer current, and fill selected areas with RGB 70,70,70 gray.
8. Contract the selection set 1 pixel, and fill with RGB 40,40,40 gray.
9. Select on the `Dents` layer where there is no gray, and then go to Select, Inverse to get back to where you were, with all the grayed areas selected.
10. Apply a Drop Shadow Layer Effect to the selected areas. Select Hard Light, light gray color, and 40 percent Opacity. Change Angle of Light to 120, and check Use Global Light. Set Distance to 1, Spread to 0, Size to 0 or 1, Quality to Normal, and Contour to 0 percent. Check Layer Knocks Out Drop Shadow.

11. Bring the `Grime` layer down in Brightness/Contrast to about –40 each.
12. Place `GrimeMR1.jpg` over layer 0, which is the basic metal texture. Change Hue, Saturation, and Lightness to +101, +86, and 0, and set Opacity for this layer to 10 percent. Drag the Hue slider around to see the color effects you can get in the overall layer with these settings.

These steps create `SpacesuitTextureBasic.psd`. If this material is flattened, with Hue up 8 and Saturation down 28, you have the material used as the foundation of the spacesuit material used in `Astronaut1.psd`. Both of these textures are shown in Figure 9.1 and are available on the companion CD-ROM under `Files\Astronaut`.

ON THE CD

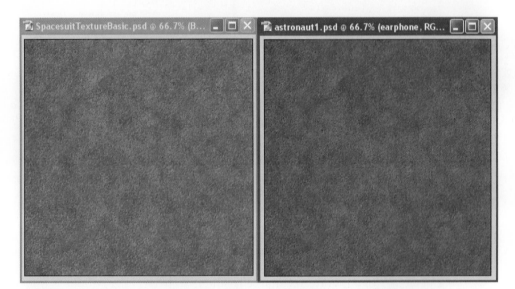

FIGURE 9.1   The astronaut texture before and after a Hue/Saturation adjustment.

Using a Layer Style to Create Raised Pixels

The panels on the health patch in Chapter 4 were created with Layer Styles. Here, Layer Styles are used to add depth to the spacesuit texture. Figure 9.2 shows what this Layer Style looks like. It uses Drop Shadow, Inner Glow, Bevel and Emboss, and Satin effects.

The Drop Shadow effect puts a shadow underneath what we are painting, leading the viewer to believe that our pixels have height. In the Drop Shadow settings, Blend Mode is Multiply, Color is black, Opacity is 36 percent, Angle is 120 degrees, Use Global Light is checked, Distance is 2 pixels, Spread is 18 percent, Size is 3 pixels, Contour is Linear, Noise is 0 percent, and Layer Knocks Out Drop Shadow is checked.

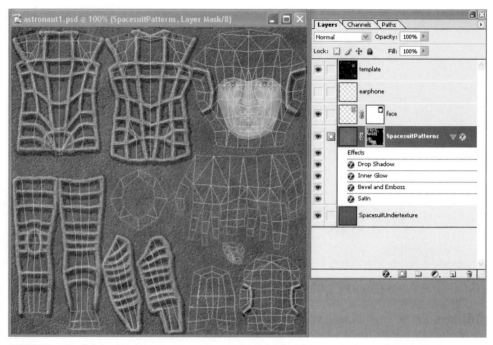

FIGURE 9.2   The finished astronaut texture is accomplished with Layer Styles and Layer Masking.

The Inner Glow effect is used here to add a highlight to the pixels along their inner boundary. The glow softens at the edges, suggesting a three-dimensional shape. In the Inner Glow settings, Blend Mode is Vivid Light, Opacity is 70 percent, Noise is 2 percent, Color is gray, Technique is Softer, Source is Edge, Choke is 8 percent, Size is 5 pixels, Contour is Linear, Anti-Aliased is unchecked, Range is 31 percent, and Jitter is 0 percent.

The Bevel and Emboss effect adds its own shadows and highlights, further caus-ing pixels on this layer to pop out at the viewer. In the Bevel and Emboss settings, Style is Inner Bevel, Technique is Smooth, Depth is 91 percent, Direction is Up, Size is 3 pixels, Soften is 2 pixels, Angle is 120 degrees, Use Global Light is checked, Alti-tude is 30 degrees, Gloss Contour is Linear, Anti-Aliased is unchecked, Highlight Mode is Normal, Color is white, Opacity is 49 percent, Shadow Mode is set to Multi-ply, Color is black, and Opacity is 74 percent.

The Satin effect is used here to soften some of the brightness created by the Inner Glow. Satin is helpful in adding and managing soft highlights. In the Satin set-tings, Blend Mode is set to Multiply, Color is black, Opacity is 14 percent, Angle is 19 degrees, Distance is 3 pixels, Size is 4 pixels, Contour is Gaussian, Anti-aliased is unchecked, and Invert is checked.

When you apply this Layer Style to the entire layer, you do not see much difference. In the next section, a Layer Mask is used to paint away the entire layer, and then a brush is used to paint it back in, one detail at a time.

Using a Layer Mask to Draw the Ribs

In Figure 9.2, the astronaut template is on the top layer, the SpacesuitUndertexture layer is on the bottom, and a copy of this layer has been named SpacesuitPatterns. The only change to the SpacesuitPatterns layer is that it has a Layer Style applied, and it is tinted slightly green. (You can accomplish this by turning down Hue to 40 and turning up Saturation to 40.) This layer has a Layer Mask added to it. Just as with the health patch in Chapter 4, Layer, Add Layer Mask, Hide All is activated to erase the SpacesuitPatterns texture throughout; then white is used with a soft, 13-pixel brush to draw the ribbing in, using the UV edges as guidelines. The ribbing is smaller on the back of the head because the head is smaller, and it's done with a 7-pixel brush.

Texturing the Astronaut's Helmet

The texture for the astronaut's helmet is based on the steel plate texture. In this case, an interesting dent was found in the original texture. A dents layer was created and, using a color sampled from the dent indicated by the arrow in Figure 9.3, more dents were drawn in the darker areas of the texture. These areas were then enhanced with a Drop Shadow and Bevel and Emboss. Some color was added to this texture by copying the original steel plate layer and adjusting Hue/Saturation while the Colorize box was checked. This layer's Opacity was turned down to 19 percent.

ON THE CD

HelmetTexture.psd shows how the layers were set up, and HelmetTexture.jpg is the actual working texture. STEELPLT256.jpg, HelmetTexture.psd, and HelmetTexture.jpg are available on the companion CD-ROM under Files\Astronaut.

Texturing the Astronaut's Face

You can get a texture looking the way you want on a model in a few general ways. You can create the facial skin as a uniform texture that you apply with only a UVW map, and the eyes and lips can receive their own textures. A more involved method is to unwrap the face and paint it by hand in Photoshop, using layers and varying opacity to simulate the skin and facial features. A final method is to unwrap the face and piece it together by using photos of real faces. You can combine the last two methods, painting digital photos, or you can use the photos simply as reference images for your hand-painted work. Of all the methods, applying a digital photo to unwrapped face UVs is the fastest, assuming that you have a good model, a good set of UVs, and a decent photo to work with.

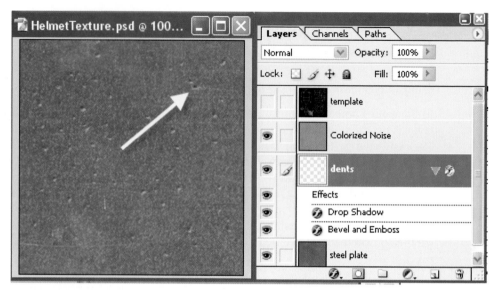

FIGURE 9.3 Using Layer Styles to create dents in steel.

Using a Photo Reference

It's a good idea to have a photo or sketch as a reference every time, whether you decide to create the character face from scratch or by manipulating the photo. You might end up with several photo references, perhaps using skin from one photo, the eyes from another photo, and so on.

Creating a Face by Applying a Photo to the UVs

The texture you apply depends on what the UVs you are using look like. If the UVs include the side of the head (ears), you need to have a digital photo of the side of the head of your subject. If the model was created from a template based on the photo, you can often get by with just rescaling the face photo to fit the UVs, as is the case in Figure 9.4. This photo was nonuniformly scaled to fit the texture, and then a Layer Mask was used to paint away the portions of the photo that should be hidden by the spacesuit. This method is impressive in the speed with which you can accomplish it and the results it provides, particularly if there is uniform lighting on the subject when photographed. Of course, you can then enhance the image by adding scars or other details, changing the skin or eye color, or pushing pixels around with the Liquify tool.

When the match is not as close, you may have to cut out the eyes, nose, mouth, eyebrows, and skin selections and then paste them into place so they align with the UV template. Here you will probably need some nonuniform scaling. Then you can finesse the missing sections of skin into place with the Clone Stamp tool. When

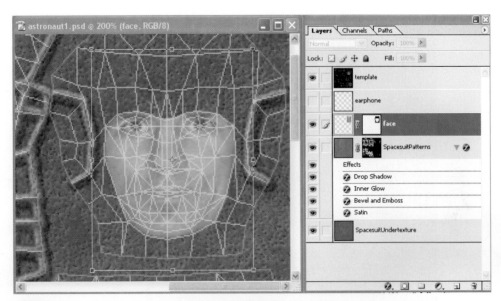

FIGURE 9.4   You can rescale the face photo to fit the UVs.

cloning flesh, keep the Opacity at 25 to 50 percent to make the process more forgiving, because face textures rarely match up as well as you'd like. Using the Dodge and Burn tools to alter the darker and lighter areas with a soft brush (again, with lowered Opacity) can work wonders on a jigsaw face. The textured astronaut character is available on the companion CD-ROM in the file `AstronautMesh.max`, as is the final texture file, `Astronaut1.jpg`. `Astronaut1.psd` is the layered texture that was used to create `Astronaut1.jpg`. All of these files are located in the `Files\Astronaut` folder.

TEXTURING THE ROBOT

The robot texture will consist of a base metal layer and peeling paint over the top. We'll use scratches, grime, and Layer Effects to create a texture that suggests old, weathered, and worn steel panels and rivets.

Creating a Base Metal Texture

The first step of this texture lies in the base metal layer. In addition to your own digital photos and created textures, 3ds Max comes with some quality textures. You can find these textures in the `Maps` folder where 3ds Max is installed. In Figure 9.5, `STEELPLT.jpg` is being used as the base metal. This bitmap is 756 × 512 pixels, so you need to crop it down to bring it to 512 × 512. After you've applied the template for the robot character, places for panels become evident. `STEELPLT.jpg` is located in

ON THE CD   `Files\Astronaut` on the companion CD-ROM.

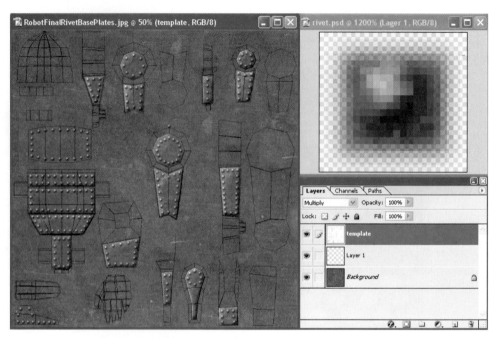

FIGURE 9.5   Pasting rivets onto steel.

Creating Panels

You create panels through Layer Styles, as described for the spacesuit patterns layer for the astronaut texture; a Layer Style is created to bring the painted areas out toward the viewer, and then a Layer Mask is added to allow the texture to be painted on or removed. Finally, the texture is painted away and then painted back on where the panels should be created.

Creating Rivets

You can create rivets with a Layer Style or hand-draw them (as the one at the upper right of Figure 9.5 was) and then cut them from their own file and paste them into the robot texture as needed. This ultimately makes for a lot of layers. Moving around the rivets on the template is made easier if you ensure that Auto Select Layer is turned on while you have the Move tool active in Photoshop. Auto Select Layer automatically selects a layer based on the pixels that your Move tool is over when you click.

Creating Scratched and Peeling Paint

Creating a layer of scratched and peeling paint over the steel and rivet foundation can add realism and believability. You can draw scratches by hand, and then you can fill in the areas where the scratches are not filled in with the paint bucket. Shadows and highlights add thickness to the paint and authenticity to the texture.

Setting Up Layers

After you've established the panels and rivets, you can merge these layers by turning off any layers you don't want to merge and then selecting Layers, Merge Visible Layers. As you can see in Figure 9.6, this then becomes the foundation layer called `BareMetalPlusRivets`; `PaintedMetalPlusRivets` is a duplicate of the foundation layer that has been painted green, where the foreground color is set to a shade of green and Mode set to Color on the Standard toolbar. The `GrimeMD1` layer is there to make the metal look more dirty and weathered. Grime in this case is simply a digital photograph of grime on a steel panel of a trash dumpster. This layer has been desaturated and set to 50 percent opacity. The `Big Scratches` layer is where scratches in the texture were drawn in white with the more irregularly shaped brushes available in Photoshop, such as the Fuzzball brush.

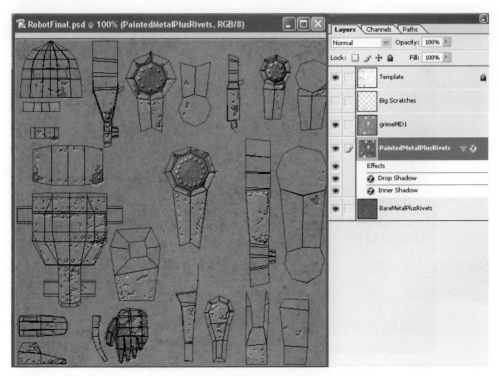

FIGURE 9.6   The final texture for the robot has a layer of grime over a layer of paint and bare metal.

Scratching the Paint

When creating scratches, paint those areas that are most exposed and would likely get the most wear and tear. In this texture, that means the rivets and the edges of the components. To apply the scratches to the painted layer, I selected the scratched areas with the Magic Wand tool while Contiguous was turned off so that every scratched area was selected. While this selection was still active, I activated the `PaintedMetalPlusRivets` layer and used the Erase tool to erase paint in those scratched areas (see Figure 9.6).

ON THE CD

There is a Layer Style applied to this layer to create shadows and highlights, which will be discussed in the next section. `RobotFinal.jpg` is the working version of the robot texture, created from `RobotFinal.psd`. `RobotFinal.jpg` and `RobotFinal.psd` can be found in the `Files\Robot` folder, and `GrimeMD1.jpg` can be found in the `Files\Astronaut` folder on the companion CD-ROM.

Adding Shadows to the Paint Job

You can paint shadows at the edge of the paint, or you can take care of this with a Layer Style. Figure 9.7 depicts the process of applying shadows. Just as you'd apply a Layer Style to edges of text, the Layer Style here is applied to the edges of the

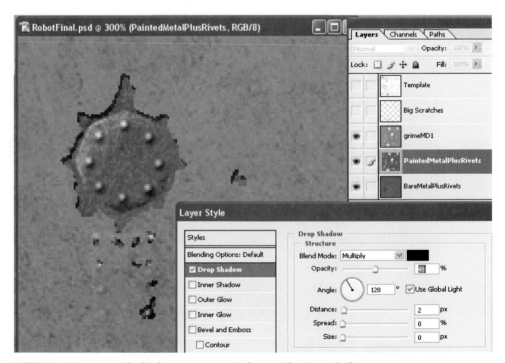

FIGURE 9.7 You can apply shadows to your paint layer with a Layer Style.

scratched-out areas, where there are no pixels. The drop shadow here has been slightly exaggerated to make it more visible in the figure. Of primary importance is the direction of the light source. This should be coming from above, and the angle should be consistent with the other art you create for the game.

Adding Highlights to the Paint

Where the light hits an edge, a highlight is formed. Even though no Inner Highlight Layer Style is available, we can use an Inner Shadow to accomplish our purposes. In Figure 9.8, a highlight has been added to the opposite side of the unpainted area by checking the Inner Shadow box and setting the Blend Mode to Luminosity, with Color set to white. Keep Angle the same as it was for the Drop Shadow, and adjust Opacity, Distance, and Size as necessary. The highlight was slightly exaggerated for clarity in this figure.

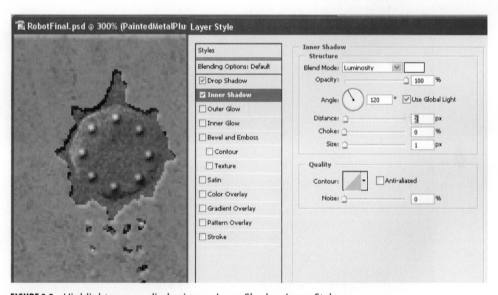

FIGURE 9.8   Highlights are applied using an Inner Shadow Layer Style.

MODELING TEXTURES IN 3DS MAX

You can create textures from scratch, using digital photographs, or combining the two. Yet another method is to create or acquire a sculpted mesh, to which a starting material is applied. Omni or Spot lighting is applied until the image looks right, and a single frame image is saved as a TIF or JPG. The Rendering dialog box in 3ds Max allows you to select a single frame, any desired pixel resolution, and the file type to save the image as. You can then modify the file in Photoshop as necessary. 3ds Max has a wide range of tools for creating textures in the actual mesh. The two images shown in Figure 9.9 started as planes. The steel texture on the right was created by setting the plane segments to 20 × 20. Some of the polygons were beveled, and a MeshSmooth modifier was applied. The reptile texture on the left was converted to an Editable Poly and subdivided with the Cut tool. Some of the sections were beveled, and Edge Tesselation was applied. The entire model had the MeshSmooth modifier applied to it.

To take this idea further, you can unwrap the model to a UV template, paint the template, and apply the result to the model again. This is how the reptile texture was created. First, the model was unwrapped using the Unwrap UVWs modifier. The UVs were used to create a template, which was then imported to Photoshop and painted with darker green paint in the lower faces and lighter green paint in the more elevated faces. This texture was then reapplied to the model in 3ds Max. At this point, you can create another rendering of the model in its textured state for the final texture bitmap.

FIGURE 9.9   You can model textures in 3ds Max and then render them as a texture file.

TROUBLESHOOTING

After a texture is on a model, problems with the unwrap can become more apparent. Misaligned Unwrap modifiers can be disorienting to deal with, and distorted textures can ruin a model's believability.

Misaligned Unwrap

If you have an Unwrap UVW modifier that has become misaligned, meaning that the seams for the UVs appear to have become offset from the actual model location, unfreeze and unhide everything, and make sure all the modifiers are "on" in the modifier stack.

Distorted Textures

If you are going to use rivets or some other round design in your texture, be careful about using the Normal map to unwrap the model. If the model is not flat to the front or back view (or whichever view you use), you can get texture distortion, which is more obvious if the texture has circular elements, because the oblong shape is a dead giveaway. This can also be the case if you have not carefully corrected the UVs by moving vertices in the UVW Unwrap dialog box. In either case, it ruins the believability of the effect. In those instances, it's better to unwrap using a Planar map aligned to the model with Best Align than using Normal map.

SUMMARY

Character texturing begins with a template that lays out the UVs for the model in such a way that they are as flat and as recognizable as possible. Layer Styles and Layer Masking are powerful tools for creating and enhancing textures. Shadows and highlights can give thickness to a layer of paint or make a handmade scratch look like it cuts into the surface. Scratches, ribs, dents, grime, and dirt layers can make a surface look more authentic. Digital photos are a quick way to create a face texture, whether the image has to be stretched to fit the UVs, or it has to be cut and pasted into different pieces that fit and then blended together. 3ds Max is a great texture creation tool; you can model, render, and hand-paint textures in Photoshop and then reapply them to a model.

10 CHARACTER RIGGING

In This Chapter

- Rigging—Overview
- Minimizing Vertex Collapse
- Fitting the Biped to the Character Mesh
- Examining the Skinning Process
- Moving and Rotating Bones to Check Vertex Assignments
- Rigging a Robot
- Using the Default Player Biped with a Custom Mesh
- Combining Bones with Biped

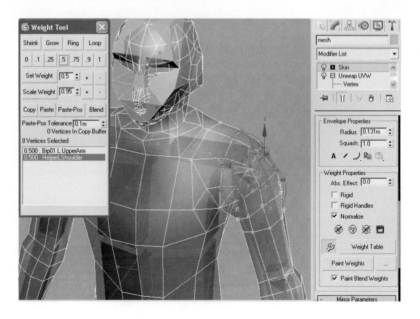

RIGGING—OVERVIEW

Rigging is the process of creating and applying a skeletal structure to your character mesh so that when the different bones move, the mesh moves with them in a convincing way. You can achieve the skeleton part of the equation with either biped or bones. The skeletal system is connected to the character mesh by using the Skin modifier. By taking care in how you create the mesh, how you create the skeleton, and how you tie the two together, you increase your chances of success when it comes to the final stages of animating and exporting to the Torque Game Engine. The difficulties of rigging are hard to appreciate until you have actually rigged a reasonably complex character yourself. It is a realm full of tricks, compromises, pitfalls, and challenges.

Deciding Between Bones and Biped

Biped is a precanned humanoid skeleton system that is adjustable to most of the models and situations you might run up against. Bones require more work than the biped, because you have to build the skeletal structure bone-by-bone yourself, and then you must create inverse kinematic (IK) relationships between the bones. Although creating a bones skeletal structure by hand is ultimately more flexible, biped is the more straightforward method. The 3ds Max help has several tutorials on how to set up a bones rig; also, the sections in this chapter on helper bones and using the Skin modifier apply equally to both biped and bones. Therefore, biped will be the primary skeletal system addressed in this chapter.

Setting Up the Mesh as a 3D Template

Before you start this process, you should back up your character mesh. Open a copy of the character mesh, which should by now be approximately 2.5 meters tall, facing the back viewport, and converted to an Editable Mesh. Any UV maps, unwrapping, and texturing should already be applied.

Although you can adjust your mesh to fit a biped, the normal procedure is to let your mesh define what the biped will look like. This is easier if you make the mesh transparent and frozen. You can't select frozen objects, so it's not possible to accidentally select some of the faces of your mesh. By making the mesh transparent, you can see the bones inside the mesh to select and manipulate them. To do this, right-click the mesh, select Properties from the right-click menu, and check the boxes for Freeze and See-Through; then uncheck the box for Show Frozen in Gray. Turning off Show Frozen in Gray allows your mesh to keep some of its shading information so that you can keep a sense of its form as you fit the biped to it. Make sure the viewport is set to display Edged Faces, because edges give you a visual cue as to where key joints are in your mesh.

Making a Biped

To create a biped, select Create Panel, Systems, and click the Biped button. Click-drag, similar to when you are creating a box primitive, to set the size of the biped. On the panel to your right, in the Create Biped rollout, you will see that you can also type in a height for the biped. Test out the different structures you can make with a biped by changing the number of links for fingers, tail, spine, and so on.

Modifying the Parameters of a Biped After You've Created It

You can change the body type of the biped, the number of links for different bones, the name, and the height of the biped at the time of creation or afterward. In Chapter 1, "Introduction to 3ds Max," we discussed the idea that if you create something like a box primitive in 3ds Max, after you click on something else, you lose the menus that allow you to modify the box. So, to modify the box after it has been created, you must select the box and activate the Modify panel to once again have access to the parameters and segments of that box. The same is true for biped, but it is slightly more complex. To modify the structure or the name of a biped after you've created it, you must select a bone on the biped, activate the Motion panel, and activate Figure mode, which is a mode specifically designed for modifying the number, size, and rotation of the different bones in the biped.

Select a bone on the biped and activate the Motion panel. On the Biped rollout, click the Figure mode icon to turn it on. The Structure rollout shows up below, allowing you to change the height of the biped or the number of links associated with different body parts. What you want for your astronaut character is a default biped with only two spine links and one toe link. Figure 10.1 shows what the menus look like if you are in Figure mode and how the menus change if you turn off Figure mode.

Understanding the Biped

It is a worthwhile exercise to simply create a biped and experiment with moving the various bones so that you can visually understand how rotating or moving one bone affects other bones. This is best done with Figure mode turned off. Rotating the hips rotates the upper thighs and all the way down to the feet, if the feet are not somehow anchored to the ground. Rotating any of the spine bones also rotates the entire upper body, from that spine bone and upward. Moving a foot or hand moves the rest of that limb, up to the hip or clavicle bone. Several tutorials are available in the Tutorials section of the 3ds Max Help drop-down menu if you feel you need further information on biped skeletal animation.

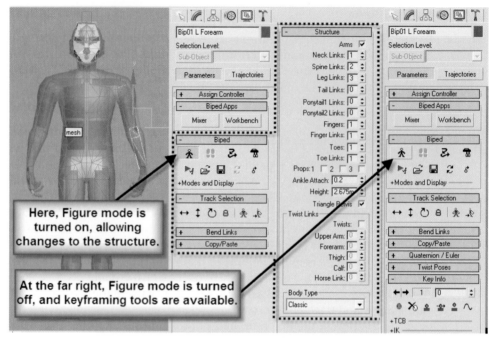

FIGURE 10.1   From the Motion panel, you can turn Figure mode on or off.

Understanding the Biped Center of Mass (COM)

The biped is actually a hierarchy of objects, with one special parent object called Bip01. This object is also known as the Center Of Mass (COM). It appears as a blue tetrahedron that is generally not visible unless you are in wireframe mode, because it is buried in the pelvis of the biped. Because the biped has so many parts, naming and keeping track of them can be tricky. If you want to rename the biped to a different root name than Bip01, select a bone, and in the Motion panel, in the Biped rollout, expand the Modes and Display menu and change the root name there. All the other bones associated with this biped now carry the new root name.

Rotating the Biped

When you are rotating or moving the biped as a unit, make sure you are in Figure mode. Before you rotate the biped so that it is facing the back view, make sure that your Angular Snap toggle is turned on. This helps you to make the rotation of the biped an exact 180 degrees. Under the Track Selection rollout, click Body Rotation. Click and drag on the rotation gizmo to cause a full 180-degree rotation on the biped. Alternatively, you can select the COM object (Bip01) and use the Rotate tool to rotate the biped.

Moving the Biped

Moving the biped is similar to rotating the biped. Make sure you are in Figure mode, and select Body Horizontal or Body Vertical from the Track Selection rollout. Alternately, you can select the COM object (Bip01) and use the Move tool to position the biped. Move the biped so that the bottom of the feet and the pelvis line up with your character mesh as closely as possible.

MINIMIZING VERTEX COLLAPSE

The subject of vertex collapse is slightly advanced. If this is your first time rigging a character, try working with the standard biped setup until you have a little practice. Delving into helper bones, prerotated biped bones, and proxy objects may be too much for right now.

Even though we haven't discussed assigning the mesh vertices to the different bones yet, the subject of vertex collapse has to do so much with bones that we must address it first. In areas like the elbows, shoulders, hips, and knees, mesh vertices collapse when the joints rotate. The problem is illustrated in Figure 10.2. When the elbow is rotated, the vertices collapse and cause an unnaturally thin elbow area. This happens because when the bone rotates, it also rotates the vertices of the mesh. If the forearm is rotating and the upper arm is not, there is going to be a collapse as the forearm vertices meet the upper arm. The first step to minimizing this problem is carefully assigning vertices to the bones using the available tools. Additional methods are discussed in this section.

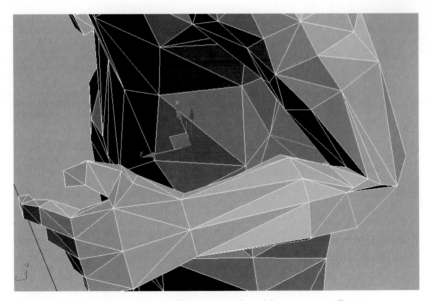

FIGURE 10.2   Shoulders, hips, and elbows are vulnerable to vertex collapse.

Minimizing Collapsed Vertices by Modeling

Two approaches are often successful in minimizing collapsed vertices by way of modeling. The first method is modeling the character in a "ready" pose, with knees, elbows, and other joints slightly bent, so that the creasing or collapsing of vertices that occurs during full movement is not as pronounced. Modeling, and unwrapping, a character this way is a little harder, although some tricks can make this work better. The second method is hiding the deformations with the model itself. The character may have shoulder pads or armor that covers most of the shoulder area where the vertices are most affected by movement. Where vertices in the shoulder area must be divided between the clavicle and upper arm bones, the shoulder pad or armor might be assigned to the clavicle only so that it does not collapse.

Minimizing Collapsed Vertices by Prerotating Biped Bones

Biped is trying to mimic the human skeletal system, and the Skin modifier is trying to mimic that incredible organ that stretches perfectly over the human body. Neither of these is an easy feat. Getting the left arm of the biped to turn and hold a gun that is tucked under the character's right arm requires a real stretch. And, by the time you get it there, the twists and turns you have to make on the biped's upper arm, lower arm, and hand can end up making a mess of the mesh. It's possible to make this work, but let me tell you a helpful technique. In Figure mode, after you've sized the biped to fit your mesh, rotate the upper-left arm +90 degrees around X and –5 degrees around Y. Then rotate the left forearm +4 degrees around Z, and rotate the left hand –90 degrees around X, –20 degrees around Y, and about –20 degrees around Z. The end effect of this is that the upper-left arm is rotated into a position that is more forgiving for a rifle-carrying pose. The elbow joint can now bend directly to the right side and thus ends up putting less twist on the shoulder vertices. Unless you are looking for this modification, it is difficult to even tell it has been done.

Minimizing Collapsed Vertices by Using Helper Bones

 If this is your first time rigging a character, you may want to skip this section on using helper bones for now and give it a try later when you have had a little experience with creating a more standard character rig.

Helper bones are simply bones you create and place in problem areas such as the hips, shoulders, and elbows to help the mesh to adjust smoothly to the skeleton. A standard bone is created at the joints for hips, shoulders, and elbows. This extra bone is constrained with an Orientation constraint to the bones on either side of it. Then, when the bones on either side of the helper bone move, it bridges the angular gap between them. The forearm bone in Figure 10.3 is set to transparent so you can clearly see this in action; the forearm is bent at 90 degrees, but the helper, which is the gray bone sitting at the joint of the elbow, is only bent at 45 degrees. When the character mesh is skinned to the skeleton, its vertices in these joint areas are applied to the helper bones, minimizing resultant distortion.

In this section, we engage in parenting objects and creating parent-child relationships. If you need review on creating parent-child relationships, see Chapter 5, "Animating Game Art."

FIGURE 10.3   Helper bones bridge the gap between the bones on either side of them.

Creating a Helper Bone

You can create bones from the Character pull-down menu by selecting Bone Tools and clicking the Create Bones button, or from the Create panel under Systems, Bones. Because you should set 3ds Max to a metric scale for this operation, adjust your default bone Width and Height to 0.1m or so. (It is also possible to create the rig with generic units in 3ds Max, where you work as if every unit is a meter.) Click on the screen once to place the bone's first joint, and then click again to place the next joint. You need only one bone per problem area, so place your first bone, right-click to escape the bone creating process, and delete the bone tip that is automatically formed at the end of the bone. The process of adding helper bones to a biped is on the video `FittingBipedAndHelperBones.wmv`, in the `Videos` folder on the companion CD-ROM.

A bone is placed on the biped where the problem joints are. When placing a helper bone for the elbow, for example, take care that the pivot point of the helper bone is positioned exactly where the pivot point is for the elbow. Parent the helper bone to the bone it is helping; that is, the helper bone for the elbow should become a child of the forearm bone, using Select and Link. Remember that Select and Link operates by clicking and dragging with the left mouse button on the *child*, and releasing the mouse button when the cursor is over the *parent*.

Adding Orientation Constraints to the Helper Bone

You can add an Orientation constraint to the helper bone so that it is influenced by the orientation of the bone above it and the orientation of the bone below it. To do this, select the helper bone and then, from the Animation drop-down menu, select Constraints, Orientation Constraint. Then click on the bone above the helper bone. When you constrain a helper bone to a biped bone, the helper bone generally flips into a new orientation; you can remedy this by checking Keep Initial Offset. (See the motion menu in Figure 10.4.) This is all that is necessary for the first half of this process.

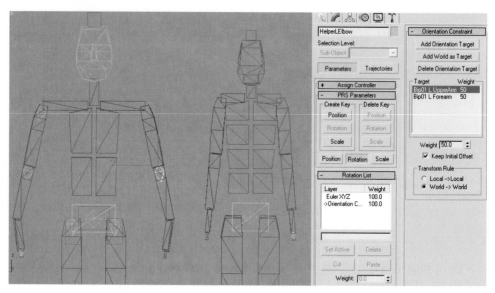

FIGURE 10.4   The helper bone with Orientation constraints to the bones above and below it.

You should now be in the Motion panel. Figure 10.4 shows a biped with helper bones added on the left, and a stock biped with no helpers on the right. The Motion panel has been expanded to two columns so that you can see how the Orientation constraints work. You can see in the menu a rollout for Rotation List, which lists the different constraints that are on your helper bone at the moment. Orientation constraint should be on this list. Further down the panel is an Orientation constraint rollout, which has a list box in it; the bone that is above your helper bone should be in this list; notice that by default the bone above your helper bone is influencing the helper bone 50 percent. Click on Add Orientation Target, and select the bone below your helper bone. By default, both bones now influence your helper bone 50 percent each. Figure 10.4 shows what the Motion panel should look like when this is done. Note also from this figure that Keep Initial Offset is checked. It is worth noting that in the PRS Parameters rollout, the Rotation button is turned on, enabling all the Rotation rollouts in the menu below.

This means that the helper bone is really finding a middle rotational orientation between the two bones it is constrained to. If the mesh vertices in the elbow area are assigned to the helper bone, the vertex collapse is more subtle and acceptable. This technique works for both Biped and Bones. It is a good idea to name these helper bones so that you can easily identify and access them later. Give them a name that makes sense to you, such as `HelperRElbow` (meaning helper bone for the right elbow).

Using Proxies for the Helper Bones at the Hips

If you try to use a helper bone at the hip area, between the pelvis and the upper leg bone, the helper bone twists in both the Y axis and the X axis, causing ugly deformations to the mesh. By using proxies, or stand-ins, for the pelvis and the upper leg bone, you can avoid this problem. As shown in Figure 10.4, simply create three boxes: `ProxyRThighbone`, `ProxyLThighbone`, and `ProxyPelvis`. Apply an Orientation constraint to each proxy so that it is oriented 100 percent to its parent bone. Use the same pivot point for both of the thighbone proxies that you used for each thighbone. Make each proxy a child of the bone it is a proxy for; for example, parent `ProxyPelvis` to the biped pelvis. Then place a helper bone for the left and right hip, so that the pivot point matches the pivot point for each upper leg bone. You can parent each hip helper bone to its proxy object. For example, you can parent `HelperLHip` to `ProxyLThighbone`. These proxies are visible in Figure 10.4 as red boxes. You should not add proxy bones to the Skin modifier because they will not receive vertex assignments. They are only there to facilitate proper functioning of the helper bones in the hip area. The process of placing and constraining proxies for the hip area is in the video `ProxiesAndLinking.wmv`, located in the `Videos` folder on the companion CD-ROM.

ON THE CD

Another important aspect to helper bones (and this applies to proxy objects as well) is that if you want to save the biped to a BIP file so that you can apply it to other bipeds, you have to insert dummy objects as proxy objects, or stand-ins, for every bone that the helper bone will be constrained to. This is not used as a step-by-step example here because it can be unwieldy, and the size and location of the dummy objects do not translate well across differently sized bipeds. An example of this is located in the `Files/Misc` folder on the companion CD-ROM and is called `BipedDummy.max`.

ON THE CD

Minimizing Deformations by Using the Joint Angle Deformer

The Skin modifier has an available gizmo called the Joint Angle Deformer, which bears mentioning because you can also use it to control the deformation of the mesh as the bones move. Because we typically delete the character mesh for the animation sequences, the helper bone technique discussed earlier is a more applicable solution.

FITTING THE BIPED TO THE CHARACTER MESH

Figure 10.5 shows three bipeds at different phases of being fit to the character mesh. The third biped is shown in profile at the far right of this figure. All of these adjustments are being performed while the biped is in Figure mode. Figure mode is a button on this panel that allows you to adjust the structure, location, and orientation of the biped itself as well as the bones in the biped. Note in this image that Figure mode is turned on. The first biped has been rotated to face the back view and has been moved as necessary to line up with the character mesh. The second biped has had its hips and clavicle bones scaled to match the character mesh, and the legs and arms have been rotated and scaled to fit the mesh. The third biped has had the spine scaled horizontally, the head scaled to fill the mesh head, and the legs and arms rotated from the side view to make sure that its bones are lined up as well as possible to the different parts of the character mesh. This third biped has also had the left arm pre-rotated and helper bones added, although these modifications are optional.

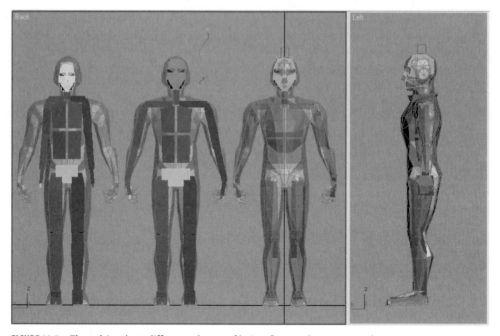

FIGURE 10.5   Three bipeds at different phases of being fit to a character mesh.

Scaling the Pelvis and Clavicles of the Biped

One of the first adjustments that must be made on the biped is scaling the hips and clavicle bones to match the width of these areas of the character mesh. This repositions the legs and arms so that later, you can match them to the character mesh. You can scale the pelvis axially by selecting the pelvis and using the Z axis of the Scale tool to make it wider or narrower according to the needs of your mesh. In this case, you can make the pelvis a bit wider. You can scale the clavicle bones axially as well; select them both, or select one, and use the Symmetrical button from the Track Selection rollout to easily select the opposite of any selected bone.

Scaling and Rotating the Legs and Arms of the Biped

After you've scaled the hips and clavicles to match the character mesh, rotate the arms and legs if necessary so that they will be aligned to the character's arms and legs. Again, make sure the Angular Snap toggle is turned on so that you can keep the left and right sides of your biped in step with one another when you rotate. You may want to lower the Angular Snap default to one-degree increments so that you can get a more refined rotation for this fit. When you've rotated the arms and legs correctly, select both sides of the upper arm bones and scale them axially if necessary so that the elbow of the biped lines up with the elbow of the character mesh. Scale and rotate the lower arm and leg bones if necessary, and rotate the hands as well. Although this example does not use the single finger on each of the biped's hands, if you did want to use it in the animation process, you'd probably want to scale it up to one big, fat finger. A one-bone foot is sufficient for a game character, but if you do want to use a two-bone foot, simply scale up the toe0 bone, as shown on the third biped in Figure 10.5. If you want a simpler foot, scale the main foot bone up until it is as big as the foot on your character mesh. The run cycle example in Chapter 11, "Character Animation," uses a one-bone foot.

Aligning the Biped to the Character Mesh from the Side View

Finally, check the right or left view to see how well the modified biped fits your character mesh. One of the first things to check is the overall position of the pelvis. Remember, you can move the biped as a unit by selecting the Bip01 COM object and moving it (while in Figure mode). You may also need to rotate the upper and lower arms, or rotate the first or second spine bones to match your mesh. Rotate or scale the neck or head if the head is not positioned correctly. Scale the head so that it nearly fills up the space for the head area of your character mesh.

Saving the Figure File

After you have gone through the trouble of fitting the biped to your mesh, you can save the Figure file so that you can access it later. The Figure file remembers the structure and positions of your biped's bones and can be used on future bipeds you might want to use with the same or similar meshes. This button looks like a floppy disk and is called Save File. You can find it on the Biped rollout; it's active only while the biped is in Figure mode.

EXAMINING THE SKINNING PROCESS

When the Skin modifier is added to a mesh, you have the option of adding bones to the modifier. Every vertex of the mesh (or the skin) is assigned to one of these bones, or to a combination of bones. Then, when the biped bones are keyframed, the mesh moves along with them.

Applying a Skeleton via Skin or Physique

3ds Max offers two methods of applying a skeleton to a mesh: Skin and Physique. We will be using the Skin modifier. Skin is supported for real-time deformation, and Physique is not. Real-time deformation uses the node transforms of the bones to drive the mesh vertices, a very effective solution. Physique animations export as morph animations, where a snapshot is taken of the position of all vertices of the mesh at each frame. This creates very large and inefficient files. Morph animation also prohibits default animations (see Chapter 11, "Character Animation"), blend animations, and transitions. So, the Skin modifier is the way the mesh is linked to the bones or biped. The help for Skin can be tricky to find, depending on your version of 3ds Max, because most references to Skin actually refer to Physique. In version 8, check under Help, Reference, select the Index tab, and look up Skin, Save/Load Envelopes.

Ensuring You're Ready for Skinning

Before you start the skinning process, make sure you have a mesh that is defined well with the biped or bones you are planning on using. If you do not have enough edges to enable the joints to move well, or if your edges are in the wrong places, you will waste time trying to adapt a poorly designed mesh to a skeleton. Build the mesh so that you can assign each vertex in the mesh to one bone or have it shared by two bones. This can minimize collapsing of joints and make the mesh look as good as possible when the character is moving. Place your character mesh next to the biped and make any necessary edits in the mesh before moving on. The final prep before adding the Skin modifier is making sure both the biped and the character mesh are standing with their feet at the origin and that the bones are as well placed and centered within the mesh as possible. Check this from the back view (which looks at the front of your character) and from the side views.

Applying the Skin Modifier to the Character Mesh

At this stage, make sure that the biped is still in Figure mode. The character mesh should be unfrozen, yet transparent so that the bones are visible. Alternately, you can work in wireframe mode if you want. Select the character mesh and apply the Skin modifier. The interface for the Skin modifier is extensive. The normal procedure is to start by adding the bones that will be assigned vertices. On the Skin menu, in the Parameters rollout, click the Bones Add button. The process of adding and adjusting the Skin modifier is shown on the video `SkinModifier.wmv`, located in the `Videos` folder on the companion CD-ROM.

ON THE CD

Deciding Which Bones to Add to the Skin Modifier

It is important that you add only the bones you are actually going to need in the animations. Keep in mind that you need to account for every vertex in the mesh, and every bone you add to the Skin modifier must have at least one vertex assignment, even if it is just a partial assignment. This means that you can add only necessary bones to the Skin modifier for vertex assignment. Keep bones such as `Bip01_Head_nub` out. For most real-time rendering purposes, the only bones you will want to add to the modifier are the head, clavicles, upper arms, forearms, hands, spines (usually a biped with two spine bones is sufficient), pelvis, thighs, calves, and feet. If you want a two-bone foot, you can include `toe0` in this list. If you are using helper bones, include them in the list. If you are using proxy bones in the hip area, don't include them in the list; they are only for keeping the hip helper bones properly constrained, so they should not receive vertex assignments. If you want to delete a bone from the list or add a bone to the list after the vertex assignment process has begun, you can do so, but if there are problems with the export, you may need to delete the Skin modifier and go through the process again.

Adjusting the Envelope

Each bone comes equipped with an envelope; you can resize these envelopes to select vertices in the mesh. After you've added all relevant bones to the Skin modifier list, turn on the Enable Envelopes button. This makes it possible to select any particular bone from the list or via the viewport. Figure 10.6 shows that the Skin modifier has been added to the character mesh, the relevant bones have been added to the Skin modifier, and the Edit Envelopes button in the Parameters rollout has been activated. The bone currently selected in this screen shot is the head, so you can see that the head bone on the mesh now has its envelope activated. Each bone, when selected either in the working area or off the side panel, has an envelope that you can adjust to vary the vertices that will be affected by that bone. *Skinning* is a process

ON THE CD

of tuning which vertices in the mesh are affected by which bones. Envelope-based vertex assignment is covered in the video `SkinModifier.wmv`, located in the `Videos` folder on the companion CD-ROM.

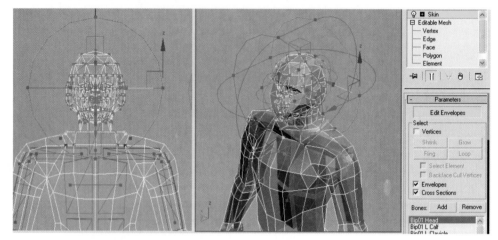

FIGURE 10.6   The Skinning process has begun with the head bone.

Each bone has two envelopes: a bright red inner envelope, and a dark red outer envelope. Each of the envelopes is shaped like a capsule, with a circle at each end, and four control points on each circle that you can select and move with the Move tool. In Figure 10.6, one of the control points of the inner envelope has been selected with the Move tool active; you can now move this control point and thus alter the head bone's influence over the surrounding vertices.

Selecting Relative or Absolute

You can use two methods to calculate how the envelopes affect vertices. The default is called the Absolute method, in which any vertex that is within the outer, dark red envelope is assigned 100 percent to that bone. In the Relative method, any vertex that is within the inner, bright red envelope is assigned to the bone; vertices that fall between the inner and outer envelopes are shared by neighboring bones, based on envelope overlaps. Even though the Absolute method is the default, you will probably want to try the Relative method, especially in areas like shoulders, elbows, and hips; sharing vertices between envelopes helps make the skin "stretch" across joints to create more realistic motion. To select Relative or Absolute, click the A or R button in the Envelope Properties section of the Parameters rollout in the Skin modifier.

Assigning Vertices to Helper Bones

In Figure 10.7, all the envelopes have been turned on at the same time so that you can see how the helper bones are taking care of the vertices in the problem areas of the shoulder, elbow, and hip. If you are using helper bones, remember that they are taking responsibility for the regular bones only at the trouble areas. For example, the helper for the shoulder area is being assigned vertices for the entire shoulder area, which includes some of the vertices that would normally be assigned to the clavicle and some of the vertices that would normally be assigned to the upper arm. Vertices in the middle area of the upper arm are assigned to the upper arm bone. As you move further down the upper arm to the elbow joint, those vertices are assigned to the elbow helper bone. Again, helper bones are optional.

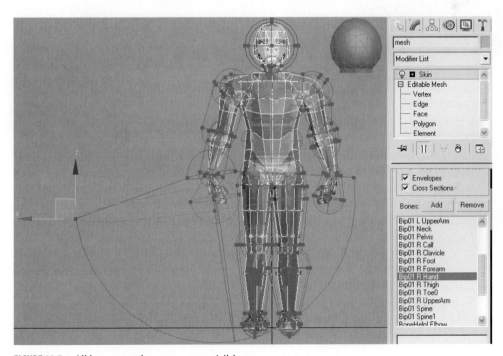

FIGURE 10.7   All bone envelopes are now visible.

Resizing Envelopes

Figure 10.7 also illustrates why the character's legs and arms cannot be too close to the body. The astronaut's legs are about as close together as you would want your character's legs to be. It is easy for a bone's envelope to capture vertices that should belong to another bone. The bones on the right side of the image have been assigned vertices, and the bones on the left side are still in process. The inner envelope of the right-hand bone has been expanded until it has contacted the outer envelope, causing the outer envelope to blow out to several times its original size. You can avoid this by resizing the outer envelope before adjusting the inner envelope. Often you can select and move an envelope control point by doing a click-drag-release type action; however, sometimes you have to specifically click and release on a particular control point to select it. You will see the move gizmo move to that point; then you can click and drag on the move gizmo to move the control point.

Adjusting the Axis of the Envelope

Besides the four control points at each cross section of an envelope, each envelope has an axis that goes through the bone. You can select this axis to activate the bone, rather than selecting the bones from the Skin bones list. You can shorten, lengthen, or reposition this axis as necessary to achieve the desired result. You accomplish this the same way as when you edit the cross-section control points, by simply moving the control points with the Move tool. The axis is actually shorter than the distance from one cross section to the other. If you want to select an axis control point, just look for the short dark line going through the center of the bone, and select one of the two dark control points at either end. Generally, it is a good idea not to reposition these except to shorten or lengthen the influence of a bone.

Checking the Side View

Working from the side view and perspective/user views is also important to ensure that the envelopes are influencing the proper vertices. In Figure 10.8, a side view shows that the envelope for the foot has flipped to a vertical orientation. In this image, the envelope is in the process of being moved to a horizontal orientation. Very short bones, like the bone in the foot, will flip like this and need to be realigned. To fix this, select and move the control point at the upper end of the envelope axis. This can be a little deceptive, because even though the proper axis control point was selected, the move gizmo is centered on one of the control points of the envelope cross section. This is one case where moving both control points on the axis, one at a time, may be necessary to properly center the envelope on the foot.

Assigning a Vertex to Every Bone

For Torque to accept the character, you have to assign at least one vertex to every bone that is included in the Skin modifier. One way to help this happen is to make sure that you keep the Weight All Vertices check box checked in the Advanced Parameters rollout. This saves you the trouble of tracking down stray vertices, which may have never been assigned a bone.

Keeping the Armpit Vertices Tied to the Spine/Clavicle Bone

This mesh has one edge, with two vertices, that defines the area where the arm meets the body. You should assign these two vertices to the spine or clavicle bones, not the upper arm.

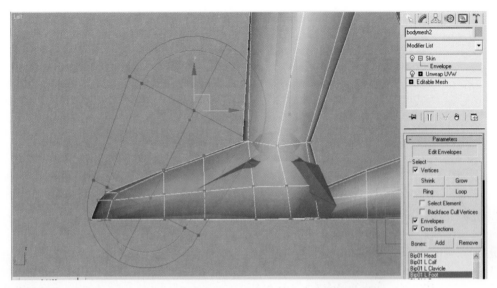

FIGURE 10.8   Correcting a rotated envelope.

Using Envelopes as a First-Pass Tool

Using envelopes for vertex assignments is a great way to start the skinning process, but don't get into the trap of thinking that you have to tweak the envelopes over and over until the vertex assignments are perfect. Spend some time on each envelope, in both front and side views, and then move on to other vertex assignment tools found in the Skin modifier, such as the Abs Effect and the Weight tool.

Moving the Bones After Skinning Has Started

You can effectively "turn off" the vertex assignments if you need to move or rotate the bones so that they fit the mesh better. Do this from the Skin Modifier menu, in the Parameters rollout, by unchecking the Always Transform box. After you've repositioned your bones, turn this check box back on to proceed as usual.

Assigning Weights to Vertices with Absolute Effect

Ultimately, you may need to select vertices individually and assign their weight using the Weight Properties group of the Parameters rollout for the Skin modifier. A box called Abs Effect allows you to select one or more vertices (assuming you have enabled Vertices selection from the Parameters menu earlier) and assign how much effect the currently selected bone will have on them. For example, if you have a vertex that is assigned to the pelvis and you want to assign it to the upper leg, activate the Upper Leg envelope, select the vertex, and enter 1.0 in the Abs Effect box. When you press Enter on the keyboard, the vertex should be assigned to the new bone. If you want to assign the vertex 50 percent each to the pelvis and the upper leg, it has to be at least partially assigned to each first. If it is assigned 100 percent to the leg bone, the best workflow is to then activate the Pelvis envelope, select the vertex, and enter 0.5 in the Abs Effect box. When you press Enter, the vertex should be equally influenced by both bones. You can also use Abs Effect to assign weights to several vertices at once. Working with the Abs Effect box is demonstrated in the video SkinningAbs.wmv, located in the Videos folder on the companion CD-ROM.

ON THE CD

Assigning Weights to Vertices with the Weight Tool

Figure 10.9 displays the Weight tool and the button that launches it. The Weight tool is similar to the Absolute Effect box, but with more flexibility; it is a useful tool for refining the rough work that the envelope assignments have already accomplished. Before you can launch this tool, you must turn on the Edit Envelopes button, and you must have at least one vertex selected. Like the Absolute Effect tool described in the earlier section, the Weight tool resides in the Weight Properties group. Click the button that looks like an open-ended wrench to bring up the dialog

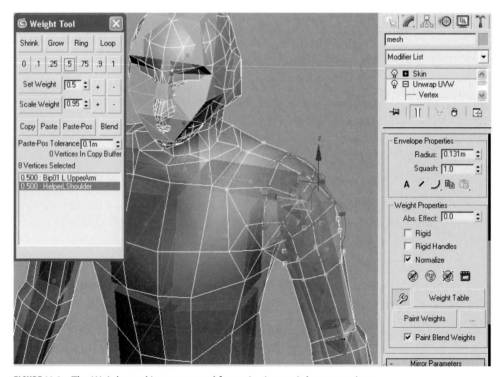

FIGURE 10.9   The Weight tool is a great tool for assigning weights to vertices.

box. One of the most useful ways to use the Weight tool is to select two vertices in any given loop in the mesh and then click the Loop button. The rest of the vertices in the loop should appear, saving you selection time. In this image, a loop of eight vertices has been selected and weighted equally between two different bones. You can generally assign all the vertices in any given loop the same weight values. The Weight tool is demonstrated in the video `SkinningWeightTool.wmv`, located in the `Videos` folder on the companion CD-ROM.

ON THE CD

If you select a group of vertices that the Weight tool indicates are influenced entirely by the upper arm bone, and you want the vertices to be influenced solely by the shoulder helper bone, you can select the shoulder helper bone in the viewport or the side panel and set the weight to 1.0 in the Weight tool. Alternately, if you want the two bones to share the selected vertices, you can assign 0.5 to the shoulder helper bone and then select the upper arm bone in the Weight tool listing and click the 0.5 button to ensure all the vertices are assigned evenly. Don't make assumptions when dealing with groups of vertices in the Weight tool; it can display only one assignment percentage at a time, so what you see listed may not be accurate for all the vertices.

The weights for the upper body vary depending on your character mesh and the positions you anticipate the mesh adopting. For the astronaut, the vertex assignments are shown in Figure 10.10. The arrows point to a vertex that is a part of a larger loop of vertices. Because of the way the astronaut mesh was modeled, most of the loops have eight vertices. All of the vertices in each loop can receive the same weighting as shown in the figure, with the exception of the loops that end up in the armpit area. (For the armpit area, see Figure 10.11.) Where Figure 10.10 states "Helper," it refers to the nearest helper bone; thus, any helper references in the shoulder area refer to the shoulder helper bone, and any helper references in the elbow area refer to the elbow helper bone. These values are only a suggestion, but they help to show how to balance vertices between bones. If you don't have helper bones, you still need to balance weights between the clavicle and the upper arm until the mesh looks as good as possible when you have moved it into the different required positions.

Figure 10.11 starts at the armpit area and works down to the knee. The mistake that a lot of people make when weighting vertices in the armpit area is weighting them partially or fully to the arm. If you move your own arm, you will see that the armpit area next to your chest doesn't move much. You should tie these vertices to the spine bone, the clavicle, or both. As with the previous figure, you can see the gradual progression down the body as helper bones bridge the angular spread between the regular biped bones. You could put a helper bone at the knee joint as well, although the vertex collapse of the knee area is not as noticeable as it is in the other areas.

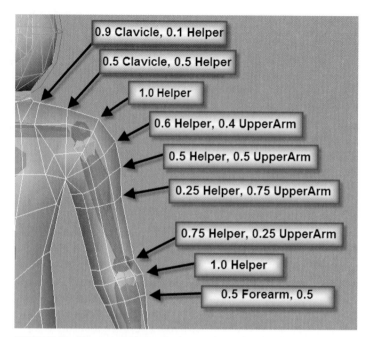

FIGURE 10.10   Vertex weighting for loops along the shoulder and arm.

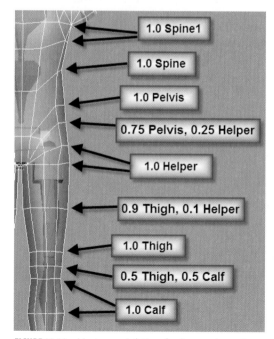

FIGURE 10.11   Vertex weighting for loops along the side of the body.

MOVING AND ROTATING BONES TO CHECK VERTEX ASSIGNMENTS

The mesh deformation needs for a FPS game are much simpler than if you were going to animate a high-resolution mesh for a movie. The arms don't move much because your character will most likely be holding a gun the entire time, and the leg movement requirements are pretty straightforward. Some riggers and animators create full-blown stretch animations so that the mesh vertex assignments can be optimized for many different bone positions. You may not need to go to this length, but you do need to move the arms and legs through the ranges of motion you antic-ipate animating later. This includes, at minimum, a run, a backward run, a strafe, a jump, and a death fall.

Understanding Forward Kinematics and Inverse Kinematics

Forward and *inverse kinematics* refer to two different ways of moving linked bones. The way forward kinematics works is that if you move or rotate an object, anything that is linked to that object moves or rotates accordingly. In this way, you could make a character walk by rotating the upper leg bone, which in turn rotates the lower leg bone, and the foot. Then you would need to rotate the lower leg bone separately. Finally, you would have to rotate the foot separately. At the end of the process, you may find that you have to rerotate the upper leg because you guessed wrong about where the rest of the leg would end up.

Inverse kinematics (IK) is more goal-oriented. This means that you can move the foot, and the upper and lower legs will follow in a more natural and useful way. This can save a great deal of time, because you are generally working only with the hand or foot of the skeleton, and can let the arm and leg bones naturally follow along. As you are keyframing different movements to check the character mesh de-formation, try moving the hand or foot of the biped to get a feel for how this works.

Avoiding the Chewing Gum Effect

A simple and preliminary way to check vertex assignments is to simply try rotating different bones to see how the mesh responds. Make sure the Angular Snap tool is activated, turn off Figure mode, set the character mesh to frozen and transparent, and set the viewport to Smooth + Highlights. Start with one of the upper arm bones. This allows you to easily select and move various bones to see how the mesh reacts. If you notice a bone exerting more influence on the vertices than you think it should, see if adjusting the size of that bone's envelope helps. A full range of motion should be used from the front and side viewports.

Figure 10.12 shows the foot bone selected and being moved up and out in front of the body. A *chewing gum effect* is created when some of the vertices of the mesh (the heel of the foot and the back of the knee) stay with the moving bone, and some of the vertices of the mesh stay where they are. This is a sign that you have not properly assigned the mesh vertices to the bones. This figure also serves to make clear that when you are moving the biped to check vertex assignments, you have selected a bone, and Figure mode is turned off. Any movement you make, as long as you do not set keyframes, can easily be written over by simply activating Figure mode and then deactivating it again. If you have made keyframes, select and delete them before returning to Figure mode; those bone movements will be cleared.

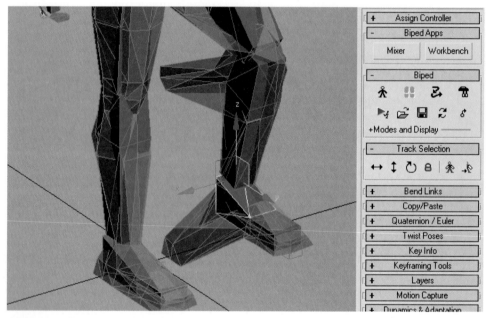

FIGURE 10.12   The chewing gum effect comes from poorly assigned mesh vertices.

Changing the Skeleton While Skinning

Because it is the joints in a skeleton that are really key, it is important that you scale the bones to hit the joints within the mesh exactly. Finding out halfway through the skinning process that the joints don't match up as well as you thought they did is no fun; the sooner you catch the mistake, the better. If you do need to adjust the biped skeleton after the skinning process has begun, make sure to uncheck Always Deform in the Advanced Parameters rollout of the Skin modifier; this allows you to adjust the biped while in Figure mode. After you have scaled or rotated the bones as necessary, check Always Deform to continue skinning as normal.

Looking for Vertex Collapse

If all the bones are pulling on the right portions of the mesh, it's time to consider the most troublesome joints: the elbows, shoulders, and hips. A character will always have some collapsed vertices, because you are using mechanical techniques to imitate a complex organic body. Therefore, don't rotate the limbs any more than is necessary for their animation requirements. Careful assignment of vertices via envelopes, the Weight tool, and helper bones can minimize joint compression.

Keyframing the Biped to Check Mesh Deformation

For a more thorough method to check how well your mesh is assigned to your biped bones, you can keyframe the biped. This is a two-part technique. The first part of the technique is to make sure you are not in Figure mode and, with one of your biped's bones selected, arrange the Motion panel so that the Track Selection and Key Info roll-outs are both visible. While on frame 0, select the bone you are interested in animating and click the red Set Key button in the Track Selection rollout. Drag the Time Slider to frame 10, and move the bone into any pose you feel you will encounter when it comes time to animate the character. Click Set Key again. Drag the Time Slider to frame 20 and move the bone, and then click Set Key once again. Figure 10.13

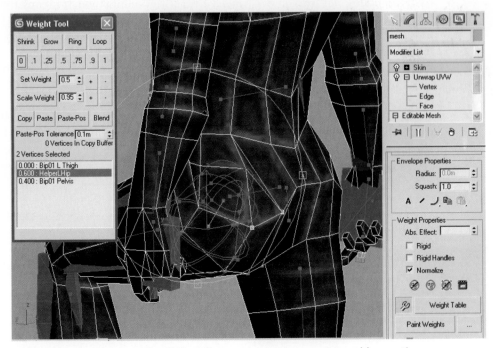

FIGURE 10.13   The Weight tool and Abs. Effect can be used to reassign problem vertices.

demonstrates vertex assignment while the legs are in a simulated running motion. The texture is visible in this version so that stretching is more apparent. Two vertices are selected; the Weight tool is providing feedback as to the vertex assignments, and the Absolute Effect textbox lets us type in any value from 0.0 to 1.0 for whatever bone is currently selected. This process is demonstrated in SkinningAbs.wmv, located in the Videos folder on the companion CD-ROM.

ON THE CD

Creating Optional Controller Objects

You can create a controller object for the hands and feet of your biped so that you can easily select and move them. A controller can be any object such as a rectangle that a hand or foot of the biped is parented to. This is just like putting handles on your character. Because controller objects are often positioned outside of the character mesh, they are easier to select than the actual bone, which is usually hidden inside the mesh. There are no controller objects on the astronaut, but you can add them if you like. At this point in the process, our spaceman character is ready for animation.

RIGGING A ROBOT

The classic robot is made of hard surfaces, so there is no stretching of the skin across multiple bones. 3ds Max allows rigid vertex assignments, which means that all the selected vertices are specifically assigned to *one* bone (whichever bone has the most influence). You can create a robot from multiple meshes; you can then attach these meshes into one Editable Mesh and convert the components to elements within the Editable Poly or the Editable Mesh. Having these separate components distilled into elements makes them easy to select, because an element selection option is available in both the Skin modifier and the Unwrap UVWs modifier.

Each body part is a separate unit, and each body part is tied to a specific bone. It's obvious which bones might go to which components in most cases; the upper arm bone, for instance, would have the vertices of the upper arm mesh assigned to it. The pelvis, spine bones, clavicle, and neck bones are a little more ambiguous. Normally, all these bones are included in even an economical biped, but what components of the robot mesh should be assigned to each?

You can either assign the pelvis to the overall torso of the robot or to a separate lower torso mesh. This depends on how you plan out your mesh. You can assign the spine bone(s) to a single torso component, or separate them so that one spine bone controls a lower torso component and one spine bone controls an upper torso component. For the neck bone, you can assign it to a separate neck mesh or assign at least a partial vertex of the torso mesh. You can assign the clavicle bones to vertices in the torso. Of course, you can make a robot that is partially rigid and partially nonrigid, in which case you can have nonrigid vertex assignments throughout the torso to give the robot some flexibility.

With a robot rig, you can turn Select Element on and select the component to select all the vertices at once. Turning off envelopes and cross sections prevents accidental vertex assignments and allows you to quickly key in vertex assignments. In Figure 10.14, Envelopes and Cross Sections are turned off, Select Element is turned on, and Rigid is checked. Assigning the entire element of the upper left arm a value of 1.0 ensures that all those vertices will follow when the upper arm rotates. This type of skin assignment goes very fast because of the element selection and the fact that every component is 100 percent tied to a single bone.

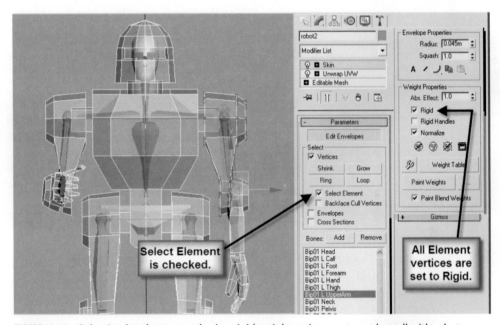

FIGURE 10.14   Selecting by element and using rigid weight assignments works well with robots.

USING THE DEFAULT PLAYER BIPED WITH A CUSTOM MESH

You can use the default player biped (hereafter referred to as the Kork player biped) that comes with the Torque Game Engine in combination with your own custom mesh to take advantage of the animations that are already keyframed for that biped. There are advantages and disadvantages to doing this.

Taking Advantage of Using the Kork Player Biped with Your Character Mesh

By using the Kork player biped, you can take advantage of the existing animations for the Kork player, such as the running, jumping, and dying sequence files, which would otherwise take considerable time to develop. You can also avoid having to do script file editing; as long as your file is exported as `player.dts` and you put it in the proper folder, the new mesh automatically replaces the original Kork player mesh in the game. Particularly if you are new to Torque or 3ds Max, this is the quickest way to make your character mesh come alive in the Torque Game Engine.

Dealing with the Disadvantages of Using the Kork Player Biped with Your Mesh

With the Kork player biped, you have no access to the original animation files that describe the various bone positions, so you are stuck with animations that you can't edit. This means you can't use character meshes that include any bones not used in the Kork player biped. It also means you can't add additional bones, such as helper bones, to minimize collapsed vertices. Depending on the character mesh you use, you may find that your character's left shoulder self-intersects and that your character's right hand intersects the torso. This is because the biped is set up to look like it is carrying a crossbow; thus, the arm positions and upper body twist are pronounced. Using a mesh that is less robust or that has plenty of room between the upper arm and body minimizes the risk of self-intersections with the Kork player biped.

Stripping Down the Player.max File

Chapter 12, "Character Exporting," goes into more detail about how to prepare a character to be exported, but a brief overview pertaining to the Kork player file will be presented here. Save a copy of `Player.max` and open your own working copy. Two meshes are used in the Kork player file: `Multires::bodymesh` and `bodymesh`. Delete them both. To get the file to work as quickly and clearly as possible, skip making your own level of detail mesh for now; instead, use the marker called `Detail3` and verify that it is a child of `Bip01`. Delete any other detail markers. Change the name of your mesh to `bodymesh3` to correspond to the marker `Detail3`. The next step is to apply the Skin modifier to `bodymesh3` and assign mesh vertices to the bones in the Kork player biped.

Applying the Skin Modifier to Your Mesh but Using the Kork Player Biped Bones

According to the minimal biped configuration, you should have some 29 bones in the entire biped, but only 19 of these are actually used in the Skin process. Depending on your mesh, it may work out that one of these bones does not actually get vertices even partially assigned. In this case, your mesh imports to the Show tool, but you can't import any of the DSQ animations. The solution is to open the Skin modifier one more time and make sure each bone has at least one vertex assigned to it, at least partially. One way to check this is to select the suspicious bone and click the Weight Table button (located next to the Weight tool) to check what vertices are assigned to it.

Minimizing Vertex Collapse with the Kork Player Biped

You can minimize vertex collapse using the Kork player biped in two ways. You can use these methods independently or combined.

Utilizing the Prerotated Technique

The first way to minimize joint collapse when using your custom mesh with the Kork player biped is to perform the upper arm and hand rotation on the left arm of the biped as discussed at the beginning of this chapter in the section "Minimizing Collapsed Vertices by Prerotating Biped Bones."

Reverse-Engineering the Mesh in Root Pose

The second way to minimize vertex collapse is to make your initial mesh position match that of the Player Biped in its root pose, or *ready* position. Imagine if you could model your character mesh so that it was already in this *ready* position; you'd have almost no vertex collapse issues initially, because the mesh would perfectly conform to the position of the biped. Although it would be hard to model a mesh so that it was already an action pose, it would not be hard to generate the same result with a few extra steps. First, after you have unwrapped the UVs, make sure you save them to a file so that you can restore them if necessary. Then skin your mesh to the player biped with Figure mode turned on, and when all the mesh vertices are assigned, turn off Figure mode. The player biped jumps to its ready position. Now select the character mesh, right-click on the Skin modifier in the modifier list, and select Collapse All.

Now you have an Editable Mesh that is positioned just like the player biped; all this mesh needs at this point is a little bit of clean-up. Inspect the mesh for self-intersections and collapsed joints. Correct these manually by moving vertices and edges, using all four viewports when necessary. One rule here is that you can't delete or add vertices, or your saved texture won't work as well (or at all). Finally, with the player biped positioned perfectly inside the mesh, and Figure mode turned off, apply a Skin modifier once again to your mesh. This time, the mesh has been prepared for the position of the bones, and the animations won't cause much noticeable mesh distortion.

With these changes, your character mesh should be all set to work with the Kork player biped. Export a DTS shape named `player.dts` to the `data\shapes\player` folder. (Save the old `player.dts` to another name first.) The 3ds Max file and the character texture should be in the same folder you export to. The next time you launch the FPS sample game, your character mesh should appear. You can find more information on exporting characters in Chapter 12.

COMBINING BONES WITH BIPED

What if you wanted a character with wings, eight legs, a cape, or some other keyframable accessory? Besides the option of creating a character exclusively with bones, you can add additional bones to your biped, just as we did with the helper bones in this chapter. The parts of the mesh that represent additional limbs or features can have their vertices assigned to the new bones. In Figure 10.15, three bone chains have been added to the character to serve as the skeleton for a cape. The character mesh has been turned off for clarity. A simple cape has been created from a segmented box. The left bone chain is parented to the left clavicle, the right bone chain to the right clavicle, and the middle bone chain to the neck. These bones have

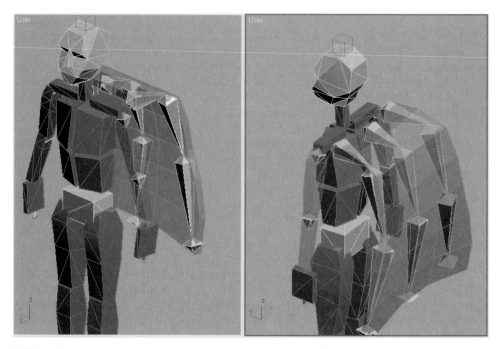

FIGURE 10.15 You can create a cape, wings, or additional limbs with bones.

been properly named (CapeL1, etc.) and included in the Skin modifier bone list. Attach the cape mesh to the character mesh. You can create a simple IK and controller for the bone chains to enable easier manipulation for keyframing the cape movement for the various animation cycles.

SUMMARY

We have looked at how to set up the biped to fit the mesh and how to minimize problems like collapsed vertices by using prerotated bones and helper bones. We have also reviewed how to apply a Skin modifier to the character mesh so that it recognizes the biped bones, and how to use both envelopes and weighted vertex assignments to control this relationship. We ended this chapter by looking at how rigging a robot might be different from rigging a standard character, how we can use the default player animations with our own character mesh, and how we can add bones to our biped skeleton if we want additional keyframable features. In the next chapter, we will put this rig to work, as we keyframe a run cycle.

CHARACTER ANIMATION

In This Chapter

- Implementing Character Animation Concepts
- Distinguishing Animation Methods
- Animating with Biped
- Creating the Root Pose
- Animating the Root Cycle
- Animating a Run Cycle
- Animating a Back (Backwards Run) Cycle
- Animating a Side (Strafe) Cycle
- Animating Jump, Fall, and Land Cycles
- Animating the Death Fall

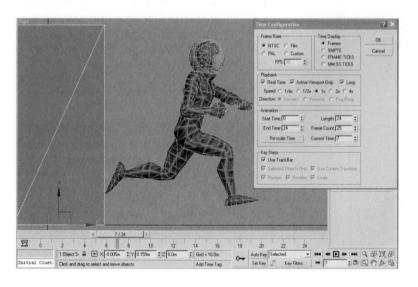

IMPLEMENTING CHARACTER ANIMATION CONCEPTS

The following concepts only scratch the surface, but they are of particular importance for generating action cycles for a game character.

Applying Counterpose

In a run, when the right leg is forward and the left leg is back, the left arm is forward and the right arm is back. When the right hip is forward, the left shoulder is back. This is called counterpose because the body parts are in opposite positions. In fact, much of what the human body naturally does is done in counterpose. With our character holding a rifle, the arm movement is somewhat constrained, but it is possible to rotate the entire upper body to counter what the hips are doing and thus make the overall movement more realistic.

Avoiding Twins or Twinning

When both sides of the character move the same way, the result doesn't look authentic; an example would be if both of the character's arms lift up at the same time in the root animation. Try to avoid "moving in twins"; instead, lift one arm, bend one leg, lift one shoulder, and so on, to give the character a more natural movement.

Using Arcs for Natural Movement

As you are keyframing the hands and feet, remember that natural movement is described in arcs. The legs don't move in a linear path between keyframes; they move in arcs, and you need additional keyframes to describe this. This is especially the case when you have a launch point for the foot and you have an airborne keyframe; the foot does not move directly from point A to point B but describes an arc in the motion between the two points. To create this effect, add a keyframe between these two points that creates an arc.

Applying Secondary Motion

When you see someone running and his backpack is bouncing along on his back, you are seeing a good example of secondary motion; it is connected to the motion of the running body, but the movements are slightly delayed and added on to the movements of the runner. Secondary motion can also happen when a character's head bobs while running, or the arms come down slightly after the body lands. Subtle application of secondary motion to the character can make the overall animation more believable.

Exaggerating Movement

For in-game animation, you can exaggerate all movements to a point. The root pose is meant to be one where the character is waiting, resting, or watching. If the character looks like he is breathing hard, it adds to the tension of the game and makes the character seem more alive. If you were to keyframe real-life breathing movement, it might be too subtle to even notice in a game, especially at a distance. Therefore, you have to exaggerate many of the movements that a character makes so that he is clearly defined and easily recognizable.

Planning the Animation Cycles

Deciding how long to make your different cycles depends on how many positional stages you want for each cycle and how quickly you want each cycle to execute. The example run cycle in this chapter has six key positional stages and is 24 frames long. It could just as well be 30 frames long, or any number divisible by 6; what's important is that you have a logical plan for how to divide the frames into the main positional stages of the run. A 30-frame run cycle makes the character appear to be running slower than a 24-frame run cycle, and a 12-frame run cycle produces a run cycle that is extremely snappy. You may decide that you need ten positional stages for your cycle; you can set each stage to three frames each and then decrease it to two or increase it to four based on how slow or fast you feel the cycle looks in the game.

DISTINGUISHING ANIMATION METHODS

You can create animations for the Torque Game Engine in a few different ways. You can create animations that affect all or part of the character's body. You can keep all the animations in one file with the character mesh, or you can create separate animation files for each type of movement that the character performs. You can create animations with biped or with a custom bones rig.

Choosing Between Full Body, Lower Body, and Blend Animation

Torque allows for three general types of character animation: full body, lower body, and blend. Although you could easily get by making all your animations full body, each type of animation has a specific application.

Full Body Animations

Normal, full body animations are those in which you are making changes to the entire rigged character, and all the bone positions are exported to the DSQ file. Although you do have the option of making some of your animations lower body only, or blended, there's nothing wrong with making all of your character animations full body.

Lower Body Only

Lower body only animations are those in which only the lower body bones are being animated; thus, they are the only bones that are exported. You can handle this by adding the upper body bones to the Never Export list in the export config file when exporting. Typically, this could include run, side, and back animations; however, you may want to make these "running" animations full body to include the spine, clavicle, and arm movements that make a run look more realistic.

Blend Animations

Blends are animations noted as Blend in the general rollout of the Sequence object. These animations change only those bones that are actually animated in the blend animation; the blend animation doesn't affect the position of all other bones in the character. An example of a blend animation is a "look" animation, which has the player tilting his head and perhaps lifting or lowering his gun; you would add this animation to whatever animation is being played at that moment, whether the player is running or in a root animation.

Exporting All Animations Together or Separately

Even though it is possible to export all animations from a single file, exporting them into separate files is the recommended method, because it gives you more flexibility to go in and make changes on a file-by-file basis. This means you will have a DTS export of your character mesh, and a DSQ export for each different animation, from the run to the backward run to the jump. Initially, however, it makes sense to work from a single file for two reasons: first, so that you can observe how well the character mesh works with the skeletal animations and make adjustments as necessary in the model, texture, or vertex assignments; second, so that you only have to create the markers and hierarchical links once. When you feel comfortable with this master file, you can make a copy called Root, Run, and so on, and complete your animations in those files.

Choosing Between Biped and Bones Animation

Biped is more developed than bones for dealing with character animation. It is already set up with working limbs and joints, and a host of tools can control movement. One of the advantages that biped gives you for doing game animations is an animatable pivot point for the foot. (This means you can rotate the character's foot around the heel, ball, or toe much easier than you could with a bones setup.) Another advantage is the ability to easily lock the foot to the ground so it doesn't pass through the ground plane. Therefore, this chapter animates with biped. If you are interested only in bones animation, please read this chapter anyway, because many techniques and principles still apply.

ANIMATING WITH BIPED

Animating with biped is fairly straightforward, but several tutorials are available via the 3ds Max Help drop-down menu. Keep in mind as you animate biped bones that you should perform all bone rotations while you're in the Local Reference Coordinate System. (This setting is located on the Standard toolbar.)

Dealing with Nonintuitive Dependencies in the Biped Skeletal System

By default, there is a hierarchical dependency in the biped skeletal system. Clavicle bones are parents of upper arm bones, which are parents of lower arm bones, which are parents of hand bones. This means that if you animate hand and finger positions on the same key that you use to animate clavicle positions, and you delete the clavicle key, you also delete the hand and finger keys. To get around this, in the Motion Panel, Keyframing Tools rollout, in the separate tracks group, turn on Arms. This keeps you from inadvertently losing keyframes for the hands and fingers if you delete a clavicle keyframe that happens to reside in the same keyframe. This also stores and makes accessible the keyframes for the hands and fingers in their own tracks in the Dope Sheet, should you want to adjust the tension, continuity, and bias (TCB) aspects of the animation curve for one key or several keys at once. This concept pertains to the legs as well. If you decide to generate separate tracks for legs, be sure that you also turn on Set Parents mode in the Keyframing Tools rollout, or you will not be able to save keys. Don't turn these settings off and on multiple times; instead, set them at the beginning of a session and keep them there to avoid generating multiple keys for bone movements.

Creating and Importing BIP Files

You can create a BIP file from your animation that you can use to apply the same movements to any other similarly equipped biped. You may also import a BIP file of a run cycle or other actions and apply it to your biped. You can then blend these BIP files with other BIP files, or edit them to remove unneeded frames. If you want to save a BIP file of a character that was rigged with helper bones or proxy objects, make sure that all nonbiped/nonbone objects are dummy objects, as mentioned in Chapter 10, "Character Rigging."

CREATING THE ROOT POSE

The root pose is the position that the player is in when exported as a mesh. Normally, the root pose is the pose from which the root animation starts.

To create a root pose, first work on the lower body positions. Select one of the biped's feet, activate the Motion panel, and make sure that Figure mode is turned off. In the Key Info rollout, click the Set Planted Key button. Now select the other foot and click Set Planted Key again. To bring the body of the biped down a little, in the Track Selection rollout, click the Body Vertical button and move the biped COM object down a little bit, so that the knees are slightly bent. The feet should stay put, since they are planted. Keyframe this latest movement by clicking the Set Key button in the Key Info rollout.

Now select the biped's left foot, and move it slightly forward, so that the left foot's heel is about even with the right foot's toes. Click the Set Planted Key button again to lock down the new foot position. Now the body seems off balance, so in the Track Selection rollout, click Body Horizontal and move the biped's body forward, so it is evenly balanced over both feet. Click the Set Key button in the Key Info rollout once again to lock down the COM object. These adjustments help to make the biped look more natural and capable of breaking into a run at any moment.

For any given model, depending on the length of the arms, the geometry of the weapon, and the girth of the character's body, you need to consider how the character will be able to hold the weapon. Assuming that you have your own custom weapon and character mesh to work with, you would want to merge the weapon mesh into the character file so that you can see both meshes together. Concentrate on figuring out how to manipulate the biped so it holds the weapon properly. You can complete this stage with the biped out of Figure mode and the Auto Key turned on. At any time, you can delete keys and return the biped to Figure mode to get back to a generic relaxed state.

Figure 11.1 depicts this process; the weapon and its MountPoint have been merged into a rigged character file. The arms are positioned so that the weapon looks like it is being held. Also note in this figure that the MountPoints for the weapon and the character are being matched up, so that the weapon will be in the character's hand when the game starts. The laser rifle used in this image was scaled slightly to fit the character better; it is exactly 1.41 meters long.

The spine and the clavicles were rotated to bring the left shoulder forward of its normal position and to bring the right shoulder back. The left arm and hand of the biped are easy to adjust so that they hold the weapon; you can do most of this positioning by moving the right hand of the biped until the elbow is slightly behind the body of the character. You may need to rotate the upper-left arm so that there is just a small gap for the stock of the weapon to fit in.

The left hand and arm were a little more involved to position. A forward kinematic method was used to position these bones, rotating the upper arm bone away

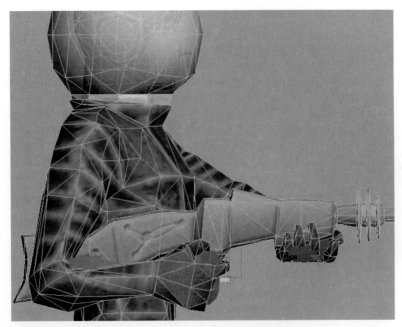

FIGURE 11.1   Matching up the weapon and the character to make sure everything fits.

from the body, bending the elbow toward the weapon, rotating the hand bone to cradle the weapon, and making adjustments to all three bones until they were in a suitable position.

It's good to remember that no law states that your player needs to be carrying a rifle or any other two-handed weapon. The robot that is provided on the companion CD-ROM carries a single-handed weapon that works fine. As long as your weapon conforms to the export requirements, it can have any shape or size you want. AstronautRootPose.max is available in the Files\Astronaut folder on the companion CD-ROM.

ON THE CD

ANIMATING THE ROOT CYCLE

The *root cycle* is what the character does when he is not engaged in a run, jump, strafe, or any other action. Study the root animation of the default Kork player in the Torque FPS demo game or in the Torque Show Tool Pro to get an understanding of what this animation looks like. Typically, the feet do not move, but the character may shift weight between legs, slightly move the hands and arms, slightly move the head, lower the center of gravity somewhat, and otherwise show himself to be "ready" for action, not unlike an athlete getting ready for the action to suddenly start in a game. Often in games, the root pose animation makes the player look like he is out of breath. As with other game character animations, you can exaggerate these movements beyond normal human movements to bring more life to the character and make the game more immersive.

Here you go from a simple pose of a biped within a character mesh to an animated biped. Normally, the best way to approach this is to make a copy of your `RootPose.max` file and call it `RootAnim.max`. Keep the character mesh intact for now; you can freeze the mesh and set it to see-through so that the bones are easy to select.

A simple root animation was applied to the astronaut character; the biped COM was keyframed to move it down at frame 10 and then back up to the start position at frame 20. The lower spine bone was rotated slightly at frame 10 to give the impression of being out of breath, and it was returned to the default position at frame 20. Each time something was moved, the Set Key button was pressed so that a keyframe was established.

When the animation is completed, you can save the file as `RootAnimExport.max` and delete the character mesh before you actually export. `RootAnim.max` can be your actual working copy where you can see what the animation is doing to the mesh, and `RootAnimExport` can be the one you export from. Alternatively, you can work purely from the biped without a mesh.

ON THE CD

You can take your biped animation and apply it to a bones animation using the FBX exporter. This is documented in the 3ds Max tutorials that come with 3ds Max 8. `AstronautRootAnim.max` is available in the `Files\Astronaut` folder on the companion CD-ROM.

ANIMATING A RUN CYCLE

The *run cycle* is the foundational cycle that brings a character to life in the game. A template and step-by-step instructions have been provided for this cycle; if you are new to character animation, this section gives you some practical experience that you should be able to apply to the other cycles.

Keyframing the Biped to Run

The most obvious movement in a run takes place from the side view. Adjusting the spine, feet, and biped COM to conform to the template from the side view gives you a decent run cycle all by itself. Because the biped is set up for IK, moving a hand or foot moves and rotates the rest of the limb into proper position. Usually after the foot is moved, you need to rotate it as well. You can also animate the hands this way, although you need to keep in mind what is going on with the weapon as you make changes. In such a case, it might make sense to have a weapon mesh parented to the character's right hand while you animate so you can adjust one or both hands as necessary.

ON THE CD

The run cycle template is located in Files\Astronaut on the companion CD-ROM and is called BasicRunTemplate.jpg. You may apply the template to a plane in a new file or get a head start by opening the file AstronautRunAnimStart.max. In this file, the biped is positioned for you in the start position at frame 0. The first 12 frames should allow for an initial crossover position where one foot is planted, a driving position where the free leg drives forward, a glide position where both feet have left the ground, and ending up once again at a crossover position where the character has landed, but the bone positions are opposite of when they started. At this point, the cycle is halfway complete. Then the cycle is repeated, with the bone positions reversed, until the character is back to the original position, from frames 12–24. The process of creating the run cycle is demonstrated on the video RunCycle.wmv, in the Videos folder on the companion CD-ROM.

Figure 11.2 shows a method of keyframing the biped with a template to make the process more exact. This figure starts with the biped in the root position, with the left foot slightly forward. The BasicRunTemplate.jpg bitmap is applied to a plane behind the biped in the right view. The easiest way to do this is to apply the material to the plane and then resize and move the plane until it matches your character. This bitmap has been lightened so that it is easy to see the positions of your biped against it. If you need more contrast, open the file in Photoshop and click Images, Adjustments, Brightness/Contrast, and increase the Contrast value.

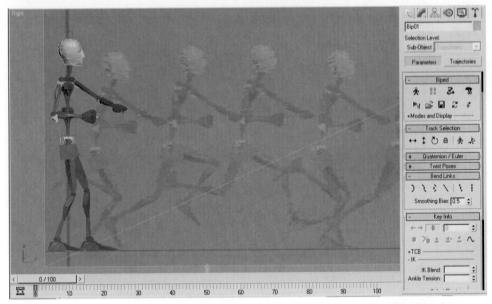

FIGURE 11.2 A run template is applied to a plane and resized to match the size of the biped.

Figure 11.3 depicts the right foot being raised into position. You can set feet in biped as planted, sliding, or free. Because this foot is in the air, you can move it with the Move tool and then click the Set Free Key. The body has been moved forward by pressing the Body Horizontal button under the Track Selection rollout and then moving the biped COM a little bit forward and down. (See Figure 11.4 for a better look at this.) Every time you move the biped COM, click the Set Key in the Key Info rollout. The left foot should still have a planted key on it from when you created the root pose. The upper and lower spine are rotated slightly to fit the template; each time they are rotated, the Set Key button is pressed.

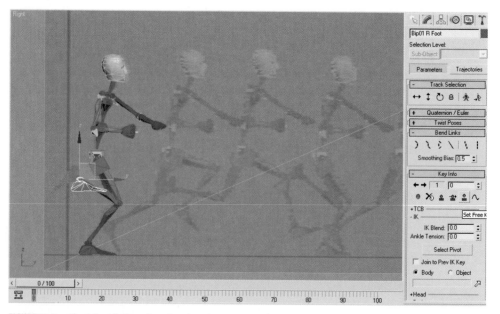

FIGURE 11.3 The biped's free foot has just been moved into position; the next step for this foot is a rotation.

Figure 11.4 depicts the way the main body of the biped is moved; from the Track Selection rollout, you click the Body Horizontal or Body Vertical button. Then you move the biped COM to the desired location. It is simpler to move the body first and then position the feet (and hands if you are animating them as well) as necessary. After you have moved the biped COM, make sure to click the Set Key in the Key Info rollout. Note that this screen shot was taken on the fourth frame of the run cycle.

In Figure 11.5, the keyframes at 4, 8, and 12 have been established by animating only the two feet and the biped COM. At frame 12, the run cycle is at the halfway point. Frames 12–24 are the same as frames 1–12, but instead of the right leg reaching forward, it is the left leg that moves forward.

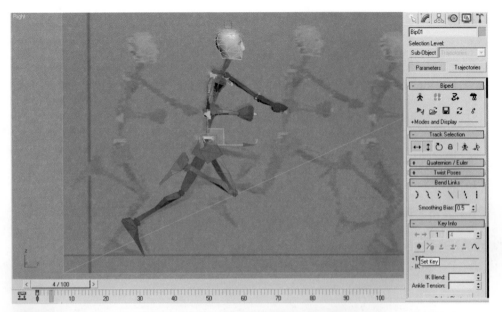

FIGURE 11.4   The COM object has been moved horizontally and vertically. Set Key is about to be clicked.

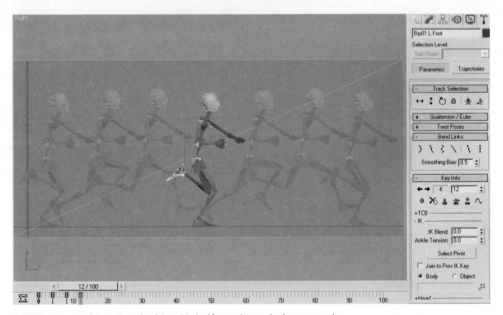

FIGURE 11.5   At this point, the biped is halfway through the run cycle.

It is okay to animate the biped by itself, but it can be helpful to keep the mesh around to see how it is behaving in the actual run (see Figure 11.6). Here the mesh has been turned on, and the cycle is being previewed. If your total number of frames is 100 and your cycle is only 24 frames, the 76 dead frames at the end ruin the continuity of the run as you try to study it. In this figure, the Time Configuration button has been clicked, and the Length has been changed to 24, so that the animation cycle plays smoothly, over and over. Another feature evident in the Time Configuration dialog box is the ability to change the playback Speed setting in the Playback group. This value affects only the animation speed in the viewport and has no effect on the speed of the animation in the game.

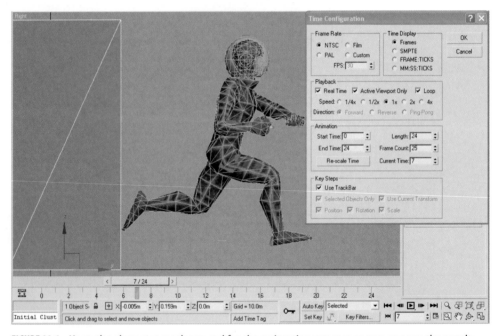

FIGURE 11.6   Keep the character mesh around for the animation process so you can see the result.

In Figure 11.6, the astronaut character is running ahead of the bounding box. If this file is exported, it causes the astronaut's run to stutter in the game. It is important that the bounding box track with the player's main direction of motion (horizontally, not vertically). You can achieve this by keyframing the bounds box so that it stays with the character or by parenting the bounds box to the biped pelvis bone. If you use the latter technique, you should adjust the inheritance for the bounds box so that only the main direction of character movement is inherited. You can do this through the Hierarchy panel, under Link Info, in the Inheritance rollout. In Figure 11.7, only the Y direction movement is being inherited, because the Y direction is the main direction of movement of the run animation. For the sideways run animation (or the "strafe"), only the X direction of movement would be inherited. It is important to turn off Z inherency in the Move group so that when your biped bends his knees in the game, his feet stay on the ground.

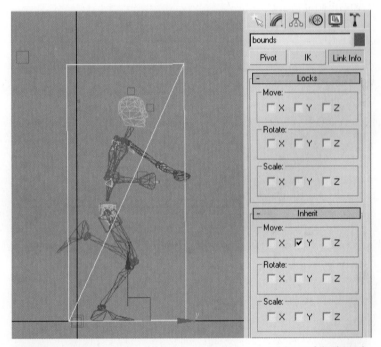

FIGURE 11.7   The bounds box and the cam marker are children of the biped hip bone and only inherit its Y movement.

Constraining the Cam Marker

You can employ the same technique on the cam marker that you did on the bounds box to achieve an up and down bobbing effect for the third-person camera. Parenting the cam marker to the Bip01 Pelvis and then turning off all the Inherit values except for Y causes the cam to stay level while tracking the character's movement; this emphasizes any up and down movement of the character and makes for a more interesting third-person view. Without this effect, it looks as though your character is not really moving in the third-person camera.

Viewing and Adjusting Trajectories

The Motion panel has two sides: Parameters and Trajectories. If you activate Trajectories, you can see and make changes to the trajectories of feet, hands, and other objects. Figure 11.8 shows how this works. Any object that you select while the Trajectories button is turned on displays its keyframes in a trajectory spline. In this image, Auto Key is turned on, allowing the trajectory and actual keyframes to be adjusted. Frame 10 is being moved higher so that the path of the foot forms a smoother arc. At a minimum, you should look at and adjust the trajectories for both feet and the biped COM object.

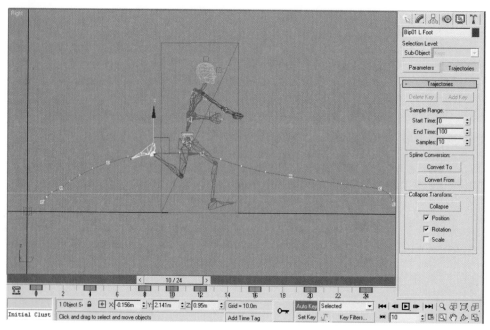

FIGURE 11.8 Adjusting trajectories helps you to create proper arcs in your movements.

Improving the Run Cycle

After you have a simple run cycle working, save a copy of the file and try some further ideas for a more complex movement. From the side view, you can try rotating the spine to a more bent position at the landing stages and rotating the spine back to a more vertical position for the gliding stages.

In the front view, the supporting foot tends to land somewhere closer to the midline than many people realize; this helps balance the body while it is on only one leg. Position the foot nearer the midline at the planted keyframes. Also, most runners exhibit a slight pelvic movement; the hip is a little higher on the supporting side, so it dips a bit on the side of the passing leg. If the left leg is planted, the left side of the hip is up, so the spine, as it leaves the pelvis, curves toward the passing leg and then back toward the supporting leg. What this achieves for the human run is a better balance, where the center of gravity is more evenly set over the planted foot.

The shoulders and upper body turn with the arms. When the left leg is forward, the left arm is back, and the upper body is turned toward the left, in counterpose. The entire body is twisting opposite at each stride. The head can stay still or even bob a bit down immediately following each landing and come up a bit just after each launch to illustrate secondary motion. The shoulders can come down a bit just after each landing and then come up again just after launch. This can be done with a slight rotation on the clavicle bones. The pelvis also twists forward on the side where the leg is driving forward.

In all this, you have to be careful about your mesh vertex assignments. Some movements in the skeleton look completely natural but may cause the mesh to contort based on how you assign the bones. If your complex run doesn't work out the first time around, you still have the simple run to fall back on. `AstronautRunAnim.max` is available in the `Files\Astronaut` folder on the companion CD-ROM.

ON THE CD

ANIMATING A BACK (BACKWARDS RUN) CYCLE

When you have completed a run cycle, try to create the *back* cycle, or the backward run. This movement is distinguished by the character leaning backward and pushing off of one foot at a time. The push-off comes from the ball of the foot or the front of the foot, and each foot usually lands on the front or flat (depending on how many bones are in your foot). The distance covered in this complete cycle is usually about half the distance covered with a forward run. As with the run cycle, make sure the bone positions at the last frame of the cycle match up to those in the first frame of the cycle. `AstronautBackRunAnim.max` is available in the `Files\Astronaut` folder on the companion CD-ROM.

ON THE CD

ANIMATING A SIDE (STRAFE) CYCLE

The cycle described in the original `player.cs` file as *side* is actually a sideways run, or what many consider a strafe. The basic body dynamics are that the character drops his center of gravity, launches off of one foot, and leaps to the side where both feet are airborne; the character then lands with the leading foot while the launching foot closes. In the example character, the `cam` marker and the `bounds` box are parented to the pelvic bone, and inherency for both of these objects is set to move in the X direction only. By default, the Torque engine reverses this animation if the character moves in the other direction; this solution is not ideal, because the sideways run is not really a symmetrical movement. If you want to change the core functioning of the Torque Game Engine so that you can have a specific left and right strafe,

ON THE CD

you can find directions on how to do it via the GarageGames.com Web site. AstronautSideAnim.max is available in the `Files\Astronaut` folder on the companion CD-ROM.

ANIMATING JUMP, FALL, AND LAND CYCLES

To understand these cycles better, launch the Torque Show Tool Pro and study these three sequences as performed by the default Kork player. The *jump* cycle involves the character crouching slightly and then launching off of one leg as the arms and torso twist, adding momentum to the jump. The *fall* cycle involves the character positioning both feet forward slightly, with one leg extended and the other leg with a 90-degree bend at the knee. For this cycle, visualize a character sliding down a steep slope. The *land* cycle involves going from a normal stance to a deep crouch, where the feet actually slide forward slightly; visualize a character jumping from a wall and absorbing the impact with his legs. `AstronautJumpAnim.max`, `AstronautFallAnim.max`, and `AstronautLandAnim.max` are all available in the `Files\Astronaut` folder on the companion CD-ROM.

ON THE CD

ANIMATING THE DEATH FALL

The death animation can be anything from a complex movement, where the character grabs his chest and slowly crumbles to the ground, to a simple head-first fall. Set the death fall as a Complete Cycle, not a Cyclic Sequence. This is because you want this animation to run its course and then stop; the dead player falls, lies still, and then is automatically deleted from the game, just as a duplicate is spawned into the game. Because this animation does not repeat, and because the defeat of any character in the game is pivotal to the game, this animation should take up more frames than the others. If you look at the Sequence Info for the original Kork run cycle in the Torque Show Tool Pro, the entire cycle is only 11 frames long and takes a mere 0.767 seconds to play, whereas the `player_diehead` animation is 60 frames long and takes 3.967 seconds—more than five times as long. This extended animation gives any players watching a chance to see what happened before it is all over. `AstronautDeathAnim.max` is available in the `Files\Astronaut` folder on the companion CD-ROM.

ON THE CD

SUMMARY

Keeping in mind counterpose, secondary motion, and the other basic character animation concepts helps you make your character animations stronger. Three different types of character animation are available with the Torque Game Engine, but full-body animation is the most applicable for most situations. Animating the biped is much like regular Auto Key animation, as discussed in Chapter 5, "Animating Game Art," but it has an additional emphasis on using the Set Key from the biped motion menu and setting planted, sliding, or free keys for the biped's feet. From the root cycle to the death cycle, the actual bone positions are up to you; use the default cycles from the original Kork player and the astronaut as a starting point, and create your own cycles.

CHARACTER EXPORTING

In This Chapter

- Exporting Character Shape (DTS) Files
- Exporting Character Animation (DSQ) Files
- Using the Torque Show Tool Pro
- Scripting Characters
- Troubleshooting

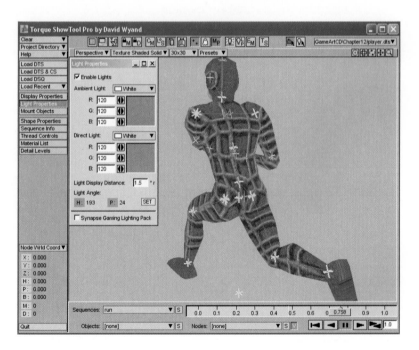

EXPORTING CHARACTER SHAPE (DTS) FILES

Exporting a character DTS file requires a specific set of markers, a more involved method of creating detail meshes, a more complex hierarchy, and a configuration file to manage what is exported and what the exporter ignores. This section looks at each of these areas in detail.

Required Markers for Character Export

If you have gone through Chapter 6, "Exporting Game Art," you are familiar with some of the export requirements such as detail meshes, detail markers, and a bounds box. When exporting a character, you need to consider three new markers. The eye marker tells Torque where the player's eye camera is located (the view in first person mode), the cam marker tells Torque where the third person camera should be located, and the mount0 marker defines the position for the weapon to attach to the character.

Checklist for Exporting a Simple Character

This example assumes that you are exporting a simple character mesh that uses biped for the skeletal component.

- The character mesh is an Editable Mesh.
- The Skin modifier references only the bones that are actually used in the animations.
- Every vertex in the mesh has been assigned.
- All bones must have at least one vertex at least partially assigned to them.
- The character is facing the back view.
- The character is standing at 0,0,0.
- A box called bounds encloses the character.
- The Start01 marker is the parent of Bip01 and Detail2.
- Eye is a child of Bip01 Head, and mount0 is a child of Bip01 R Hand.
- The bounds box and cam are both children of Bip01 Pelvis.
- Bone names do not end in numbers, so they are not mistaken for detail objects.
- One config file resides in the folder you are exporting to.
- The 3ds Max file resides in the folder you are exporting to.
- Any additional meshes being exported with the character (such as the helmet we are exporting with our astronaut character) end in the same number as the character mesh detail number. In our case, the character mesh is called bodymesh2; the detail marker for this character is called detail2; thus, the helmet should be named helmet2.

Position of the Character's Markers

Figure 12.1 shows the astronaut character ready for export and the locations of the markers. The marker in front of the character's head is the eye marker, and the marker above and behind the character's head is the cam marker. The mount0 marker is placed near the character's right hand and may ultimately have to be moved slightly to ensure that the gun lines up properly with the character's hand.

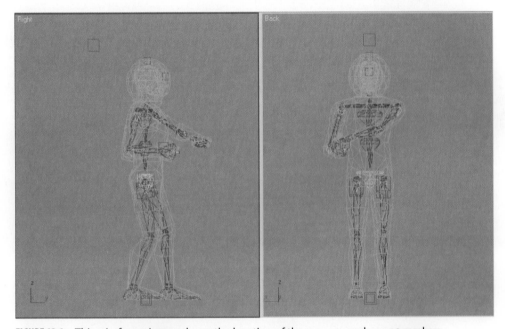

FIGURE 12.1   This wireframe image shows the location of the eye, cam, and mount0 markers.

The Character Hierarchy

Figure 12.2 shows the bare-bones astronaut hierarchy without regard for levels of detail, which will be addressed later in this chapter. This figure is complex, mainly because of the underlying biped structure. This hierarchy is the one used for the actual export of the root pose. Note in this figure that both the bounding box and the cam marker are children of the Bip01 Pelvis. This allows for proper movement of the character and helps to create the up and down bobbing movement of the third-person camera, as discussed in Chapter 11, "Character Animation." Any changes made to nonmesh markers or bones in the hierarchy should be consistent across all your files, whether they are used for DTS export or DSQ export. When the hierarchy doesn't match up between the shape file and the animation file, the animation usually doesn't play. Although this example uses Start01 as the start point in the hierarchy, you can also use Bip01 as the start point.

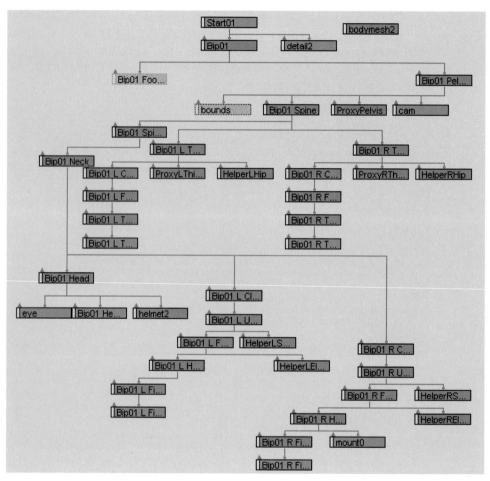

FIGURE 12.2 A simple character shape hierarchy.

Bounding Box

The bounding box determines float distance above ground. This means that if your character is climbing stairs, a much larger bounding box causes your player to float higher above the stairs than a smaller bounding box. Keep the bounding box small to minimize this float effect, yet large enough to encompass the main body of the character mesh.

Levels of Detail

You can create a low-resolution version of your character mesh for when the mesh is farther away from the camera in the game. Just as our lower resolution meshes worked with the other game art, the LOD process allows the Torque Game Engine to render fewer polygons and makes the game more efficient. There are two methods of creating character LOD: the Multires method and the manual method. If one of the methods does not work for you, use the other one.

Both methods create the same result: a set of detail markers that access variations on the character mesh. For example, if you have three detail objects, called detail128, detail64, and detail2, the Torque Game Engine uses the mesh that is associated with detail128 whenever the character is close enough to the camera to be 128 pixels high or higher. Detail64 is activated when the character is from 64 pixels high to 127 pixels high, and detail2 is only activated when the character is so far away that it is between 2 and 63 pixels high.

The Multires Method for Creating Levels of Detail

You can use the Multires modifier in 3ds Max to create your LOD meshes on the fly at export. You must create the detail markers by hand, but you generate the detail meshes based on the User Properties values assigned to the character mesh. This method of creating multiple levels of detail for your character is demonstrated in the video MultiresLOD.wmv, on the companion CD-ROM.

ON THE CD

Start by creating the detail markers. For example, you might have detail128, detail64, and detail2. Parent all three detail markers to Start01 or Bip01, whichever is at the top of your hierarchy. (The DTS export works either way.) Select the character mesh (let's call it bodymesh), and select Snapshot from the Tools drop-down menu. Set the Snapshot value to Single, and set the Clone Method value to Mesh. Name this new mesh Multires::bodymesh.

From the MAXscript drop-down menu, select Open Script. Locate AdjustLODs.mcr (this file ships with Torque and is part of the torque_max_filepack.zip file) and run the macro. If you have problems running this macro, select all of the lines except the top two lines and the last line in this code. Drag the selected code to your Standard toolbar, or better yet, create a custom toolbar for this new button. Add a Multires modifier to Multires::bodymesh, and click the Generate button on the Multires modifier to activate it. Parent MultiRes::bodymesh to bodymesh. Note that neither of these meshes is part of the larger hierarchy.

Now run the AdjustLODs.mcr script you installed earlier. This should generate three buttons for you, one for each level of detail. Click each one and enter values for the percentage of vertices to be visible. For example, set detail128 to 1.0, set detail64 to 0.5, and set detail2 to 0.2. After you've set these values, click Apply Settings. Right-click the Multires::bodymesh and select Properties. Click the User Defined tab, and you should see something similar to this:

```
MULTIRES::DETAILS = 1.0,0.5,0.20
MULTIRES::SIZES = 128,64,2
```

If these lines are not there, type them in, with spaces only around the equals signs. Use Ctrl+C to copy the two lines to the Clipboard. Next, right-click bodymesh and select Properties. Click User Defined, and apply these same two lines with Ctrl+V. At this point, the levels of detail should be properly applied. Make changes in the above text as necessary if you need more levels of detail or different values.

Your DTS shape should be exportable now. If you get an Assertion error during vertex merge error when you export, see the "Troubleshooting" section at the end of this chapter.

Even after you export the DTS shape, it may not be properly set up for Torque. You can run Unmess.exe to clean up the DTS file. Unmess.exe is included in the file pack that comes with Torque. To use unmess.exe, place it in the same folder as your DTS shape. Let's assume your DTS shape is called player.DTS. Use a text editor to create a batch file called unmessDTS.bat. This batch file needs only one line:

```
unMessDTS Playerlod.DTS Playerlod.DTS
```

The first entry runs the EXE file, the second entry is the input file name, and the third entry is the output file name. After you run the batch file, your DTS shape should be ready for Torque.

The Manual Method for Creating Levels of Detail

You can do this whole process manually. In fact, this is how it was done before the Multires method was created to simplify it. Let's assume that your original character mesh is named bodymesh128. Make a snapshot of bodymesh128 and name it bodymesh64. Apply a Multires modifier to bodymesh64, click the Generate button, and scroll the Vertex Percent value until it is around 50. Right-click on the Multires modifier in the modifier stack, and select Collapse All. Then repeat this process, this time calling the snapshot bodymesh8 and scrolling the Vertex Percent to 15 or 20.

This leaves you with three bodymeshes, one of which is already skinned. Bodymesh64 and bodymesh8 have had the Multires modifier collapsed and now need to be skinned to the same biped that bodymesh128 is skinned to. When working with any given mesh, hide the other meshes so that they are not a distraction. Apply the Skin modifier to each mesh, one at a time, and assign vertices as usual, making sure every bone gets at least a partial vertex assignment. This should go fast, because these are simpler meshes.

When you did a simple export of the character mesh, you needed only one detail marker and one mesh. Because this example covers three levels of detail, there are three detail markers and three meshes necessary. All three detail markers should be parented to the Start01 marker. If you are not using a Start01 marker, you can optionally parent the detail markers to Bip01. None of the character meshes should be part of the larger hierarchy; they exist on their own.

Then, if you end up with an invisible player in your game, it is likely because you do not have your details set up right. Do you remember the details from the first simple shape example? You need at least one detail, called detail2. This goes hand in hand with your player mesh, which should be named bodymesh2. If you have any other detail markers but no meshes to correspond to them, the game may be playing a character that appears invisible, because the mesh for it does not exist!

MountPoints

Your character needs a special marker for the weapon called mount0. Position mount0 somewhere near your biped's right hand, or wherever you want the weapon to be mounted in the game. The weapon has a corresponding marker called mountpoint, which positions itself at mount0. Wait until the character has been positioned in a root pose that you are satisfied with before creating and parenting the mount0 marker to the biped's right hand; inadvertent movement of the biped's hand can affect the orientation of the mount0 marker and thus affect the orientation of the weapon, which should generally be pointing straight ahead. If this marker ends up in some unusual orientation, it is always an option to delete it and create another one.

It is also possible that the gun will be facing the wrong way when you finally get the character into the game. To solve this, rotate the mount0 marker 90 degrees in any axis necessary for the gun to face the way the character is looking, and re-export your DTS shape.

Additional Meshes and Collisions

If you have an additional mesh you want to connect to the character, make sure that it is an Editable Mesh and that it has a UVW map or an Unwrap UVW modifier applied to it. A bitmap should also be associated with the file. The mesh should have the same trailing number as the character mesh; that is, if your character mesh is called bodymesh2, your character's helmet should be called helmet2. Finally, make sure the mesh is parented to the biped bone system at an appropriate bone. For example, the astronaut's helmet is parented to the head bone of the biped, so that if the head moves, the helmet moves with it. If it were a jet-pack, you'd probably want to parent it to one of the spine bones.

Based on the method for creating collisions for simple shapes and health patches, you may be wondering how to set up a collision mesh for a character. The answer is, you don't need to; the mesh handles collisions on its own. A character has no need for a separate collision mesh or collision markers.

Config File

Make sure you have *one* config file in the export folder. For a full-body animation, your config file should look similar to the default `player.cfg` file shown in Listing 12.1. This file has headings for AlwaysExport, NeverExport, and Delete. A lower-body only animation has the upper body bones called out in the NeverExport list, so that they are not included in the DSQ file.

LISTING 12.1 Config File Sample

```
AlwaysExport:
eye
cam
mount0
//mount1
//jetnozzle0
NeverExport:
Bip01
Bip01 L Finger*
Bip01 R Finger*
Dummy*
Bip01 L Toe*
Bip01 R Toe*
start01
mountpoint
DELETE*
//Ski0
//Ski1
Light0
Light1
//Mount1
//Mount2
+Error::AllowEmptySubtrees
+Error::AllowCrossedDetails
+Error::AllowUnusedMeshes
-Error::AllowOldSequences
-Error::RequireViconNode
-Param::CollapseTransforms
//=Params::T2AutoDetail -1
```

You should use this config file as-is unless you have different export needs because you want to include Toe0 (as in the case of a two-part foot) or if you want to include or exclude other bones.

Export of the DTS Shape

When the markers are in place, the hierarchy is complete, and all the key files are present in the export folder (the 3ds Max file, the config file, and any necessary texture files), it is time to export the DTS shape for the character. Figure 12.3 shows a typical setup for this export. The Dump File Control rollout has all options checked to generate the most complete export report possible. This file will be named dump.dmp and will be written to your export folder. The dump file can be viewed with any text editor and searched for clues if there are problems with the export. The Configuration Control rollout is for saving your DTS export configuration; it has nothing to do with the config file you create in the export folder. When you are ready to export the DTS file, click the Whole Shape button in the Utilities rollout.

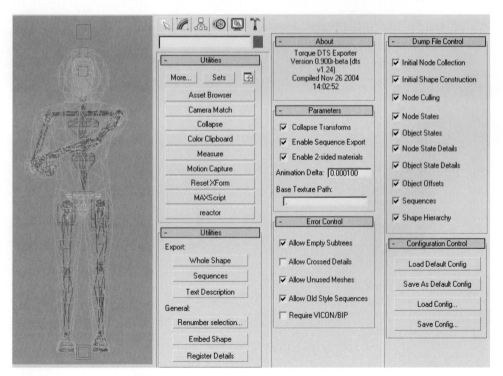

FIGURE 12.3   A look at the DTS export menus. Clicking Whole Shape exports your character.

EXPORTING CHARACTER ANIMATION (DSQ) FILES

Characters require the same general markers and meshes as the other art assets, but there are some important differences, particularly to get the animations to properly export. As mentioned in Chapter 11, the best way to manage your animations is to create them in separate files, although it is possible to export your animation sequences as part of the DTS export. The process we will be using is to export a DTS file of your character mesh and create a DSQ export for each animation, from the run to the backward run to the jump. The 3ds Max file you are using for the different animations does not need the character mesh; all you need is the biped and the other associated markers and Sequence objects.

There is an order to setting up your exports so that you do not end up re-creating markers and linkages. Start by defining your character shape file with all the markers and parent-child relationships so that you can export the DTS file. Then use a copy of that file to animate the root animation, and move on to separate copies of the other animations. Delete the mesh when you are ready to export the DSQ file.

The hierarchy when exporting a character animation is much the same as the hierarchy shown in Figure 12.2, except that the animation will have a Sequence object. Figure 12.4 illustrates the changes between the two files; this image shows the position of the bounds object in the hierarchy, the Sequence object, and the deletion of the character mesh and any other associated meshes. Because it is helpful to have a version of the character animation with the mesh intact, it is recommended that you save a copy of the file before deleting the character mesh and exporting the DSQ file.

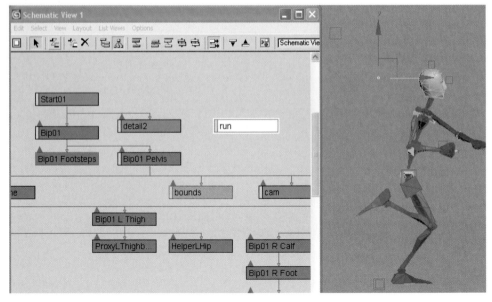

FIGURE 12.4   The run sequence is almost ready to be exported.

Sequence Object Setup

For a typical animation export, you first have to make sure your Sequence object export settings are correct. If the Sequence object is selected and the Modify panel is selected, your screen should look something like Figure 12.5. For a run or strafe cycle that will repeat over and over, use a Cyclic sequence. A Complete cycle is only applicable to an animation that should play from start to finish and then stop, such as with a death fall.

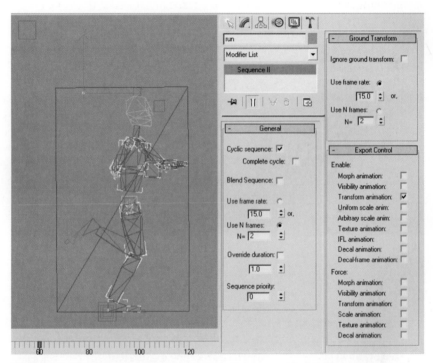

FIGURE 12.5   Modifying the parameters of the Sequence object before exporting the sequence.

Blend sequences allow you to animate just the lower or upper portion of the character. An example of a blend sequence is a look animation. The lower body of the character may be in the middle of a run or root animation, but the look animation, which uses only upper body movements, blends with current actions. More information about blend sequences is available on the GarageGames Web site. For most character animations, you only need to check the Transform Animation check box.

Footprints and Foot Sounds

Each Sequence object comes with a Triggers track. You can use the Triggers track to place triggers that indicate where the feet should leave footprints and generate footfall sounds. You place these triggers in the Curve Editor, by selecting the Triggers track, inserting two keys, and assigning values to those keys. In Figure 12.6, a key was assigned at frame 4 with a value of 1.0, and a second key was assigned at frame 22 with a value of 2.0. The default setup for the Torque Game Engine is that a value of 1 generates a footprint for the left foot, and a value of 2 generates a right footprint. Make sure the key values are exactly 1.0 and 2.0.

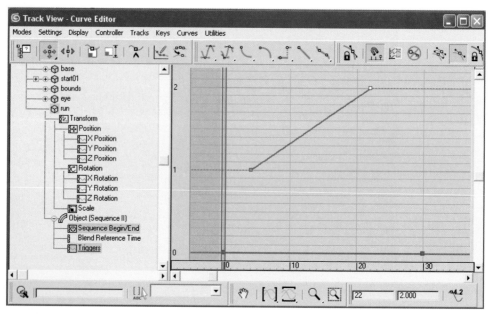

FIGURE 12.6   Keyframing footprint triggers with the Curve tool.

Export of the DSQ Animation

You export the DSQ animation from the Torque DTS Export menu. If you are animating your character while the mesh is still present, delete the mesh from the biped before exporting the DSQ file. Make a copy of the 3ds Max file with the character mesh intact in case you want to work with it again, delete the character mesh, and click the Sequences button from the Utilities rollout. Save the file as `player_root.dsq`, `player_forward.dsq`, or whatever is appropriate for your character name and animation.

USING THE TORQUE SHOW TOOL PRO

The Show Tool is a great time-saver for character previewing. Here, you can preview your character in full animation while having the ability to completely rotate your view. You can quickly detect all sorts of issues with the model, the rig, the texture, and the animation. Many of these problems are difficult to see properly inside of 3ds Max or in the Torque Editor because of the numerous distractions and viewing hindrances. In Figure 12.7, the lighting is being adjusted while effects of the run cycle on the texture are being studied. You can play the animation loop at full speed or slowed down, or you can scroll it by hand; you can zoom in, rotate, and relight the image.

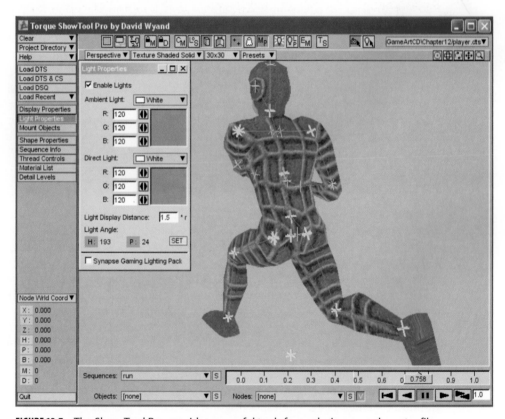

FIGURE 12.7 The Show Tool Pro provides powerful tools for analyzing your character files.

You can use the Project Folder tab to select the location of your DTS and DSQ files. Load DTS and Load DSQ allow you to load shape and animation files. You can select loaded sequences from the drop-down list in the lower left of the dialog box and play them from the Control Panel on the lower right. You can use the mouse wheel to zoom the image in and out; click and press left to rotate your view, click and press right to pan your image around the screen.

SCRIPTING CHARACTERS

If you are just interested in replacing the default player in Torque, you only need to replace the original shape file, textures, and animations in the \data\shapes\player folder with your own versions. As long as your DTS and DSQ files keep the same names as the originals, Torque detects them and replaces the original character with your character. If you want to use your own folders and file names for characters, or if you want more than one unique character mesh in the game, you need to change some of the character scripts, as described in this section. The script changes necessary for weapons export are detailed in Chapter 6. The companion CD-ROM has example scripts and files for the astronaut, the robot, and their weapons using unique folders and file names. The video SettingUpGameFiles.wmv demonstrates the process of setting up the scripts and shapes for your own installation of Torque. This file is located in the Videos folder on the companion CD-ROM.

ON THE CD

The Player.cs Animation Script

Two different player.cs script files are available. One of these typically resides in the \data\shapes\player folder, and the other resides in \server\scripts. This section pertains to the player.cs script that resides in \data\shapes\player, which we will refer to as the player animation script.

The player.cs animation script is the means by which you tell Torque what animations your character can play. This file lists the base shape, which is the player mesh and associated markers, as well as each animation sequence, followed by the actual name of the Sequence object. Deleting any entry from this list causes any other animations listed lower in the file to fail. The player.cs file holds the key to what your sequences should be named for each animation and what the Sequence objects for each animation should be named; for example, the root animation sequence should be named player_root.DSQ, and the root animation Sequence object should be named root. The following lines of code show an abbreviated player.cs file, which is set up for a character with only four animation sequences.

```
datablock TSShapeConstructor(PlayerDTS)
{
    baseShape = "./player.DTS";
    sequence0 = "./player_root.DSQ root";
```

```
        sequence1 = "./player_forward.DSQ run";
        sequence2 = "./player_back.DSQ back";
        sequence3 = "./player_side.DSQ side";
    };
```

If one of your characters were a robot, and you wanted to change the folder name and the file name for your player, you would want to make sure that all necessary files are located in the \data\shapes\robot folder. These would include any DSQ sequence files, a DTS shape file, any character textures, debris_player.dts, splash.png, and footprint.png. You can copy these nonanimation files from the player folder and use them wherever you need them. Here you can see the robot animation script, which has just a root and run animation sequence:

```
        datablock TSShapeConstructor(robotDTS)
        {
            baseShape = "./robot.dts";
            sequence0 = "./robot_root.dsq root";
            sequence1 = "./robot_forward.dsq run";
        };
```

ON THE CD

The example in Files\Astronaut on the companion CD-ROM has an abbreviated set of animation sequences and is named astronaut.cs. You can abbreviate your character animation script file any way you want as long as you do not skip sequence order. If this file (astronaut.cs) skipped from sequence3 to sequence5, none of the sequences listed after sequence3 would play. Therefore, it is important that all sequences listed are sequential, even if some of them are substituted with sequences that do not fit the traditional setup found in the original player.cs. It may be that some of the sequences are not important to you for the game you are developing. The following example replaces the look sequences that are normally sequence4 and sequence5 with a root sequence, so that sequence6 through sequence9 will play:

```
        datablock TSShapeConstructor(AstronautDts)
        {
            baseShape = "./astronaut.dts";
            sequence0 = "./astronaut_root.dsq root";
            sequence1 = "./astronaut_forward.dsq run";
            sequence2 = "./astronaut_back.dsq back";
            sequence3 = "./astronaut_side.dsq side";
            sequence4 = "./astronaut_root.dsq root";
            sequence5 = "./astronaut_root.dsq root";
            sequence6 = "./astronaut_fall.dsq fall";
```

```
        sequence7 = "./astronaut_land.dsq land";
        sequence8 = "./astronaut_jump.dsq jump";
        sequence9 = "./astronaut_diehead.dsq death1";
    };
```

The Player.cs Datablock Script

This script is located in \server\scripts\player.cs and tells Torque where to find the DTS shape and the player animation script. The following changes are necessary if you want to change the folder name and location for the player. Note that the name of the file does not change, only the references within the file.

Find:

```
// Load DTS shapes and merge animations
```

Edit:

```
exec("~/data/shapes/player/player.cs");
```

To read:

```
exec("~/data/shapes/astronaut/astronaut.cs");
```

Find:

```
datablock PlayerData(PlayerBody)
```

Edit:

```
shapeFile = "~/data/shapes/player/player.dts";
```

To read:

```
shapeFile = "~/data/shapes/astronaut/astronaut.dts";
```

Scripting for Different Character Meshes in the Game

The default first person shooter demo basically has two Korks in the game. One is the computer-run AI character, who in this case simply runs circles around the village. The second is the player character, which also uses the Kork mesh. One of the first steps toward creating a working game is being able to replace these two default meshes with two of your own characters.

For the AI player, create a folder in \data\shapes called, for example, robot. This folder must have a file called robot.dts and all the associated files mentioned in the earlier section "Scripting Characters."

Player2.cs

In the \server\scripts folder, make a copy of player.cs and call it player2.cs. Player.cs will remain unchanged (unless you want to use a different mesh for it), but player2.cs requires two basic modifications:

Find:

```
// Load DTS shapes and merge animations
```

Edit:

```
exec("~/data/shapes/player/player.cs");
```

To read:

```
exec("~/data/shapes/robot/robot.cs");
```

Find:

```
datablock PlayerData(PlayerBody)
```

Edit:

```
datablock PlayerData(PlayerBody)
```

To read:

```
datablock PlayerData(Player2Body)
```

Edit:

```
shapeFile = "~/data/shapes/player/player.dts";
```

To read:

```
shapeFile = "~/data/shapes/robot/robot.dts";
```

Edit:

```
debrisShapeName = "~/data/shapes/player/debris_player.dts";
```

To read:

```
debrisShapeName = "~/data/shapes/robot/debris_player.dts";
```

Game.cs

In game.cs, you need to execute both player.cs and player2.cs. Change the script as shown here:

Find:

```
exec("./player.cs");
```

Add:

```
exec("./player2.cs");  // Added so player2.cs gets loaded
```

AIplayer.cs

In AIplayer.cs, make the change shown here to the DemoPlayer datablock so it uses the player2 body:

Find:

```
// Demo Pathed AIPlayer
```

Edit:

```
datablock PlayerData(DemoPlayer : PlayerBody)
```

To read:

```
datablock PlayerData(DemoPlayer : Player2Body)
```

TROUBLESHOOTING

Some of the most common character export problems and solutions are listed next. For further resources, check the Frequently Asked Questions (FAQ) about Torque DTS setup and exporting, found at the GarageGames Web site at http://www. GarageGames.com. Do a keyword search using the word *FAQ*, or keyword search the particular issue you are having.

Assertion Failed on Skin Object

If you get this error message, it probably means that you forgot to convert your Editable Poly to an Editable Mesh. Remember, the Torque Game Engine recognizes only Editable Meshes.

Improperly Assigned Vertices

In a case in which one or more mesh vertices have become attached to the wrong bone, first make sure that all the envelopes are properly sized. If this does not fix the problem, you have two easy options. The first is to select the bone you want to assign the vertex to, select that vertex, and then assign it manually. Assign a weight of 1.0 to force the current bone to take possession of the selected vertex or vertices.

Character Is Invisible in the Game

If your character is not visible in the game, it is likely that you forgot one or more detail markers. In a simple scenario, if you have a character mesh called body2, you need a marker called detail2. Without the marker, Torque cannot display the mesh. If you have an additional mesh called body64, you need a marker called detail64 to see that mesh. There have also been cases of 3ds Max momentarily forgetting the mesh, where the character mesh becomes invisible even inside of 3ds Max. To remedy this, select the character mesh from the Select By Name button in the Standard toolbar, and select the most recent modifier applied to the mesh from the Modify panel; then try your DTS export again.

Character Is Not Animating

The first reason for nonanimating characters has to do with the Sequence object and the sequence file. It could be that you did not properly create and keyframe the Sequence object in 3ds Max, you did not properly name the sequence file, the sequence file is not in the proper location, or you did not properly reference the sequence file in `player.cs`.

A second reason that your character may not animate is if you left the 3ds Max file in Figure mode when you exported the animation sequence. Turn Figure mode off and try exporting again.

A third cause for nonanimating characters is that the hierarchy has been changed between the shape file export and the animation file export. Just moving the cam marker from being a child of `Start01` to being a child of `Bip01 Pelvis` is enough to cause an animation to fail. Check both hierarchies, and make the hierarchy of nonmesh objects (markers and bones) consistent between shape and animation files. Mesh objects should not matter, because they are deleted in the animation file prior to export.

Cannot Collapse bip01 L Finger00 Because It Is a Bone

This error probably means that you have included the finger bone in the list of bones used in your Skin modifier, yet this bone did not receive mesh vertex assignments. Remove this bone from the list of bones in the Skin modifier and re-export. In some cases, you may have to delete the Skin modifier and start over.

Helper Bones and Proxy Objects Are Distorted in the Animation Files

If you have exported your DTS and DSQ files without a proper configuration file, or if the configuration file is not located in the same folder as your 3ds Max file, you may have problems with the character mesh being very distorted due to the helper bones and proxy objects not being properly exported. To fix this, make sure that the configuration file is located in the same file as your 3ds Max file when you export DTS and DSQ files. If you read the `dump.dmp` file (located in the folder you are exporting to), and near the top of the file you see the line `Config file not found`, yet you can see that there is a proper configuration file in the folder, the probable solution is that you need to save the DTS and DSQ files to a folder that also contains the 3ds Max file.

Weapon Is Invisible or Intermittently Visible in First Person Mode

It is possible that you did not set up your weapon properly, so verify that the weapon is an Editable Mesh, that it has a marker, and that both the marker and the weapon have the same detail number. Also check the location of the eye marker; if the eye marker is placed too far ahead of the player, it may not completely see the weapon. Place the eye marker near where the actual player's eye would be.

Weapon Is Pointed the Wrong Way or Is Otherwise Misaligned

If your crossbow or gun is turned the wrong way, it might be caused by a bad orientation of your mount0 helper dummy in the character file. Try rotating the mount0 dummy 90 degrees in whatever direction necessary until the weapon looks right in the game. Because the mount0 dummy is parented to the player's hand bone, don't put your mount0 dummy into the hierarchy until you've positioned the arms and hands, because arm and hand position changes can affect the weapon orientation. You may need to delete the old mount0 dummy and go through the parenting and export process again.

Footprints Are Not Visible in the Game

Make sure that the footprint.png file is in your player folder. Check that the trigger track has been properly keyframed with a value of 1.0 and 2.0 for left and right foot trigger points, respectively. Make sure that Ignore Ground Transform is turned off for the Sequence object. If you still cannot get footprints, select all of the animated bones and slide them down to between frames 1 to 30 to see if that corrects the problem.

Character Stutters Forward and Backward During Run

It could be that you have not matched the position of your bounds box with the biped. You can link the bounds box to the pelvis of the biped (but turn off any inherited transforms other than in the Y direction, as described in Chapter 11), or you can keyframe the bounds box to match the player position.

Character Does Not Fall Down in Death Cycle

If a character's death animation ends up with the character going though the frames of the animation but not lying down, it is probably because the bounds box is moving with the character. If your bounds box is parented to the hipbone of the biped, use the Link Info tab of the Hierarchy panel to turn off all inheritance for the bounds box. If your bounds box is keyframed to stay with the character, delete those keyframes so that the bounds box stays put while the character falls.

Assertion Error During Vertex Merge

If you get the error message Assertion error during vertex merge: Must weld verts on mesh bodymesh when you try to export a character that has had levels of detail created through the Multires modifier, it probably means that you have unwelded vertices in your character mesh. One way to check this is to select your bodymesh object, right-click and select Hide Unselected, and then activate the Modify panel. Select the Editable Mesh at the bottom of the modifier stack and go into Vertex sub-object mode. Select all the vertices in the mesh. The total number of vertices in the model should be listed at the bottom of the Selection rollout. Now in the Weld group of the Edit Geometry rollout, type an appropriate number next to the Selected button; for example, 0.005 (meters). Now zoom in on the face of your character and click the Selected button so that the weld takes place.

If you see the lips or other features within your mesh start welding together and looking distorted, your weld setting is too high and needs to be brought down a bit. If there were no disagreeable changes in the mesh, check the number of vertices in the model. If it is lower now, you most likely had some stray vertices that needed welding, and now you are okay to try exporting the DTS shape again.

Of course, now your mesh has changed, so you need to delete the Multires:: bodymesh object and walk through the entire Multires setup process once again. If you find that your levels of detail are working now, check your character texture; you likely had some adjustments in your texture UVs that you need to correct. You can do this by putting the biped back into Figure mode, editing the Unwrap UVWs modifier on the bodymesh, and using the original character UV template as a guide for rescaling and moving the different sets of UVs. After you do this, you can go through the process of setting up levels of detail one last time. You should be in good shape.

Character Does Not Complete Animation

Whether in Torque Show Tool Pro or in Torque, the character moves only the number of frames designated by the Sequence object in the Curve Editor for Sequence Begin/End. Keep this in mind when you are making edits to the animation; whenever you change the number of frames in the animation, make sure to update the Sequence Begin/End keys.

SUMMARY

The recommended way to export a character is with a separate shape (DTS) file and separate sequence (DSQ) files. This way, you can adjust the individual files as necessary without affecting the other working files. Still, it makes sense to take the basic, meshed shape file as far as possible before splitting off copies for animation purposes, so that your hierarchy is set up correctly and does not have to be re-created for each animation file. When you're previewing the shape and the sequence files, the Torque Show Tool Pro is almost indispensable, supplying all manner of detailed information about the file. You can script your character to simply replace the default player files, or you can create your own folder and scripts to allow for one or two custom characters in the game. The troubleshooting suggestions at the end of this chapter are of particular importance if something goes wrong. If you can't find the answer you're looking for here, search the GarageGames.com Web site.

A

ON THE COMPANION CD-ROM

The companion CD-ROM is divided into five main folders: Figures, Files, Scripts, Videos, and Software.

The Figures folder has all of the figures listed in the book at high resolution in case there is something you want to see closer than was possible on the book page.

The Files folder has all of the meshes and related files discussed in the book.

The Scripts folder has the scripts, shapes, and animation files necessary for the various assets to work in the game. The characters include the astronaut and the robot. The robot animations are abbreviated with just root and run cycles so that you can create your own. The scripts for these characters are set up for the astronaut to have its own folder and name as the main player and the robot to have its own folder and name as the AI player. The robot is assigned a blaster, and the astronaut has a raygun; you can alternately replace the astronaut's raygun with a railgun by using the instructions in Chapter 6, "Exporting Game Art." The video SettingUpGameFiles.wmv addresses how to install these character and weapon scripts.

The Videos folder has how-to videos covering the major areas discussed in the book. These movies should be played using Windows Media Player. Access them via the Start.exe file on the companion CD-ROM, or directly from the Videos folder.

- ModelingAChair.wmv demonstrates how to model the chair from Chapter 1, "Introduction to 3ds Max."
- SemiOpaqueMaterials.wmv demonstrates how to create a transparent material, as described in Chapter 4, "Texturing Game Art."

- CharacterModeling.wmv demonstrates how to set up templates in 3ds Max for a character, and how to start the modeling process, as described in Chapter 7 "Character Modeling."
- FittingTheBiped.wmv demonstrates the process of creating and fitting a biped to your character mesh, as described in Chapter 10, "Character Rigging."
- FittingBipedAndHelperBones.wmv demonstrates how to fit the biped to the character mesh, as well as how to place and constrain helper bones to the biped object, as described in Chapter 10.
- ProxiesAndLinking.wmv demonstrates how to place and link proxy objects to the biped hip area so that helper bones will operate properly, as described in Chapter 10.
- SkinModifier.wmv demonstrates how to add a Skin modifier to a character mesh, how to add bones, and how to adjust bone envelopes to assign vertices, as described in Chapter 10.
- SkinningAbs.wmv demonstrates how to use the AbsEffect box to assign vertices to bones, as described in Chapter 10.
- SkinningWeightTool.wmv demonstrates how to use the Weight tool to assign multiple vertices to different bones, as described in Chapter 10.
- RunCycle.wmv demonstrates how to create a basic run cycle, as described in Chapter 11, "Character Animation."
- MultiresLOD.wmv demonstrates how to create multiple Levels of Detail for your character mesh using the Multires technique, as described in Chapter 12, "Character Exporting."
- SettingUpGameFiles.wmv demonstrates how to move the files on the companion CD-ROM to your installation of Torque so that the characters and weapons function properly.

The Software folder has a trial copy of the Torque Game Engine and the Torque Show Tool Pro, the Torque DTS Exporters, and the Dark Industries DTS Exporter. Texporter, the UVW rendering alternative, is also included in this folder, and here you can also find a link to a trial copy of 3ds Max.

INDEX

LIMITED WARRANTY AND DISCLAIMER OF LIABILITY

THE CD-ROM THAT ACCOMPANIES THIS BOOK MAY BE USED ON A SINGLE PC ONLY. THE LICENSE DOES NOT PERMIT THE USE ON A NETWORK (OF ANY KIND). YOU FURTHER AGREE THAT THIS LICENSE GRANTS PERMISSION TO USE THE PRODUCTS CONTAINED HEREIN, BUT DOES NOT GIVE YOU RIGHT OF OWNERSHIP TO ANY OF THE CONTENT OR PRODUCT CONTAINED ON THIS CD-ROM. USE OF THIRD-PARTY SOFTWARE CONTAINED ON THIS CD-ROM IS LIMITED TO AND SUBJECT TO LICENSING TERMS FOR THE RESPEC-TIVE PRODUCTS.

CHARLES RIVER MEDIA, INC. ("CRM") AND/OR ANYONE WHO HAS BEEN INVOLVED IN THE WRITING, CREATION, OR PRODUCTION OF THE ACCOMPANYING CODE ("THE SOFT-WARE"), OR THE THIRD-PARTY PRODUCTS CONTAINED ON THIS CD-ROM, CANNOT AND DO NOT WARRANT THE PERFORMANCE OR RESULTS THAT MAY BE OBTAINED BY USING THE SOFTWARE. THE AUTHOR AND PUBLISHER HAVE USED THEIR BEST EFFORTS TO EN-SURE THE ACCURACY AND FUNCTIONALITY OF THE TEXTUAL MATERIAL AND PROGRAMS CONTAINED HEREIN; WE, HOWEVER, MAKE NO WARRANTY OF THIS KIND, EXPRESS OR IMPLIED, REGARDING THE PERFORMANCE OF THESE PROGRAMS. THE SOFTWARE IS SOLD "AS IS" WITHOUT WARRANTY (EXCEPT FOR DEFECTIVE MATERIALS USED IN MAN-UFACTURING THE DISC OR DUE TO FAULTY WORKMANSHIP); THE SOLE REMEDY IN THE EVENT OF A DEFECT IS EXPRESSLY LIMITED TO REPLACEMENT OF THE DISC, AND ONLY AT THE DISCRETION OF CRM.

THE AUTHOR, THE PUBLISHER, DEVELOPERS OF THIRD-PARTY SOFTWARE, AND ANYONE INVOLVED IN THE PRODUCTION AND MANUFACTURING OF THIS WORK SHALL NOT BE LIABLE FOR DAMAGES OF ANY KIND ARISING OUT OF THE USE OF (OR THE INABILITY TO USE) THE PROGRAMS, SOURCE CODE, OR TEXTUAL MATERIAL CONTAINED IN THIS PUB-LICATION. THIS INCLUDES, BUT IS NOT LIMITED TO, LOSS OF REVENUE OR PROFIT, OR OTHER INCIDENTAL OR CONSEQUENTIAL DAMAGES ARISING OUT OF THE USE OF THE PRODUCT.

THE SOLE REMEDY IN THE EVENT OF A CLAIM OF ANY KIND IS EXPRESSLY LIMITED TO REPLACEMENT OF THE BOOK AND/OR CD-ROM, AND ONLY AT THE DISCRETION OF CRM.

THE USE OF "IMPLIED WARRANTY" AND CERTAIN "EXCLUSIONS" VARY FROM STATE TO STATE, AND MAY NOT APPLY TO THE PURCHASER OF THIS PRODUCT.